Contents

2
Plant Nutrition and Fertilizers   23

3
Grasses   46

Lawn Care
A Handbook for Professionals

Henry F. Decker
Buckeye Bluegrass Farms, Inc.

Jane M. Decker
Ohio Wesleyan University

Prentice Hall, Englewood Cliffs, New Jersey 07632

LIBRARY OF CONGRESS
Library of Congress Cataloging-in-Publication Data

Decker, Henry F.
    Lawn care : a handbook for professionals / Henry F. Decker, Jane
M. Decker.
        p.   cm.
    Bibliography: p.
    Includes index.
    ISBN 0-13-526708-0
    1. Lawns. 2. Turf management.   I. Decker, Jane M. II. Title.
SB433.D377 1988
635.9'647--dc19   87-35204
                                                  CIP

Cover design: Wanda Lubelska
Manufacturing buyer: Peter Havens

 © 1988 by Prentice-Hall, Inc.
A Division of Simon & Schuster
Englewood Cliffs, New Jersey 07632

Printed in the United States of America
10 9 8 7 6 5 4 3 2

ISBN   0-13-526708-0

Prentice-Hall International (UK) Limited, *London*
Prentice-Hall of Australia Pty. Limited, *Sydney*
Prentice-Hall Canada Inc., *Toronto*
Prentice-Hall Hispanoamericana, S.A., *Mexico*
Prentice-Hall of India Private Limited, *New Delhi*
Prentice-Hall of Japan, Inc., *Tokyo*
Simon & Schuster Asia Pte. Ltd., *Singapore*
Editora Prentice-Hall do Brasil, Ltda., *Rio de Janeiro*

4

Pesticides 102

5
Weeds and Herbicides   118

7

Fungi and Diseases   200

8
Special Turf Practices 230

Figures

Grassy Weeds

Broadleaf Weeds

Insects, Fungi, and Turf Care

Preface

This book is dedicated to the many young people we have taught or trained in botany and horticulture, including turf management, in colleges and for lawn care companies. The basic arrangement of the book grew out of a teaching program we were hired to prepare in the formative years of one of the nation's largest lawn care services.

Aside from the obvious benefits of producing oxygen, reducing erosion, and providing a premier playing surface, a fine turf is, after all, beautiful. It is often an integral part of aesthetic landscaping. When asked in a national poll what they prefer most in their environment, people overwhelmingly selected trees and grass. For all the damage man does to the land, it can usually be healed quickly by grading and grass, and the effect is often more pleasing and more beneficial than the original landscape.

Pesticides play an important role in turf management. They provide an effective, economical means for controlling insects, diseases, and weeds that would otherwise destroy a fine turf. The use of pesticides, however, is a sensitive environmental issue that the young turf worker should understand and appreciate. Chapter 4 is entirely devoted to pesticides. Environmental issues are easily polarized, on the one extreme by those who simply distrust all industry but on the other extreme by turf personnel who are careless and unknowing. Pesticides must be used with intelligent concern, their routine use avoided, and cultural methods of pest control substituted whenever possible. It will always be better to have a well-trained, licensed applicator treating a lawn rather than an inexperienced homeowner.

A lot of help for professional lawn workers is on the way, and the future is bright: Chemists are beginning to develop safer and more accurate pesticides, breeders are providing grasses that have improved insect and disease resistance and that require less water, and more turf personnel are receiving superior in-depth training. We hope this book will play a part in this bright future.

We would like to thank our illustrator, Cynthia Cummins, whose discerning eye and skilled hand have vastly enhanced the quality of this work.

1

The Soil

A COMPLEX LIVING SYSTEM

Soil is formed from weathered and disintegrated rock. Its quality, quantity, and depth over the mantle, or bedrock, of the earth vary from area to area, but it is the ability of this earthen crust to support life that distinguishes soil from simply powdered rock. Soil is, after all, a complex living system. Turfgrasses germinate, grow, mature, and survive or die on soils, which anchor them; serve as a reservoir for essential nutrients, water, and gases; and insulate their roots against adverse environments such as freezing temperatures.

The soil sustains plant and animal life. Without it, higher plants could not exist, and without plants as a food source, animals could not survive. Thus soil is a crucial natural resource, and its loss from the land by erosion is a severe problem worldwide. Since we all depend on the soil for our well-being, it is crucial that we understand it. Handling this living medium successfully is an important skill for everyone involved in agriculture and horticulture.

SOIL FORMATION

Soil is formed by crumbling and disintegration of the earth's bedrock in chemical and physical processes called *weathering*. Soil formation has occurred for hundreds of millions of years, and it continues today. At the same time that soil is being formed from below it is being lost from the surface layers by erosion. Thus soil is a transitory resource and is being continuously, in a sense, "harvested." Though erosion is a natural process, it has been greatly accelerated by the activities of humans, and the rate of harvesting is often greater than the rate of replenishment from bedrock. For example, it is estimated that a single duststorm in the dry West can blow away more topsoil than can be made in two centuries. Erosion control is a serious national problem.

Soil material can be formed in one place and then transported to another site. When streams and rivers cause erosion upstream, they move and deposit the sediments farther downstream. Soils formed in this way are called *alluvial* soils, and they are some of our most fertile ones. The areas where they are found are floodplains and bottomlands or, if the fine sediments were carried into the mouth of the river, deltas, such as the Mississippi River Delta.

Lacustrine soils are found particularly in northern areas of the United States, such as Washington, North Dakota, Minnesota, and around the Great Lakes. During the Pleistocene Ice Age, meltwater from the glaciers formed large lakes. With the retreat of the glaciers and drainage or evaporation of the water, sediments deposited in the bottoms of these lakes were exposed as lacustrine soils. Much the same process of sedimentation occurred in the formation of *marine* soils. As the land was uplifted or the oceans receded, the sediments that were deposited formed soils. Marine soils characterize the coastal plains of the Atlantic and Gulf states.

Fine soil materials can also be carried and deposited by wind. Huge quantities of soil were moved in this way by the dust storms of the West in the 1930s and deposited to the east in the states of the Mississippi Valley. Soils of windborne origin deposited shortly after the retreat of the last ice sheet, some 10,000 to 15,000 years ago, are called *loess*.

SOIL HORIZONS

When a vertical cut is made through the various layers, or *horizons,* of the soil, the soil profile is exposed. Most soils exhibit three principal horizons, which are denoted by letters, beginning at the surface. The *A horizon* is the zone of leaching, from which some soluble materials have been lost. However, it contains many living organisms such as plant roots, microorganisms, and animals, and particularly the upper part of it may be rich in decomposing humus. The *B horizon* is the zone of accumulation. It is rich in materials such as clay and iron and aluminum oxides, which have washed down from the A horizon above. Fewer living organisms are present in the B horizon than in the A. The *C horizon* consists of unconsolidated rock materials that have only begun to weather and are outside the region of biological activity. Sometimes carbonates accumulate in this horizon. The underlying bedrock is known as the *R horizon*.

The thickness of the soil horizons varies greatly in different areas, particularly in soils that have been subject to cultivation. Frequently the A horizon is referred to as the *topsoil* and the B horizon as the *subsoil.* However, this terminology is not exact. For example, if the A horizon is deep, part of it may contribute to the subsoil layer. Conversely, although the soil to plow depth is commonly referred to as topsoil, plowing at the usual depth of 7 to 10 inches may actually turn over subsoil.

THE FIVE COMPONENTS OF SOILS

Soils in general are composed of *mineral matter, organic matter, living organisms, water,* and *air.* Of these components about 50% of the volume of a typical good topsoil consists of water and air (in a ratio of about 1:1) and the other 50% is composed of solid matter (mineral and organic matter in a ratio of about 9:1).

Minerals, derived largely from the underlying parent rock, are the largest component of most soils, calculated on the basis of volume. The most abundant elements are oxygen, silicon, aluminum, and iron, with potassium, calcium, magnesium, and sodium also of significance. The mineral content determines one of the most important characteristics of soils, namely, texture. It also affects soil structure. Organic matter, including largely decayed humus, consists of the remains of dead plants, animals, and microbes, the living organisms of the soil. Water and air fill the small pores of the soil.

SOIL TEXTURE

Texture refers to the size of the individual mineral particles in a soil, which vary from coarse *sand* to fine and almost flour-like *silt* to very fine *clay.* These types are defined in Table 1-1. Clay particles are microscopic, so small that clay is considered *colloidal*—that is, it will suspend as finely divided, discrete particles in a continuous medium such as water. A *solution* is homogeneous, but a colloidal suspension contains discrete particles. These fine clay particles are extremely important in soil, since they provide a large surface area over which chemical reactions can occur, and they thus contribute greatly to the high fertility of soils. Particles coarser than sand are called gravel.

Most soils consist of particles representing all three size ranges and thus contain sand, silt, and clay. However, the proportions of these in soil mixtures vary greatly and determine in large part the suitability of soils for plant growth. Soils containing roughly equal parts of sand, silt, and clay are intermediate in type and are known as *loams.* These intermediate types are often considered good soils for the growth of plants, since the sand component, for example, lends some looseness and air-holding

TABLE 1-1.   Soil Particle Size According to the
U.S. Department of Agriculture System of Classification.

Particle Type	Size (mm)
Gravel	>2
Very coarse sand	1–2
Coarse sand	0.5–1
Medium sand	0.25–0.5
Fine sand	0.1–0.25
Very fine sand	0.05–0.1
Silt	0.002–0.05
Clay	<0.002

capacity to the loam, whereas the clay component contributes nutrient storage and water retention. Several intermediate soil types have been named, as the soil texture triangle in Figure 1-1 indicates.

PORE SIZE AND REACTIVITY

The size of the particles in a soil, or soil texture, determines one of its most important features, namely, *pore size.* Coarse-textured sandy soils contain much larger pores (called *macropores*) than do silts or clays, simply because the larger sand particles do not pack together so tightly. Since the large pores drain readily and contain mostly air, sandy soils tend to be well aerated and tend not to become waterlogged. However, water retention is so low that plants, including many turfgrasses with their shallow root systems, frequently do not thrive. Clay soils, with their smaller *micropores,* may retain so much water that they become waterlogged and plant roots die from lack of oxygen. Thus the loams, with a mixture of both macropores and micropores, are more suitable for plant growth.

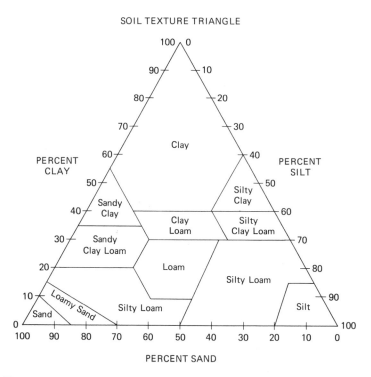

Figure 1-1 The soil texture triangle. To determine soil texture type of a given sample, read the triangle in the following way: Find the correct figure for percent silt on the right side of the triangle and the correct figure for percent clay on the left. Project a line inward from the silt line and parallel to the clay side; project a line inward from the clay line and parallel to the sand side (horizontal). The point where the two lines intersect is the soil texture type.

It is important to bear in mind that pore size is affected by the way in which the soil is managed. Soils that have been heavily plowed or rototilled have less pore space than undisturbed soils of the same type. For example, a bluegrass sod grown on undisturbed loam was shown to have 57% pore space, whereas that grown on previously cropped and tilled soil had pore space reduced to 50%. Thus it should be understood that, although it is necessary to prepare a proper bed prior to establishing a new turf, one should avoid excessive plowing, disking, rototilling, and so forth.

Another factor influenced by the size of soil particles is chemical reactivity. Sands and silts tend to be quite unreactive because they consist of large particles and are mostly ground and unaltered quartz, or silicon dioxide (SiO_2). Clays, on the other hand, are more complex; they consist of several minerals, and the many tiny, colloidal particles present a tremendous surface across which chemical reactions occur. Thus clays are highly reactive, serving as reservoirs of chemical elements used by plants for their growth and contributing to fertility.

CLAY

If clay is examined under a microscope, it can be seen to consist of flat sheets. These are stacked up to form a *crystal unit,* or *layer,* something like the pages of a book, and many crystal units are in turn stacked up to form the entire clay crystal.

Typically, the sheets of a clay crystal are made up of silicon or of aluminum (sometimes with magnesium). Three of the most common clays are *kaolinite, montmorillonite,* and *illite.* In kaolinite the crystal unit consists of a silica sheet and an alumina sheet, or a ratio of silicon to aluminum of 1:1, as shown in Figure 1-2. These double-layered crystal units are held together by oxygen-to-hydroxyl (OH—) linkages into a firm, rigid structure that does not shrink or swell. This inability to expand is a drawback in that it prevents the easy exchange of mineral nutrients along the inner surfaces of the crystal. Thus kaolinite is less reactive than other clays, and exchange of nutrients tends to be restricted to just its broken edges.

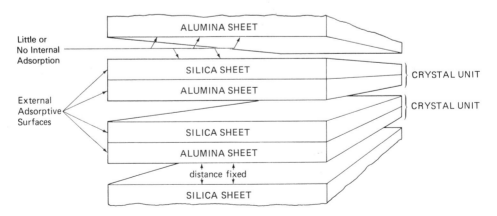

Figure 1-2 The crystal structure of kaolinite.

In the clay mineral montmorillonite, the silica to alumina ratio is 2:1, arranged in a "sandwich" of three sheets, as shown in Figure 1-3. The outer sheets of each crystal unit contain silicon and the inner sheet contains aluminum. The crystal units are held together only by weak oxygen-to-oxygen linkages, so that the spaces between "sandwiches" are expandable, unlike those of kaolinite. Thus the functional surface is readily increased, and a fine clay may have fifty times the surface area of a sand of the same weight. In these spaces water and mineral nutrients such as potassium, magnesium, and calcium are held in a form readily available to plants, and montmorillonite is therefore considered a chemically reactive clay. It is similar to (but more readily expandable than) vermiculite, a clay mineral used as a fertilizer carrier and a component of greenhouse potting soils.

Illite is a fine-grained mica with a crystal structure similar to that of montmorillonite. Though illite also has a 2:1 ratio of silica to alumina, it is less expandable when wet and less reactive. This is because, in addition to the oxygen-to-oxygen linkages between crystal units, it contains potassium atoms, which stabilize the crystal and prevent its expansion. Whenever an unfertilized soil contains a high amount of potassium, chances are great that the major clay present is illite.

These clays are widespread in the temperate regions of the United States, and they extend also into more southern areas. In general, montmorillonites predominate in the Midwest and into the western deserts, whereas soils in the southern states tend to contain kaolinite clays, although montmorillonites and illites are not uncommon there also.

In tropical and subtropical humid regions of the world, including some of our southern states, the predominant clays do not contain silica, but rather are oxides and hydroxides of iron and aluminum. These clays are less sticky when wet and even less reactive than kaolinite, and they are characteristic of the weathered and leached, reddish-brown soils of the Southeast.

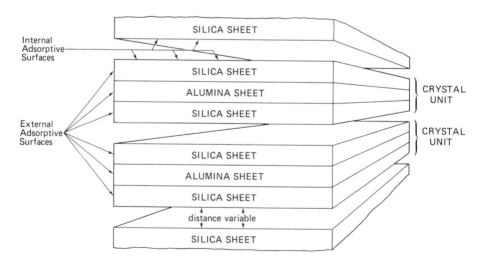

Figure 1-3   The crystal structure of montmorillonite.

CATION EXCHANGE

Many chemical compounds are composed of electrically charged particles called *ions.* Ordinary table salt, sodium chloride, consists of a positively charged sodium ion, Na^+, and a negatively charged chloride ion, Cl^-. Because of their opposite charges, these two ions are attracted to each other and form the compound, sodium chloride. However, in water sodium chloride breaks down, or disassociates, and is said to be *ionized.* An ion bearing a positive charge is called a *cation,* and an ion bearing a negative charge is called an *anion.*

A simple experiment can be used to demonstrate the important soil process of cation exchange. Suppose that one puts a small amount of a loam soil in a cup or beaker and adds to it a clear, pure solution of ammonium acetate ($NH_4C_2H_3O_2$). This is stirred and mixed for a few minutes. Then the muddy suspension is poured through filter paper in a funnel and the clear filtrate is collected below in another beaker. If the filtrate solution is analyzed chemically, it can be found to contain traces of calcium, magnesium, potassium, and other positively charged ions. Since the original ammonium acetate solution was pure, where did these cations come from? The answer, of course, is that they came from the soil. Detailed experiments indicate that the ammonium ions, NH_4^+, of the ammonium acetate replaced, or exchanged positions with, Ca^{2+}, Mg^{2+}, K^+, and other cations held on clay particles of the loam. In other words, these inorganic cations, which had been attached to the internal and external surfaces of clay crystals, went into solution in the soil water, where they would be available for uptake by plants. The process that occurred is cation exchange.

Cations are bound in soils because clay and humus particles are negative in charge and hence attract the positively charged cations. Since the binding sites on the surfaces of soil particles are limited, however, excess cations go into the soil solution. Thus one of the most important functions of soils is to act as a reservoir for plant nutrients. When potassium chloride (K^+) or ammonium phosphate (NH_4^+) or lime (Ca^{2+}) is added to the soil, the cations added exchange positions with those already present on soil particles or go into the soil solution directly, contributing to the supply of nutrients available for uptake by plant roots. However, it should not be inferred that adding fertilizer is required for cation exchange. In a fertile soil the process occurs continuously between all absorptive bodies present in all directions—from clay particles to humus particles to root surfaces and vice versa. It is a natural activity in a complex, active, moist, living soil.

Cation Exchange Capacity

The extent to which cation exchange can occur in a soil is referred to as its *cation exchange capacity* (CEC) and is measured in milliequivalents (me) per 100 g of dry soil. One milliequivalent is defined as 1 mg of hydrogen or the weight of any other ion that will combine with or displace it. Cation exchange capacity varies from soil to soil, depending on the amounts and types of clays and other soil components present. It is a reasonably good indication of soil fertility, and the fertility increases up to certain limits in direct relation to the fineness of the soil particles, from sand to silt to clay to humus. Data for some surface soils in the United States are shown in Table 1-2.

TABLE 1-2. Cation Exchange Capacity of Some U.S. Soils (in milliequivalents). Adapted from Donahue, Shickluna, and Robertson, *Soils,* 3rd ed., © 1971, p. 59. Reprinted by permission of Prentice-Hall, Inc., Englewood Cliffs, New Jersey.

Florida sandy soil	1.0
Texas sandy soil	1.9
South Jersey loam	11.9
Illinois silt loam	26.3
Alabama clay	34.3
Florida mulch	100.8

Of the three clays described, the montmorillonites tend to have the highest cation exchange capacity and kaolinites the least, with illites intermediate. High cation exchange capacity is due to the property of plasticity, the ability to expand and present internal absorptive surfaces, as is seen in montmorillonites and illites. Furthermore, cation exchange capacity is greatly increased in these clays when some of the aluminum and silicon ions are replaced by other ions. In this process of *ion substitution* a cation of lower positive charge may replace one of higher charge, such as the substitution of Mg^{2+} for Al^{3+}. Each time this occurs, one unsatisfied negative charge is generated. Substitution is of great magnitude in the clays of $2:1$ type, and it contributes greatly to their ability to hold negatively charged ions in cation exchange.

Cation exchange capacity depends, then, on the number of unsatisfied negative charges present on soil particles and on the surface area presented, the plasticity, and the expandability of the particles.

Typical cation exchange capacities of some soil components are shown in Table 1-3. Such figures show us that the CEC of a soil is due as much to the percentage of organic matter as to the percentage of clay types in the soil. Colloidal organic matter, or humus, may have a CEC of 200 me or more, and if, for example, the organic matter in a sandy soil is increased by 1%, the CEC of the soil is increased by two or more milliequivalents. This relationship does not hold true, however, for organic matter present in highly acidic soils, in which the cation exchange capacity is low.

SOIL STRUCTURE

Another important characteristic of soils is their *structure.* This term refers to the groupings, or aggregations, of solid particles in the soil. Clay particles, for example,

TABLE 1-3. Typical Cation Exchange Capacity of Some Soil Components (in milliequivalents).

Kaolinite	8
Illite	30
Montmorillonite	100
Vermiculite	150
Humus	200

do not exist singly in suspension but rather in loose groupings. The most desirable soil is one with a granular structure—porous and with rounded aggregates. A well-granulated soil contains pores that are large enough to hold sufficient quantities of water and air but not so large that most of the water will drain out. It is likely to contain a significant amount of organic matter, which is important in producing good soil structure and in increasing cation exchange capacity and fertility.

Soil aggregates are in a sense fragile: they can be destroyed just by the splashing of raindrops or irrigation water on bare ground. The result is crusting, the formation of a hard surface layer that can impede the growth of small young seedlings. This problem can be severe, especially in small-seeded crop plants such as grasses. Planting of a sod crop is good protection even for unused land, since it prevents destruction of aggregates as well as retards erosion. Soil structure can be greatly influenced by management practices. Plowing, disking, and other tillage operations may be beneficial in that they incorporate organic matter into the soil, but they can also break down aggregates and destroy structure. When heavy equipment or trucks are run over the soil, compaction becomes a serious problem, especially on wet soils and clays. The soil becomes hard and impervious to water and deficient in pore space. Plant roots cannot easily penetrate such a soil, and growth is severely restricted.

The cohesiveness or resistance to distortion of a soil is referred to as its *consistence.* For example, a wet clay soil tends to have a *sticky* consistence, whereas a dry sandy soil has a *loose* consistence. The preferred soil for the growth of turfgrasses is one that is neither too loose and noncoherent nor too hard and cemented, in which case it can barely be crushed between the thumb and forefinger. The ideal is a soil that is *friable:* Such a soil when moist crushes easily under gentle pressure between thumb and forefinger, yet remains coherent when pressed together. A good soil also is said to have good *tilth,* referring to its physical condition in relation to plant growth. Tilth is determined by many factors, including texture, structure, water capacity and content, aeration, and drainage.

For the obvious reasons of drainage, aeration, and root growth, a friable soil with good tilth is highly desirable for the culture of turfgrasses. However, in practice such a soil is rarely obtained, particularly on lawns of newly built homes, where not uncommonly the friable topsoil is covered with the brick-like subsoil removed during excavation of the basement. The preferred practice is to remove the topsoil from the site by bulldozing prior to excavation and then to replace it after the construction is finished.

HUMUS

When living organisms in the soil die, they become part of the soil's organic matter. Such materials as fallen leaves, dead plants, insects, bacteria, and animal wastes are broken down continuously into finer and finer particles and gradually enrich the soil. Highly decomposed organic matter that is resistant to further decay and no longer recognizable as originally either plant or animal material is known as *humus.* That is, when a maple leaf and a dead beetle are decomposed, or degraded, by soil fungi and bacteria to the point where they are no longer recognizable as leaf and beetle, they are considered humus. Brown or black in color, humus is a complex mixture of amorphous materials such as lignin, waxes, and cellulose from plant cell walls and newly formed compounds like polyuronides. These are principally *organic,* or carbon-containing compounds, such that about 90% of the weight of humus consists of just carbon, hydrogen, and oxygen. Humus particles are even finer in texture than clays. Also colloidal in nature, they have great surface area and absorptive capacity, and they contribute greatly to the cation exchange capacities of soils (see Table 1-3). Except in highly acidic soils, they contain many negative charges generated by loss of hydrogen from —COOH and other parts of molecules. In view of this relationship between humus and cation exchange, proper management of soil acidity is extremely important to soil fertility.

With these important characteristics, humus has many functions in soils, including the following: It serves as a storehouse of nutrients released into the soil as decay proceeds, it increases the cation exchange capacity, it promotes granulation and porosity, it reduces evaporation and increases water retention, and it helps to prevent erosion by wind and water. Thus nearly every soil will benefit from addition of organic materials, which improve the cation exchange capacity and fertility, structure, and tilth.

The improvement of soil fertility by addition of organic matter is the principal reason why composting and organic gardening have become so popular in the United States. Orange and banana peels, egg shells and coffee grounds—all kinds of waste organic materials from kitchen and home—can be mixed with a little soil (containing the proper soil microorganisms) and composted, then spread on the vegetable garden to increase its fertility and tilth.

Prior to establishment of turf, soil organic matter can be increased in several ways. If sufficient time is available, the use of a *green manure* is recommended. This involves the planting of a crop, such as rye, oats, or soybeans, and then plowing this green manure under while the plants are still immature and succulent. A *compost* of well-decomposed plant wastes can also be worked into the soil to advantage. Composted sewage sludge has been found to be an excellent soil conditioner (in fact, fertilizer) for turfgrasses. One should be careful, however, to use only well-rotted materials and to avoid materials that have a high carbon-to-nitrogen ratio.

THE CARBON-TO-NITROGEN RATIO

Carbon (C) and nitrogen (N) are both present in organic wastes, and both are used by bacteria and other microorganisms of decay in their own growth processes. If a crop residue containing much more carbon than nitrogen, such as wheat straw with a C/N ratio of 375:1 (see Table 1-4), is added to the soil, decay microorganisms will grow and proliferate by using the carbon compounds as an energy source. Since the residue is proportionally low in nitrogen, the microorganisms will draw nitrogen out of the soil reservoir, depleting the supply available for the growth of crop plants. Thus the soil will develop a nitrogen deficiency. The C/N ratio of various plant residues is indicated in Table 1-4. If any material with a ratio higher than about 10:1 is used as a soil amendment, nitrogen fertilizer should be added to the soil in compensation. (The ex-

TABLE 1-4. The Carbon-to-Nitrogen Ratio of Some Common Compost Materials. Adapted from Raymond P. Poincelot. "The Biochemistry and Methodology of Composting," *Connecticut Agr. Exp. Station Bull.* 754, 1975.

Sewage sludge	6:1
Alfalfa hay	18:1
Grass clippings, fresh	20:1
Garbage and paper, municipal	37:1
Leaves, freshly fallen	40–80:1
Peat moss	58:1
Corncobs	104:1
Paper, mostly newspaper	172:1
Hardwood sawdust	250:1
Douglas fir bark	295:1
Wheat straw	375:1
Pine sawdust	728:1

ceptions to this rule are the materials with high lignin content, such as sawdust, bark, and paper, which are not quickly or readily decomposable and thus do not support proliferation of microorganisms.)

ORGANIC SOILS

Most of the soils of the United States are classified as *mineral soils* because they contain only a small proportion of organic matter. They are the most extensive and agriculturally important soils in the United States. However, some soils such as those found in the Florida Everglades or the peat soils commonly used for growing sod in Michigan, Indiana, and Canada contain much more organic matter. Any soil that contains more than 20% by weight organic matter is classified as an *organic soil.* If the organic material is not at all or only slightly decayed, so that original parts of plants are recognizable, the soil is a *peat,* whereas in a *muck* soil decay has occurred to such a great extent that plant parts are no longer recognizable. In some cases the organic content of these soils is greater than 90%. Organic soils vary both in the extent to which decomposition has occurred and in the types of vegetation from which they were formed.

In general, peat soils require quite different management practices than do mineral soils. They have much greater water-holding capacities than mineral soils (perhaps 10 times greater by weight and somewhat greater by volume), they are more porous, they are much lighter in weight, and they have a different nutrient content. These properties can cause some difficulty in a sodded turf. When a sod grown on peat is installed on a mineral soil base, the grass roots may not readily grow into the mineral soil, but will remain in the surface peat layer. The sod will not knit well to the base, and the shallow rooting will make the turf especially susceptible to drought. The same problem has been noted in landscape installations when the hole around a newly planted tree is backfilled with a peat or other lightweight soil mixture.

Organic soils cover some 330 million acres in North America, especially in Canada and Alaska. They are extensive in northern areas of the United States, such as Minnesota, Wisconsin, Michigan, and Washington. Other locations include New York, New Jersey, North Carolina, and the Everglades region of Florida. These soils are well known for production of certain vegetables and, especially in the case of Michigan peat, for the growing of grass sods. They are also the source of the commercial peat moss used to improve garden soils.

SOIL LIFE—A TON OF LIVING WEIGHT PER ACRE

Weathered rock does not become a soil until it supports life, of which there is a great quantity and variety in a fertile soil. A rich soil is teeming with living organisms in almost incomprehensible numbers: a teaspoonful of soil can contain as many as a billion bacteria, ten million actinomycetes, a million fungi, and several thousand algae; the weight of these microorganisms to plow depth over an acre can total a ton of active, living weight.

Upon their death, all the living organisms of the soil contribute to its organic matter and increase its fertility and tilth. However, it is important for the turf worker to understand the numerous beneficial activities of organisms while they are alive and to manage the soil with them in mind. The unnecessary use of soil sterilants, pesticides, and other toxic chemicals should be avoided, lest the soil die and lose its ability to support life.

Some of the animals that live in soil include gophers, moles, slugs and snails, centipedes, earthworms, insects, and nematodes. Though some of these organisms are considered harmful pests—such as the nematodes, which infest turf, and the grubs, which feed on its roots and destroy it—in general they have a beneficial effect on the soil. They may burrow through the soil, increasing aeration and drainage and contributing to good tilth. They ingest and excrete organic materials, thus hastening the processes of decomposition, which are continued by microorganisms. And finally at their death, they contribute again to the organic matter of the soil.

Earthworms in particular are well known and appreciated for their role in increasing soil fertility. They feed on dead plant material, including grasses, and pass the plant materials and soil minerals through their bodies. They then excrete in their casts a product from which nutrients are readily available to crop plants. The results can be detected by the increased growth of grass around the casts. In a recent study it was shown that earthworms could increase the soil-exchangeable calcium by 59%, potassium by 19%, magnesium by 39%, and phosphorus by 165%! They also increase the cation exchange capacity of the soil. In their normal burrowing activities, earthworms "plow" the soil, resulting in better aeration and thus promoting the growth of plant roots. One of the most desirable habitats for earthworms is a crop of perennial grass, that is, a turf, particularly if the soil is a loam. At both soil texture extremes, clay and sand, the earthworm population decreases to where it is nonexistent.

Plant roots and rhizomes (underground stems) are very significant living organisms in soils. They penetrate cracks in rocks and split them, contributing to soil formation; they increase porosity and aeration through their growth; and they contribute a greater quantity of decomposable material than any other kind of organism.

Microorganisms of numerous types, including bacteria, fungi, protozoa, and algae are present in vast numbers in soils. The importance particularly of bacteria and fungi in the life of the soil cannot be overestimated. Bacteria are tiny single-celled organisms, whereas fungi like the molds are filamentous in form. These organisms are perhaps best known as the source of many of our antibiotics used in medicine, such as penicillin (from the common soil fungus *Penicillium*), streptomycin (from the bacterium *Streptomyces*), and several others including aureomycin, terramycin, and neomycin. The most essential activity of microorganisms in soils, however, probably is decay. Utilizing the compounds of organic matter as an energy source, microorganisms break down these compounds into simpler materials such as nitrate, sulfur, and iron, which then may be held on the clay particles and through cation exchange become available for the growth of plants. Thus bacteria and fungi are agents of decomposition, a process that is not spontaneous and would not occur without them. These microorganisms have been called the "garbage collectors of the plant world," and without their ability to break down refuse, the earth would soon be smothered with fallen leaves, tree branches, dead animals, and other debris.

Some kinds of microorganisms promote soil fertility in another way: certain bacteria are able to extract nitrogen gas from the atmosphere and "fix" it in the form of nitrates usable by higher plants, whereas others process ammonia and other nitrogen-containing compounds. The result of these activities is that nitrogen-containing compounds usable by higher plants in their growth are made available in the soil solution (see Chapter 2).

Besides their participation in decay processes, fungi play an important role in the soil in the formation of structures called *mycorrhizae*. This term is literally translated as "fungus root." It refers to an association between a fungus and a plant root, in which the structures grow together, to the mutual benefit of both. The fungus filaments grow in and around the rootlets, producing a greatly increased absorptive surface for them. Thus, while the fungus uses plant carbohydrates as a food source, the plant benefits from greater absorption of water and minerals, especially phosphorus. The beneficial role of the fungi in this relationship is not completely understood, but it is clear that mycorrhizal plants exhibit higher growth rates and greater stress tolerance than the same kinds of plants living without their fungal partners.

SOIL WATER

Actively growing grasses may consist of as much as 90% water, most of which is absorbed from the soil by the roots and translocated throughout the plant. Water is used in photosynthesis and other cellular processes as well as in maintaining *turgidity*, or rigidness, so that stems and leaves remain positioned to capture the sun's energy. Water also acts as a solvent for nutrients as they move in the soil and throughout the plant. In addition to being used in these ways, it evaporates from leaves and stems, so it must be continuously replenished from the soil.

Both water and air are held in the soil pores, and in a typical loam their volumes are about equal. Their ratio is critical. Water is held mostly in the micropores and air in the macropores, except after a heavy rain or irrigation. Under those conditions water replaces air in the macropores also, and the soil is said to be *saturated*. If the condition persists for too long, the soil is *waterlogged* and plants cannot survive. Death occurs because they cannot obtain sufficient oxygen for the energy-producing process of respiration, which must occur at all times in all living cells. Plants differ in their tolerance to waterlogging: after about a week under those conditions, bluegrasses, for example, tend to be damaged, whereas aquatic weeds are not harmed at all. Thus such weeds as moss, algae, violets, and smartweed serve as indicator species for wet turf areas. It may be necessary to correct drainage problems in order to eradicate such weeds permanently. In the grass family rice and wild rice are classic examples of the many conspicuous plants like cattails, water lilies, and pondweeds that grow well in a water-saturated environment.

After saturation of soil pores by a heavy rain or irrigation, water drains out of the macropores in response to the forces of gravity. This process is called *gravitational drainage*, and it results in a soil that is said to be at *field capacity*. This is the point at which rapid downward drainage has ceased and air has replaced the water in macropores. Water is still present in the micropores—in fact, held there by a considerable force. In organic soils the difference between saturation and field capacity is much less than it is in mineral soils. Under hot and dry weather conditions the soil water may fall below field capacity, causing the plants to wilt. If the decline is so great that the plants become permanently wilted and cannot recover even if water is added, then the *permanent wilting point* has been reached. Water is not completely lacking in the soil at this point, but it is so tightly bound chemically and physically that plant roots cannot absorb it. A tension of about 15 atmospheres (220.4 lb/sq in.) has been measured with a tensiometer at the permanent wilting point. If the soil moisture tension becomes much greater than this, only a few bacteria and some seeds and spores can survive. The relation between saturation, field capacity, and wilting point is shown in Figure 1-4.

The amount of water required to bring a soil from the wilting point up to field capacity (the so-called available water capacity) is an important factor in turf management. It varies with soil texture and values are approximately, per foot of soil depth, as follows: for sandy soils, 1.2 in.; for clay soils, 1.5 in.; for loams, 2.0 in.

Watering to a depth of 6 in. is usually adequate for turfgrasses (see Chapter 8). In the bluegrass region it is generally recommended that if the turfgrass is wilting or near wilting, 3/4 to 1 in. of water per sprinkling is sufficient to bring the soil up to field

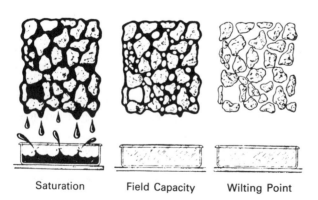

Saturation   Field Capacity   Wilting Point

Figure 1-4 A representative well-granulated silt loam soil at different moisture levels. At the wilting point, water is still present as a thin film around the solid soil particles. Adapted with permission of Macmillan Publishing Company, a Division of Macmillan, Inc. from *The Nature and Properties of Soils,* 7th Edition, by Harry O. Buckman and Nyle C. Brady. Copyright © 1969 by Macmillan Publishing Company.

capacity. As a rule of thumb, turfgrasses will grow satisfactorily if they receive about 1 in. of water per week (including rainfall) during the active growing season.

LEACHING

Soils that routinely receive more water than the field capacity often become *leached.* That is, the excess water percolates down through the soil and into the ground-water reservoir or drainage channels. In the process nutrients are washed down also and lost to the soil and its plant root systems. Leaching is characteristic of the A horizon of a soil, but its extent is greatly influenced by the amount of precipitation, which varies greatly in different geographical regions. In the Great Plains, for example, the danger of losing nutrients is minimal, but as the rainfall increases to the east and to the south, nutrient loss also increases. These losses can also be substantial on heavily irrigated land.

Inorganic elements themselves exhibit various degrees of susceptibility to leaching. Since phosphorus is tightly bound to clay particles and organic matter, very little of it is lost through leaching, whereas calcium readily leaches out and must be occasionally replenished by liming. The type of vegetation present also influences nutrient losses: a thick, well-knitted turf is probably the most resistant to leaching of any vegetation type. Thus turf once again is considered to afford excellent cover and protection for unused land.

SOIL ATMOSPHERE

The soil atmosphere comprises about 25% by volume of a typical loam and is present principally in the macropores. Like the above-ground atmosphere, it is composed largely of the gases nitrogen, oxygen, and carbon dioxide; however, the concentrations are slightly different. Whereas normal atmospheric air consists of about 78% nitrogen, 21% oxygen, and 0.03% carbon dioxide, soil air is depleted in oxygen (owing to use of this gas in respiration by plant roots) and enriched by 10 to 1000 times in carbon dioxide (owing to production of CO_2 in those same respiration processes). It also frequently contains more water vapor.

The oxygen level in particular is of great importance for the growth of plants. If the soil is compacted, compressed, or saturated with water to the point where oxygen and other gases are excluded, respiration will cease in root cells and the plants will die. This is the principal problem with waterlogged soils, from which air has been largely eliminated. The problem of compacted soils—those in which the pore space and hence water and air space is diminished—is an acute one in the turf world and will be considered more thoroughly in Chapter 8. Soil oxygen can also decline when there is great demand for it by proliferating microorganisms, which also use oxygen in cellular respiration. Such a condition occurs when large amounts of readily decomposable organic matter are added to the soil.

SOIL pH

The acidity or alkalinity of a soil solution is often expressed as its *pH*. The term is actually an abbreviation for "power of hydrogen," and it is a means of designating the concentration of *hydrogen ions* (H^+) in a solution. At *neutrality*, when a solution is neither acid nor alkaline (such as in the case of pure distilled water), the hydrogen ion concentration has been determined to be 0.0000001 g per liter. (An equal number of *hydroxyl ions*, OH^-, are present, but for ease of reference only the hydrogen ions are considered.) A less cumbersome way to express that small number is 1×10^{-7}; this is called a pH of 7. Thus a solution of pH 7, like pure distilled water, is neutral in reaction, containing the same number of hydroxyl as hydrogen ions.

If one were to add hydrochloric acid (HCl) to pure distilled water, the HCl would ionize, forming H^+ and Cl^-, and more hydrogen ions would be introduced. The pH of the solution would drop and the solution would become more acidic. Any solution with a pH lower than 7 is considered *acidic*, because it contains more hydrogen ions. At a pH of 6 the solution contains 1×10^{-6} (0.000001) g/L of hydrogen, or 10 times more than at pH 7: the solution is 10 times more acidic. A solution at pH 5 is 100 times more acidic than at pH 7.

On the other hand, any solution containing fewer than 1×10^{-7} hydrogen ions (and more hydroxyl ions) is considered *basic*, or alkaline. This would occur if we added a base such as calcium hydroxide, $Ca(OH)_2$, or lime, to the neutral distilled water. The calcium hydroxide would ionize, releasing OH^- ions, and the relative numbers of hydrogen to hydroxyl ions would decrease. A solution of pH 8, for example, contains only $1/10$ the number of hydrogen ions (or a concentration of 1×10^{-8}) found in a neutral solution. The entire pH range is from 0 to 14.

pH and Nutrient Availability

The soil pH has an important effect on availability of nutrients essential to plant growth. These relationships for mineral soils are indicated in Figure 1-5. Note that the availability of nutrients—that is, their presence in the soil solution—is directly correlated with the pH of the soil. By looking carefully at the chart, one can understand why agronomists usually recommend a pH of 6.0 to 7.0 as a range most favorable for the growth of turfgrasses as well as many crop plants.

Nitrogen, for example, starts to precipitate out of solution below a pH of 6 and above a pH of 8: it is available over only a rather narrow pH range. Potassium and sulfur also become less available as pH drops below 6 but remain stable under alkaline conditions. Availability of iron can be a particularly troublesome factor in turf management in the Midwest and increasingly so as one approaches the unleached alkaline soils near the Rocky Mountains. Note that iron availability drops markedly above pH 7. An important element in plant metabolism, it often becomes a limiting factor for growth at high pH. Turfgrasses begin to yellow, particularly between the veins of leaves, a condition known as *iron chlorosis*. Iron chlorosis is due to the failure of chlorophyll synthesis and results in stunting of growth and finally death of the plant. Clearly, impaired absorption of nutrient elements is a major cause of death when plants are grown in highly acidic or alkaline soils. Any turf manager working with peat

pH 4.0 4.5 5.0 5.5 6.0 6.5 7.0 7.5 8.0 8.5 9.0

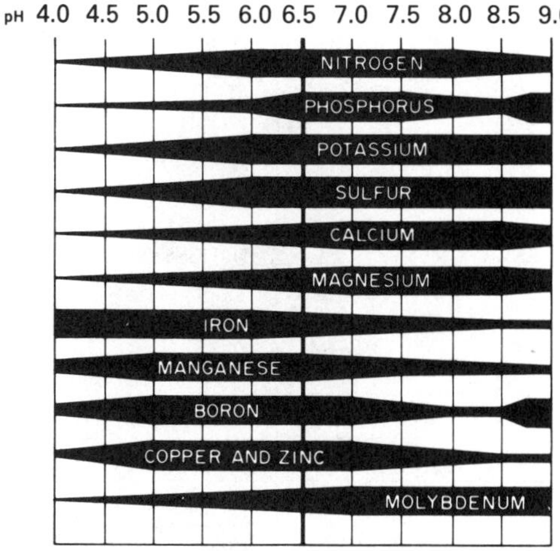

Figure 1-5 The relative availability of essential plant nutrients in mineral soils.

soils should be aware that Figure 1-5 applies to mineral soils only, and that maximum availability of elements in organic soils tends to occur at a lower pH than in mineral soils.

Acidic Soils

Soil pH does not usually fall below 4. However, in the forests of New England the humus layer may have a pH as low as 3.5. Likewise, areas subject to *acid precipitation*, may show a pH lower than 4. Acid rain and snow, arising from industrial and vehicular pollutants in the air, present a great danger to the growth of vegetation. Damage and death have been well documented in many areas of the world. In general, most plants grow best at a pH of 6 to 6.5, and a pH below 4 is considered toxic. The acid-loving rhododendrons, azaleas, and other members of the heath family are an exception, as indicated in Figure 1-6: they grow well at pH 4.5.

To raise pH (decrease acidity). The optimum pH for the growth of turf-grasses is between 6 and 7, and lime is often applied to a soil in order to raise the pH to this level. Soils frequently become too acidic after heavy fertilization, since fertilizers liberate hydrogen through ionization of inorganic compounds. When lime is added, hydroxyl ions are released and the calcium ions (Ca^{2+}) replace hydrogen ions (H^+) being held on the negatively charged clay and organic particles. Hence the hydrogen ion concentration is reduced and the soil becomes more alkaline.

Lime is available in several forms, including such materials as marl (a soft limestone consisting of highly impure $CaCO_3$), burnt lime (CaO, a caustic and concentrated material not often used), and hydrated lime ($Ca[OH]_2$, a short-lasting material produced when burnt lime absorbs water). However, the most common liming material used is ground limestone, $CaCO_3$ (calcic lime), which is plentiful and relatively inexpensive. Limestones also contain magnesium, and if the percentage of this element is high, the material is called *dolomitic lime.* Use of dolomitic lime pays an extra

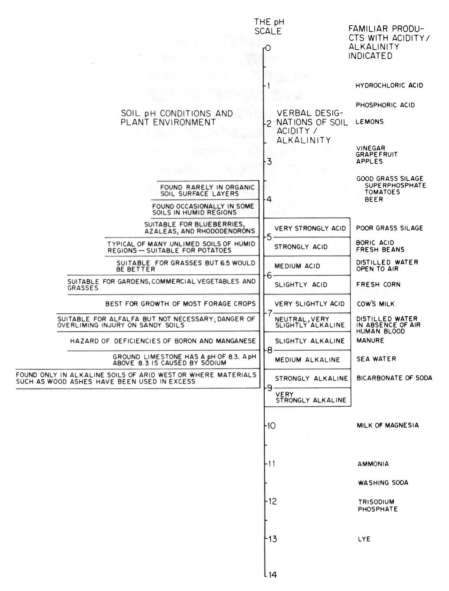

Figure 1-6   pH values suitable for various plants. Adapted from Winston A. Way, *The Whys and Hows of Liming,* University of Vermont Brieflet 997, 1968.

dividend, since magnesium is an essential element for plant growth and a component of the chlorophyll molecule. It is also an element not normally supplied in fertilizers, thus dolomitic lime improves turf in more than one way, often with dramatic effects. However, dolomitic lime is less soluble than calcic lime and takes longer to react in the soil.

The effectiveness of liming materials can be compared by noting their neutralizing value, or *calcium carbonate equivalent,* and their fineness. The standard for calcium carbonate equivalent is pure mineral calcite at 100%, a form of limestone almost never used in practice. Most agricultural limestones have a calcium carbonate equivalent of about 90. The fineness of ground lime is measured by the use of screens of varying mesh. Lime is a rather insoluble material, hence the finer the particles, the faster they will react in the soil solution. Any lime too coarse to pass through a 20-mesh screen is considered rather ineffective over the short term, whereas a lime that will pass through a 100-mesh screen is considered highly effective and will make its calcium and magnesium available to plants within a few months.

When the pH of an acidic soil is raised by liming, there are a number of direct and indirect beneficial effects. In addition to increasing availability of mineral nutrients and delivering some calcium (and magnesium in the case of dolomitic lime) to the plant, liming can reduce the availability of toxic minerals such as cadmium, nickel, and lead. A soil pH closer to neutral also stimulates bacterial activity in the soil, so that nitrogen fixation increases and decomposition increases; the latter is important in reducing thatch buildup in turf. Thus liming is an important cultural practice that improves the plant environment in many ways.

Alkaline Soils

Few soils in the United States, except in the West, have a pH higher than 8. The main factor correlated with highly alkaline soils is precipitation. As is shown in Figure 1-7, average annual rainfall may exceed 40 in. in the East but decreases to 10 or 20 in. as one moves west and approaches the rain shadow of the Rockies. This high rainfall in the humid East is sufficient to leach base-forming minerals out of the soil. However, in arid regions such as Colorado, for example, calcium and other cations accumulate, and the soil may attain a pH as high as 9.

If the soil is too alkaline for successful culture of turfgrasses or other plants, pH is usually lowered by adding an acidifying sulfur compound. These materials form sulfuric acid in the soil solution. If the problem is not severe, an acidifying organic material such as peat moss, which improves soil tilth as well as pH, can also be used. Some specific methods of lowering pH follow.

To lower pH (increase acidity). Ferrous sulfate lowers pH by producing sulfuric acid in the soil solution. It is particularly useful because soluble iron is also produced, preventing iron chlorosis. It can be applied by one of three methods: wet, dry, and foliar. For the wet method, dissolve 1 lb of ferrous sulfate in 25 gal of water and apply at the rate of $12^1/_2$ gal to 100 sq ft of area. For the dry method, spread dry ferrous sulfate evenly on a dry lawn with a fertilizer spreader, using $^1/_2$ lb per 100 sq ft or $5^1/_2$ lb per 1000 sq ft; water lawn immediately to prevent burning. For the foliar method, spray leaves with solution of 2 lb ferrous sulfate in 50 gal of water with 2 cups of a mild household detergent added as a wetting agent, or 2 oz ferrous sulfate to 3 gal water and 2 tablespoons detergent; this method may have to be repeated.

Flowers of sulfate is more effective pound-for-pound than ferrous sulfate but does not provide iron. It is used at the rate of 10 to 20 lb per 1000 sq ft for every half point that pH must be lowered.

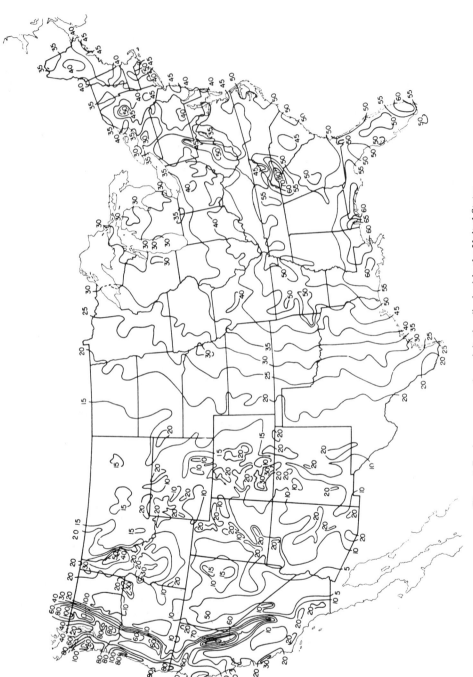

Figure 1-7 Average annual precipitation (inches) in the United States.

SPECIAL SOIL PROBLEMS

The turf manager, like other professionals in horticulture and agriculture, encounters disturbed soils much more frequently than natural ones. With an understanding of soil composition, texture, and structure, the manager is equipped to modify poor soil conditions and to prevent future problems. It is not sufficient just to plant high-quality grass seed and follow recommended maintenance procedures. If the underlying soil is poor, a high-quality turf cannot result.

If a new turf is to be installed, the soil conditions should be checked beforehand and amended if necessary. Construction practices should be monitored in order to forestall potential difficulties. In an established turf, soil can be checked by using a soil borer to bring up a small core of soil. Even pushing a spade down into the turf will indicate problems such as compaction. In an existing turf any improvements necessary will probably have to be done slowly over time by means of surface application of soil-amending materials.

A soil survey for each county in the United States has been prepared by the Soil Conservation Service of the U.S. Department of Agriculture. These are available at the local district offices, and they indicate soil texture, amount of organic matter, and other helpful information.

Poor Topsoil

Since grasses have shallow roots, it is at least relatively easy to provide them with a good soil in the root zone. Many of the problems arise during building construction and can be avoided by an alert person taking the time to make on-site inspections. For example, sometimes the friable topsoil is covered with brick-like subsoil removed during excavation of a basement. The preferred practice is to remove the topsoil from the site by bulldozing prior to excavation and then to replace it after the construction is finished. Soil imported to bring the finish grade up to level should be topsoil of good quality. If during construction rocks and debris have been buried in the topsoil or even in the subsoil, it may be impossible to develop a high-quality turf. These materials should be removed from the site before grading is completed.

Some topsoil problems can be cured by working appropriate materials, such as sand or peat moss, in to a depth of about 6 in. (However, appreciable amounts of soil should still be present in the final topsoil mixture.)

Compaction

This is a serious problem in many soils, including particularly those over which heavy equipment has repeatedly run or on which there is heavy foot traffic. Compaction alters soil structure to the great detriment of plant growth. The tight packing of particles leads to reduction of pore space (for air- and water-holding capacity), of water infiltration, and of root growth. Restoring a compacted soil is difficult, especially on an established turf, but the incorporation of such materials as peat, calcined clay, or perlite may help. The problem of soil compaction is considered further in Chapter 8.

TABLE 1-5. Salinity Tolerance of Selected Turfgrasses. Adapted from R. H. Follett, "Salinity Problems," *Proceedings of the 42nd Annual International Turfgrass Conference,* 1981, pp. 21–24. Reprinted with permission of the author.

Soil Salinity Class	Adapted Species
Nonsaline	All turfgrass species
Very slightly saline	Kentucky bluegrass, red fescue, colonial bentgrass
Moderately saline	Alta tall fescue, perennial ryegrass
Strongly saline	Zoysiagrass, St. Augustinegrass, bermudagrass, seaside bentgrass
Very strongly saline	Saltgrass, switchgrass, alkaligrass

Saline and Sodic Soils

Soils containing high levels of salts or sodium are found principally in arid and in coastal areas of the United States, often on irrigated land. Although saline soils contain enough water-soluble salts to inhibit plant growth, they tend to have a fairly normal structure and permeability and a pH below 8.5. Sodic soils, on the other hand, have poor structure, are nearly impermeable, and have exchangeable sodium at a level greater than 15% of the total cation exchange capacity. Soils high in both soluble salts and exchangeable sodium are classed as saline–sodic.

These problem soils are generally reclaimed by flushing with good quality water in order to leach out the salts, a difficult and often costly procedure. If the problem is not severe, grasses adapted to saline conditions may produce an acceptable turf. Table 1-5 indicates the salinity tolerance of some turfgrasses.

2

Plant Nutrition and Fertilizers

THE ESSENTIAL ELEMENTS

It has been shown that 16 mineral elements are required for the growth of plants. For nonwoody plants, 15% to 20% of their substance is composed of these materials; the remainder is water. As early as about 1800 botanists understood the necessity for phosphorus, potassium, sulfur, calcium, and iron as well as oxygen, carbon dioxide, and water. With increasingly sophisticated techniques, it was found that other elements are necessary, some in quite small amounts.

The nine elements required in relatively large amounts are called *macroelements:* Listed in order of decreasing abundance, they are hydrogen, carbon, oxygen, nitrogen, potassium, calcium, magnesium, phosphorus, and sulfur. Required in much smaller quantities are the seven trace elements, or *microelements:* chlorine, iron, boron, manganese, zinc, copper, and molybdenum. There is some evidence that sodium, cobalt, and silicon may also be essential for some plants. As is shown in Table 2-1, most of the essential elements are derived from the soil. Though nitrogen (N_2) and sulfur (as SO_2) are gases present in the atmosphere, they cannot be utilized by plants in these forms. They are converted in the soil solution to nitrates and sulfates, in which forms they can be absorbed by plant roots. That these elements are necessary for growth can be demonstrated by the technique of water culture, or *hydroponics,* in which plants are grown in glass containers in an aerated nutrient solution. As was demonstrated by German plant physiologists Sachs and Knop in the 1860s, culture of plants without soil is possible as long as all of the appropriate elements are supplied in the nutrient solution. Hydroponics is most commonly used commercially today in production of greenhouse crops such as tomatoes, lettuce, and strawberries.

TABLE 2-1. Raw Materials Used by Plants as Shown by the Estimated Requirements to Grow 100 Bushels of Corn. From Howard B. Sprague, *Hunger Signs in Crops*, 3rd ed., ©1964 by Longman Inc. Reprinted with permission of the publisher.

Substance	Symbol	Pounds	Approximate Equivalent
Water	H_2O	4,300,000–5,500,000	19–24 in. of rain
Oxygen	O_2	6800	Air is 20% oxygen
Carbon	C	5200	4 tons of coal
Nitrogen	N	160	Eight 100-lb bags of a 20% nitrogen fertilizer
Potassium	K	125	Three 100-lb bags of muriate of potash
Phosphorus	P	40	Four 100-lb bags of 20% super phosphate
Sulfur	S	75	78 lb of yellow sulfur
Magnesium	Mg	50	170 lb of Epsom salts
Calcium	Ca	50	80 lb of limestone
Chlorine	Cl	8	13 lb of table salt
Iron	Fe	2	2 lb of nails
Manganese	Mn	0.3	1 lb of potassium permanganate
Boron	Bo	0.06	1/4 lb of common borax
Zinc	Zn	Trace	The shell of one dry cell battery
Copper	Cu	Trace	25 ft of no. 9 copper wire
Molybdenum	Mo	Trace	A small saltspoonful of ammonium molybdate

INORGANIC AND ORGANIC COMPOUNDS

Every living plant cell requires the 16 essential elements listed previously to build its substance. Some of these are ultimately incorporated into the structures of the cell, such as the cell wall, chloroplast, and nucleus. Others are raw materials utilized in the synthesis of food materials to be used as an energy source for the living cell.

The essential elements are all considered to be *inorganic substances*, that is, substances that lack carbon. (Carbon dioxide, CO_2, and a few other simple compounds are considered inorganic even though they contain carbon.) Clay, sand, calcium, magnesium, nitrates, phosphates, hydrochloric acid, and sodium chloride all are inorganic.

Most of the materials of which living organisms are composed are *organic*, or carbon-containing compounds. The three major groups of organic compounds in plants and animals are *carbohydrates, proteins, and lipids*. Carbohydrates, which contain carbon, hydrogen, and oxygen, include the sugars manufactured during photosynthesis, starches, and the cellulose of which cell walls are composed. Proteins contain nitrogen and sometimes sulfur in addition to carbon, hydrogen, and oxygen. They are composed of building blocks called *amino acids*. Protein makes up a high proportion of the living substance of a cell, including such important compounds as the *enzymes*, which drive cellular chemical reactions. Lipids are water-insoluble substances that serve as an important food source in plants. Fats, oils, and waxes are all lipids. They are composed of carbon, hydrogen, and oxygen, but with less oxygen than is present in carbohydrates.

PHOTOSYNTHESIS

Photosynthesis is the basic process by which organic compounds are synthesized from inorganic raw materials in the plant. It occurs only in green cells and only in the presence of light. During photosynthesis the green pigment, *chlorophyll,* functions in trapping light energy, which is converted into chemical energy. Carbon dioxide and water are used, and the sugar glucose, an energy-containing organic compound, results. Photosynthesis consists of an extremely complex series of chemical reactions, but they can be summed up in the following overall reaction:

$$6CO_2 + 12H_2O \longrightarrow C_6H_{12}O_6 + 6O_2 + 6H_2O$$

In this multistep process water is split into hydrogen and oxygen, carbon is *fixed* in the form of glucose sugar, and oxygen and water are evolved. The American chemist Melvin Calvin was awarded the Nobel Prize in 1961 for elucidating the pathway of carbon in these reactions.

Grasses, like other plants, cannot indefinitely tolerate an environment in which photosynthesis is decreased or prevented, because they cannot then manufacture sufficient sugar.

RESPIRATION

The sugar synthesized in photosynthesis is used in numerous ways in the plant cell. It is the basic material used for structural components like protoplasm and cell membranes. It may be stored in the form of starch or oil. However, in all cells and as long as they are alive, sugar is continuously broken down in the energy-producing process called *respiration.* Contrary to the common misconception, respiration has nothing to do with breathing. Like photosynthesis, it consists of a complex series of chemical reactions. The overall reaction is indicated below:

$$C_6H_{12}O_6 + 6O_2 \longrightarrow 6CO_2 + 6H_2O + Energy$$

Note that chlorophyll is not required for respiration and that the process can occur in the dark. The most significant fact about respiration is that energy is produced. Chemical energy is derived from the breaking apart of glucose, and the energy is transferred into a compound called *ATP* (adenosine triphosphate). ATP is then available in the cell to drive all the many energy-requiring reactions involved in growth. Without the ATP generated by respiration, plants could not absorb materials from the soil, make protoplasm, or undergo cell division. In short, they could not survive.

THE COMPENSATION POINT

We have seen that light energy is trapped and stored in the form of sugar in photosynthesis and that the energy can later be extracted from sugar in respiration and used for maintenance and growth. How are these two processes balanced in the plant and how can we tip the balance in favor of increased growth?

It is clear that under natural conditions photosynthesis occurs only during the daytime. Respiration, however, occurs all the time, both day and night. If conditions are such that the amount of sugar made in photosynthesis during the day just equals the amount used in respiration during a 24-hour period, the plant is said to be at the *compensation point*. (Compensation point is actually determined by measuring the amount of carbon dioxide used in photosynthesis and comparing it with the amount evolved in respiration.) Such a plant can just barely maintain itself but cannot produce new cells and grow. A healthy and vigorous plant makes much more sugar in a day than is needed just for maintenance. The excess is stored and used for growth as required.

The turf manager must aim to keep grass plants growing above the compensation point. This means that during daylight hours they must receive light sufficient to promote a high rate of photosynthesis. We have probably all noted the problem of heavy shade: particularly on older lawns with large trees, the turf is thin, slightly yellowed, and grows slowly. It is living at or near the compensation point. Sometimes judicious pruning of trees will open up a turf area and permit more light to penetrate. However, if this cannot be done or is not sufficient, a shade-tolerant grass should be planted. Grasses such as fine fescue and rough-stemmed bluegrass (see Chapter 3) are recommended for areas receiving down to about 40% of full sunlight. If less than 40% sunlight is present, an alternative shade-loving ground cover such as ivy or bugleweed should be planted. Management of turf in shade is discussed further in Chapter 8.

FERTILIZERS

The best way to maximize plant growth is to manipulate the growing environment. Though an enhanced carbon dioxide level is often beneficial, it cannot easily be provided except under greenhouse conditions. On the other hand, we can provide sufficient water to a plant, using irrigation if necessary. We can likewise amend the soil in various ways if required. However, the easiest and most frequently practiced method of enhancing the plant environment is *application of fertilizers*.

Most fertilizers are inorganic materials that are added to the soil and then taken up by plant roots. They exist free in the soil solution and, after cation exchange has occurred, on the surfaces of clay and humus particles. The three most important fertilizer elements are considered to be nitrogen, phosphorus, and potassium, and fertilizers are generally denoted by the NPK concentrations. Thus 20–10–10 fertilizer contains by weight 20% nitrogen, 10% phosphorus, and 10% potassium. These three elements will be considered in the following sections.

NITROGEN SOURCES

Of all the inorganic elements absorbed by plants from the soil, nitrogen is considered foremost in importance. Over 40% of the dry matter of protoplasm is nitrogen, and it is an indispensable part of proteins, amino acids, chlorophyll, alkaloids, and nucleic acids. Nitrogen is highly mobile in plants, moving from older parts to points of active growth. Thus older leaves show the yellowing symptoms of nitrogen deficiency first. Since the growing points, or *meristems,* of grass leaves are located in the leaf bases, leaf tips show yellowing first. Turf grasses have a higher nitrogen requirement than many other plants. This is because they are maintained in an actively growing vegetative state, they have a high population density, and their flowering and dormancy are checked by mowing.

Prior to World War I most of the world's fertilizer nitrogen came from natural organic sources such as animal manures or from deposits of sodium nitrate in Chile. In 1913 a means of providing what was thought to be an "inexhaustible" source of fertilizer nitrogen was developed by Nobel laureates Fritz Haber and Carl Bosch. In their process nitrogen from the atmosphere is combined with hydrogen, usually from natural gas, to produce synthetic ammonia (NH_3). The Haber process became the basis of the modern fertilizer industry and thus was one of the great steps in the conquest of famine. However, as we have more recently come to understand after worldwide energy crises, the process requires a great input of expensive and limited energy. Natural gas reserves are rapidly dwindling nonrenewable resources, and fertilizer costs have begun to soar.

Most of the nitrogen around us exists in the form of the gas, N_2, which constitutes about 78% of our atmosphere by volume. Nitrogen gas, however, cannot be utilized directly by plants in their metabolism. Rather, plants absorb *fixed* nitrogen, combined largely with oxygen in the form of nitrites (NO_2^-) and nitrates (NO_3^-), and with hydrogen in the form of ammonium (NH_4^+). Note that these materials are all anions, not exchangeable cations. Besides the addition of nitrogen fertilizers, there are several ways in which these soluble and usable forms of nitrogen can enter the soil. Trace amounts of nitrogen are fixed by lightning during electric storms and during combustion in automobile engines. However, this atmospheric fixation is considered a negligible source of soil nitrogen. Much greater in scope are the processes of nitrogen fixation and of decay carried out in the soil by various types of bacteria and fungi. These organisms play an essential role in returning usable nitrogen to the soil. Thus they play an essential role in the cycling of nitrogen between organisms and the atmosphere and soil. An outline of the nitrogen cycle is shown in Figure 2-1.

Decomposition

Decomposition of organic material by bacteria and fungi is a major source of nitrogen compounds usable by higher plants. When these organisms change organic compounds to inorganic ones, the process is called *mineralization.* It occurs in several steps, as shown in Figure 2-2. First proteins in the dead material are used by various bacteria and fungi of decay, whose enzymes break down the proteins into the component amino acids in the process called *aminization. Ammonification* next results in production of ammonia gas, NH_3, and the ammonium ion, NH_4^+, from the amino acids. Ammonium ion is also produced through ammonification of urea, $CO(NH_2)_2$, a common component of animal wastes and of fertilizers. Maintenance of soil conditions favorable to the growth of ammonifying bacteria is extremely important to the decay process.

Much of the ammonium produced in mineralization is immediately used in the

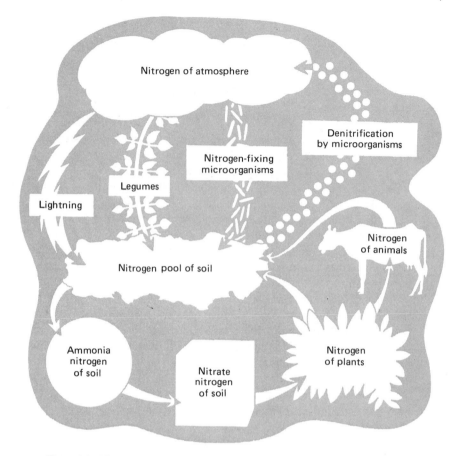

Figure 2-1 The nitrogen cycle. Galston, Davies, and Satter, *The Life of the Green Plant,* 3rd ed., © 1981, p. 183. Reprinted by permission of Prentice-Hall, Inc., Englewood Cliffs, New Jersey.

1. AMINIZATION (by decay microorganisms)
Breakdown of protein → NH_2 (amino acids) + CO_2

2. AMMONIFICATION (by ammonifying bacteria)
$NH_2 \rightarrow NH_3$ (ammonia gas)
$NH_3 \rightarrow NH_4^+$ (ammonium ion)

3. NITRIFICATION (by nitrifying bacteria)
$NH_4^+ + O_2 \rightarrow NO_2^-$ (nitrite) + H^+
$NO_2^- + O_2 \rightarrow NO_3^-$ (nitrate)

4. NITRATE ABSORPTION (by plants)
Plants absorb NO_3^-, incorporate it into protein
RETURN TO Step 1 →

Figure 2-2 A summary of the reactions of decay.

process of *nitrification.* The soil bacterium *Nitrosomonas* carries out the first step, in which oxygen is used and the ammonium ion is converted to nitrite. An additional significant product of the reaction is hydrogen ions, which contribute to acidification of the soil. (Nitrification, and the consequent acidification, occur to an even greater extent when ammonia or ammonium fertilizers are used.) The second step in nitrification occurs when the bacterium *Nitrobacter,* using oxygen, converts nitrite to nitrate. Most of the nitrogen absorbed by higher plants is nitrate, the preferred form. Thus the decomposition process results in the uptake of nitrate by plant roots. The nitrate is incorporated into plant organic material and is later recycled.

Noting the use of oxygen in nitrification, one can understand a reason why this process is depressed in poorly aerated and waterlogged soils. The reactions are greatly depressed also in soils with a pH below 5, because nitrifying bacteria do not grow and proliferate under acidic conditions.

Biological Nitrogen Fixation

Several different bacteria are capable of fixing atmospheric nitrogen directly, resulting in ammonia or organic nitrogen. Some of these organisms, such as *Azotobacter* and the blue-green bacteria, live free in the soil. Others, notably *Rhizobium,* invade plant roots and live there in a mutually beneficial, *symbiotic,* relationship. Only a few kinds of plants, such as members of the legume family (which includes alfalfa, clover, beans, peas, and vetch) are capable of harboring these beneficial bacteria. Such plants tend to boost the nitrogen level of the soil, hence they are much used in crop rotation. In recent years great interest has developed in using genetic engineering techniques to produce corn, wheat, and other plants also capable of living in symbiosis with *Rhizobium.*

Nitrogen Loss from the Soil

Although decomposition of organic wastes and nitrogen fixation may substantially enrich the soil in nitrogen, several other processes have the opposite effect. Much nitrogen is lost from the soil when ammonium ions are converted to ammonia gas, a process called *volatilization.* The problem is particularly severe in soils that are alkaline or under drought conditions. In a similar manner, *denitrifying* bacteria convert nitrate and ammonium ions into gaseous forms of nitrogen, which escape into the atmosphere. These bacteria are particularly active in alkaline soils and at high temperatures. Some soil nitrogen becomes unavailable to plants when ammonium ions are tightly bound into the structure of clay particles, and much may be lost through leaching in heavily irrigated soils. Proper turf management for retention of soil nitrogen therefore includes maintaining the soil at a pH near neutral (rather than at highly alkaline levels) and avoiding both drought conditions and unnecessarily heavy irrigation. If these situations cannot be avoided, you should plan to compensate for the lowered nitrogen level by fertilizing.

The Nitrogen Cycle and Soil Fertility

It is estimated that atmospheric fixation may add to the soil 5 to 10 lb of nitrogen per acre per year; organic matter may add 100 lb, and biological fixation may contribute as much as 300 lb, for a total of 410 lb per acre per year. On the other hand, denitrification and volatilization may account for the loss of about 50 lb per acre per year of nitrogen. Nitrogen loss by leaching is estimated at an average of 25 lb per acre per year. Thus an acre of soil under optimum conditions may gain 410 lb of nitrogen from fixation and decomposition but lose 75 lb from denitrification and leaching. The net gain of 335 lb per year, however, is probably seldom realized due to suboptimum soil conditions. Crop plants may remove from 10 to 250 lb of nitrogen per acre per year, and on bare soils nitrogen loss also occurs from erosion. One study showed that a bare, silty clay loam lost 60 lb of nitrogen per acre per year, while the same soil covered with grass lost only 2.5 lb. Considering the cost of applied fertilizer necessary to restore fertility to an eroded soil, a good case can be made for a grass cover on bare land for the purpose of erosion prevention.

Though these figures are only estimates and actual nitrogen gains and losses vary widely under different conditions, we can conclude that in most cases, at least for nonlegume crops, nitrogen fertilizer is required.

Nitrogen Fertilizers

Nitrogen is frequently a limiting factor in the growth of turfgrasses, and its application will produce a dramatic improvement in the growth and appearance of the grass. Thus nitrogen level is the most important factor to keep in mind when developing a fertilizer program for turf; levels of the other fertilizer elements are usually not critical. Turf management for fertility becomes, in essence, nitrogen management. There are two general types of nitrogen fertilizers: *soluble* and *slow release*. Examples are indicated in Table 2-2.

Soluble nitrogen fertilizers.   Soluble, or "fast-release," formulations dissolve quickly in water and become available to roots immediately. Thus a greening effect can soon be noted in the turf. However, much of the applied soluble nitrogen is

TABLE 2-2.   Some Nitrogen Fertilizers.

Fertilizer	Chemical Formula	Approximate Composition of $N-P_2O_5-K_2O$
Ammonium nitrate	NH_4NO_3	34-0-0
Ammonium sulfate	$(NH_4)_2SO_4$	20-0-0
Anhydrous ammonia	NH_3	82-0-0
Calcium nitrate	$Ca(NO_3)_2$	15.5-0-0
Diammonium phosphate	$(NH_4)_2HPO_4$	18-46-0
Potassium nitrate	KNO_3	13-0-44
Sodium nitrate	$NaNO_3$	16-0-0
Urea	$NH_2 \cdot CO \cdot NH_2$	45-0-0

leached from the soil before it can be utilized by plants. Thus much is wasted, and application is usually repeated several times per year. Some loss of soluble nitrogen from the soil occurs also by volatilization of ammonia and by denitrification of nitrate, especially when soils are dry or alkaline. Great caution must be used in applying soluble fertilizers lest the turf area be "burned." This occurs when too much material is used: The salt concentration in the soil solution becomes so high that water is "drawn" out of the plant, leading to wilting and death of the tissue.

Soluble nitrogen fertilizers can be applied in liquid, gaseous, or granular form. They include such materials as anhydrous ammonia, ammonium nitrate, ammonium sulfate, and urea (Table 2-2). Ammonium nitrate provides nitrogen both in the form of nitrate, which can be directly absorbed by plants but is rapidly leached, and ammonium, which is less rapidly leached but can be lost by volatilization.

Urea, the simple organic compound, $CO(NH_2)_2$, is the fertilizer industry's most useful nitrogen product. Some is present in the soil naturally in human and animal wastes. It is synthesized for fertilizers, as shown in Figure 2-3, by the reaction of ammonia with carbon dioxide, resulting in ammonium carbamate. Ammonium carbamate, by the loss of water, is then converted to liquid urea. Solid urea results after further concentration of the liquid form. Since the ammonia used for urea synthesis is derived from natural gas, the availability of natural gas greatly affects the cost of production of this fertilizer. Urea is water soluble and quickly converted to ammonia in the soil, thus it is not greatly subject to leaching. However, it is not effective when the soil is cold, since the bacteria necessary for its conversion to ammonia and nitrate are not active under those conditions.

Slow-release nitrogen fertilizers.   As the name indicates, slow-release materials provide a continuous supply of usable nitrogen to turf over a long period of time. This is due to the fact that such materials are slowly soluble or only gradually degraded by chemical and microbial action in the soil into forms of nitrogen usable by plants. Some slow-release fertilizers are manufactured by coating the materials with plastic or other membranes that impede the dissolving of the nitrogen in the soil solution. For example, *SCU*, or sulfur-coated urea, is made with coatings of differing thickness, which provide differing rates of release.

The most common slow-release fertilizers are organic materials of low solubility in water. *IBDU*, or isobutylidenediurea, is formed by the reaction of urea and isobutyraldehyde and has a nitrogen content of about 32%. The slow-release material most frequently used on turf is *ureaform* fertilizer. This product is the result of a chemical reaction between urea and formaldehyde. It contains at least 35% nitrogen, of which most is *water-insoluble nitrogen,* or WIN. Since release of usable nitrogen depends on microbial activity, fastest release occurs when soil conditions favor the growth of bacteria.

$$2NH_3 + CO_2 \longrightarrow NH_2COONH_4$$
ammonia + carbon dioxide   ammonium carbamate

$$NH_2COONH_4 \;\rightleftharpoons\; NH_2CONH_2 \;\leftarrow\; + \; H_2O$$
ammonium carbamate   liquid urea   water   **Figure 2-3**   Synthesis of urea.

Slow-release nitrogen fertilizers have become popular with turf managers because of the extended availability of the nutrient. Their greening effect on turf is long lasting, and they can be applied in relatively great quantities without fear of burning. However, they may lose their effectiveness in cold weather, since they require microbial or chemical action before their nitrogen is made available to plants and because significant loss by leaching can occur over the winter. Inorganic nitrogen sources, such as ammonium nitrate, may be a wiser choice in cold weather, since they are immediately available to plants. A mixture of an inorganic fertilizer with ureaform material will provide the features of both fast and slow release.

The Nitrogen Requirement for Turf

The exact amount of nitrogen required by turfgrasses is difficult to establish. Varying amounts have been specified by state experiment stations, but for bluegrass lawns the average lies somewhere between 3 and 5 lb of nitrogen per 1000 sq ft per year. Some of the so-called premium bluegrasses, such as Merion, apparently require nitrogen amounts in the higher part of the range to maintain peak performance. Fescues require half as much as the bluegrasses. In a mixture of those two grasses, bluegrass dominates at higher nitrogen levels and fescue dominates at lower nitrogen levels (see Table 3-1). Warm-season grasses may require from 4 lb to as much as 20 lb of nitrogen, depending on the species and especially on the length of the growing season. For example, bermudagrass grown under intensive irrigation and cultivation requires 8 or more lb of nitrogen per 1000 sq ft per year.

Although applications of fertilizer from spring through fall best fit the operations of a turf care company, winter applications of nitrogen (monthly, starting in October through February, at the rate of 1 lb of nitrogen per 1000 sq ft in an experiment at the Ohio Agricultural Research and Development Center at Wooster) are just as effective in maintaining a good turf. In fact, under this schedule winter color is enhanced and there is less spring growth, so that the grass does not have to be mowed as frequently. Another desirable program is to apply 2 lb of nitrogen per 1000 sq ft in September and again in April, with 1 lb in both June and August. This schedule gives good winter and summer color. If nitrogen is applied only once during the year, the application should be made just prior to the growing season. For cool-season grasses such as bluegrass and fescue, fall application is recommended, whereas spring application is best for warm-season grasses such as zoysia and bermudagrass.

Overfertilization with Nitrogen

There are several dangers to overfertilization with nitrogen. Besides the possible burning of the turf, carbohydrate depletion and enhanced susceptibility to disease may occur.

When nitrogen fertilizer is applied, the plant undergoes a spurt of growth. Carbohydrates stored in the roots are utilized in conjunction with the nitrogen for the synthesis of protein. Thus a high protein level develops in the rapidly growing shoot. However, root and rhizome growth is retarded, since carbohydrate reserves have been depleted. Under high nitrogen conditions, then, shoot growth occurs at the expense of root growth, and the plant is left in a weakened state, susceptible to extreme heat, cold, and drought. With a reduction in general hardiness, turf grasses grown at high nitrogen levels have also been shown to be more susceptible to many fungal diseases, including leaf spot diseases and several others. (On the other hand, dollar spot, rust, and red thread are more severe on nitrogen-deficient turfs, as indicated in Chapter 7.)

Overfertilization is an especially severe problem in the shade. When one sees a weakened turf under the dense shade of a tree, it is a natural reaction to fertilize it heavily, in hopes that the grass will be given a competitive advantage. Almost the reverse is true, since in the shade grasses are carrying on photosynthesis at a reduced rate due to low light intensity and fewer carbohydrates than normal are moving into the root reserves. Thus plants in shade are especially likely to suffer from carbohydrate deficiency under nitrogen conditions that are too high. Remember also that fine fescues tend to dominate in shady turf and that these grasses require only half as much nitrogen as do bluegrasses. The rule of thumb for shady turf areas, then, is to mow high (leaving more leaf area for photosynthesis) and fertilize low (see Chapter 8).

Nitrogen Fertilizers and Water Pollution

Soil erosion, a severe problem worldwide, creates a huge loss of topsoil. As soil particles are blown away or washed into rivers and lakes, nitrogen and other fertilizer elements are also carried away. The loss amounts to millions of dollars worth of fertilizer annually in the United States.

The nitrogen, phosphorus, potassium, and other nutrients lost from the land through soil erosion are in great part responsible for the nutrient pollution of our streams and lakes, as shown in Figure 2-4. The process that occurs there is called

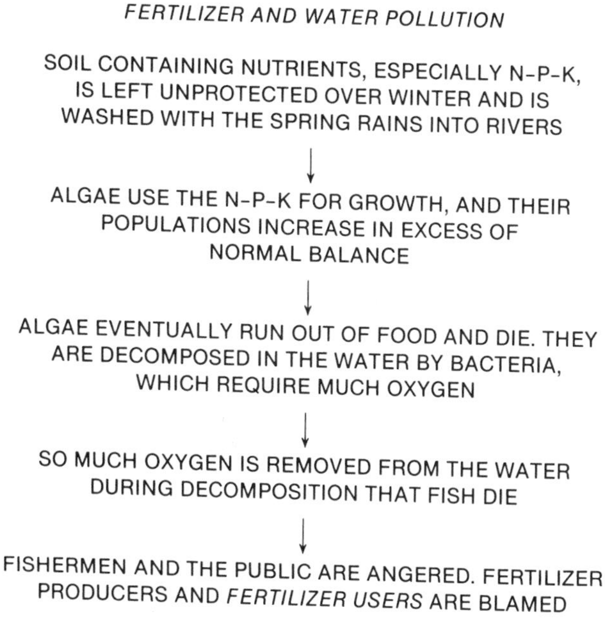

FERTILIZER AND WATER POLLUTION

SOIL CONTAINING NUTRIENTS, ESPECIALLY N–P–K,
IS LEFT UNPROTECTED OVER WINTER AND IS
WASHED WITH THE SPRING RAINS INTO RIVERS

↓

ALGAE USE THE N–P–K FOR GROWTH, AND THEIR
POPULATIONS INCREASE IN EXCESS OF
NORMAL BALANCE

↓

ALGAE EVENTUALLY RUN OUT OF FOOD AND DIE. THEY
ARE DECOMPOSED IN THE WATER BY BACTERIA,
WHICH REQUIRE MUCH OXYGEN

↓

SO MUCH OXYGEN IS REMOVED FROM THE WATER
DURING DECOMPOSITION THAT FISH DIE

↓

FISHERMEN AND THE PUBLIC ARE ANGERED. FERTILIZER
PRODUCERS AND *FERTILIZER USERS* ARE BLAMED

Figure 2-4 Fertilizer and water pollution.

eutrophication: A chain reaction begins with nutrient enrichment of the water and ends with death of fish and other wildlife. The abundance of fertilizer materials in the water causes vigorous growth of aquatic algae and other green plants. As the layer of surface algae becomes thicker and population density increases, light is excluded from the deepest algae and they die. Bacteria of decay then proliferate and use so much oxygen in their metabolism that the fish and other aquatic animals die. The pond no longer supports its normal flora and fauna. The public is often aroused when fish kills occur in this way, and blame is often placed on fertilizer manufacturers. Attention is not always paid to the importance of soil erosion in leading to eutrophication.

Turf managers should be aware of the water pollution problems that can be traced to fertilizer use. Every attempt should be made to curb runoff from bare land and to prevent soil erosion. Fortunately, a dense stand of grass absorbs large amounts of water and nutrients, so pollution problems usually do not arise from well-managed turf.

PHOSPHORUS

The main source of phosphorus for the growth of plants in the United States was bone meal until the end of the Civil War, when the commercial mining of phosphate rock began in South Carolina. Large and high-grade deposits of phosphorus were found in Florida in the 1880s, and this state is still our leading producer, with an increasing share coming today from the western states of Idaho, Montana, and Wyoming. The mined rock is processed to remove impurities and then treated with sulfuric acid to produce phosphoric acid, the intermediate necessary for making other phosphate fertilizers. The phosphate content of several of these fertilizers is indicated in Table 2-3.

A typical plant requires only about one-tenth as much phosphorus as it does nitrogen, and phosphorus is also less subject to leaching. Thus fertilizer mixtures usually contain only half as much phosphorus as nitrogen, and sometimes less. Phosphorus has an important effect on turfgrasses, particularly in rooting, tillering, and reproduction. It promotes root growth and branching and hastens maturity, hence for seedings a fertilizer high in phosphorus is recommended. Starter fertilizers typically contain more phosphorus than nitrogen or potassium and are worked into the top 1 in. of the seedbed prior to the seeding operation (see Chapter 8). Since turfgrass culture usually involves constant mowing and watering, which continuously rejuvenates the

TABLE 2-3.   Some Phosphorus Fertilizers.

Fertilizer	Chemical Formula	Approximate Composition of $N-P_2O_5-K_2O$
Ammonium phosphate	$NH_4H_2PO_4$	11–48–0
Bone meal	$Ca_3(PO_4)_2$	0–27–0
Calcium metaphosphate	$Ca(PO_3)_2$	0–62–0
Phosphoric acid	H_3PO_4	0–54–0
Triple superphosphate	$Ca(H_2PO_4)_2$	0–43–0

plants, phosphorus as well as potassium and other fertilizer elements important to young plants are continuously needed.

Phosphorus is considered an important fertilizer element not only because it is essential for plants in fairly large quantities but because it is a difficult material to manage. The crude rock is not very useful as fertilizer because it is highly insoluble and must be finely ground in order to have even minimum reaction in the soil solution. However, even the processed phosphorus fertilizers do not easily reach plants; it is estimated that during the year in which they are added to the soil, only 10% to 20% of phosphorus fertilizers are used by plants. The main problem is chemical reactions that occur as soon as the fertilizer reaches the soil, especially at low and high pH. In acidic soils phosphorus tends to become fixed as iron and aluminum phosphates, whereas at high pH calcium phosphates result. All are highly insoluble materials. The recommended soil pH for phosphorus availability is 6.0 to 7.5. The root-fungal associations known as mycorrhizae (see Chapter 1) are especially effective in absorption of phosphorus, and it has been estimated that a plant may get as much as 90% of its phosphorus in this way. Thus it is important to maintain soil conditions favoring the development of mycorrhizae.

There is an important interaction between phosphorus and arsenic of which the greenskeeper should be aware. Arsenic is used to control annual grassy weeds in turf, particularly annual bluegrass, *Poa annua*. However, it has been shown that phosphorus interferes with the absorption of arsenic by plant roots. Thus phosphorus fertilization should be reduced or omitted when arsenic is used for weed control.

POTASSIUM

Potassium is also known as *potash* because the traditional source was wood ashes, which have been used for fertilizer for centuries. In colonial times, Americans learned the value of wood ashes on corn from the Indians, and in our early history the hardwood forests of the East supported a thriving potash export business. Today potassium chloride (KCl), or muriate of potash, is the major potassium fertilizer used. The world's largest deposits of high-grade ore are found in Saskatchewan, Canada, but United States deposits are found in New Mexico, California, and the Salt Lake basin of Utah. The potassium content of some common fertilizers is shown in Table 2-4.

Most soils contain relatively high levels of potassium. Much of it, however, is present in the form of soil minerals and unavailable or available only slowly to plants.

TABLE 2-4.   Some Potassium Fertilizers.

Fertilizer	Chemical Formula	Approximate Composition of N–P_2O_5–K_2O
Potassium chloride	KCl	0–0–60
Potassium hydroxide	KOH	0–0–75
Potassium magnesium sulfate	$K_2SO_4 \cdot 2MgSO_4$	0–0–22
Potassium nitrate	KNO_3	13–0–44
Potassium sulfate	K_2SO_4	0–0–50

Less than 5% of the total potassium in a typical soil is readily available for absorption by plants. It exists in the soil solution and also as cations held on the surfaces of clay and humus particles until released by cation exchange. Because the ions are held in these ways, potassium loss by leaching is usually not a problem. Potassium deficiency may be severe in sandy soils with low clay content, however.

Potassium is an essential element required in larger amounts than any other except nitrogen and, sometimes, calcium. Its application to turfgrasses has been shown to promote root development, rapid spreading by rhizomes and stolons, and resistance to drought, heat, cold, disease, and general wear. It is especially important when the plants are young and actively growing, so for turfgrasses under constant cultivation there is a continuous need. Though potassium is not found as a component of any major material in the plant, it plays an important regulatory role in the cell, affecting photosynthesis, respiration, and water content. The last function is especially important in turfgrasses, which suffer from structural damage and water loss at each mowing. Adequate levels of potassium help to maintain cell water levels and the general *turgidity*, or rigidity, of the plant, thus preventing wilting after mowing. As with many nutrients, a relation between potassium and disease has been demonstrated. Adequate levels of potassium reduce the incidence of such diseases as brown patch, dollar spot, leaf spot, and red thread.

OTHER FERTILIZER ELEMENTS

If sufficient quantities of nitrogen, phosphorus, and potassium are supplied to turfgrasses by fertilization and other proper maintenance procedures are followed, it is usually not necessary to be concerned about levels of the remaining essential elements. Sulfur is supplied in various fertilizers and especially in lime, and turfgrasses have quite low calcium requirements in any case. Magnesium is sometimes a limiting factor for growth. However, if dolomitic lime, a mixture of calcium and magnesium carbonates, is chosen when liming is done, magnesium deficiency can be prevented. The microelements are present in fertilizers and as impurities, and the rare deficiency of these elements in turf usually results from unavailability due to pH. The micronutrient most often deficient in turf is iron, especially in soils of high pH. Iron application has been recommended for enhancing root growth, drought tolerance, and color of bentgrass and bluegrass. The color effect, especially, can be rapid, and thus iron is suggested for quick green-up.

ORGANIC FERTILIZERS

The use of natural organic wastes as fertilizers has been common practice around the world. Crop residues and animal wastes, including human wastes spread on fields as "night soil" in China and Japan, have played an important role in maintenance of soil fertility for centuries. However, when the large-scale production of chemical fertilizers began in about the 1940s, use of organic fertilizers was mostly abandoned in the United States. With the escalating cost of manufactured fertilizers and an increasing understanding of the many benefits of organic matter in soil, organic fertilizers have again become popular. Such materials as composted sewage sludge, wood products, and animal manures can be useful in this way. However, it is important to understand the dangers as well as the benefits that accompany their use.

One danger already referred to is the problem of a high carbon-to-nitrogen ratio (see Chapter 1). Some organic residues, particularly those of plant origin, have so much more carbon than nitrogen that they deplete the soil of available nitrogen during decomposition. Nitrogen fertilizer should be added if organic materials with a ratio of carbon to nitrogen wider than about 10:1 are used. Another factor to consider is the nutrient content and the rate of release of the organic materials. If nitrogen content is low or if decomposition will be slow, the material may not be of much value as a fertilizer, though it may still be a good soil amendment. It should be understood that organic compounds are never absorbed directly by plants. They must be converted to inorganic nitrates, phosphates, and similar materials before they are usable by plants. Thus whether organic or inorganic fertilizers are added to the soil, it is only in inorganic form that nutrients are available to plants. Inorganic fertilizers provide usable forms of nutrients directly; organic fertilizers provide them slowly and eventually, only after decomposition.

Some additional cautions about use of animal and human wastes are necessary. These materials can contain pathogenic bacteria, thus constituting a human health hazard. Another danger present with the use of sewage sludge is the accumulation of toxic heavy metals. Some sludges contain cadmium, nickel, lead, and similar materials toxic to plants. These metals can accumulate on soil colloids and damage the soil irreparably. Thus it is important that animal wastes be used in an environmentally safe manner. Chemical analyses of sludge are available from sewage treatment plants.

If the problems of a wide C/N ratio, low fertilizer value, and presence of pathogens or heavy metals can be avoided, addition of organic residues to the soil is a valuable practice. These materials provide at least small quantities of all the elements essential for plant growth. They also greatly improve the quality of the soil by preventing surface erosion, increasing water-holding and cation exchange capacity, and improving tilth.

FERTILIZERS AND pH

One might suppose that if all necessary fertilizer elements have been applied to a turf area, the plants will be well nourished. However, that is not always the case, mainly because of changes in soil pH.

The soil solution is complex and dynamic, constantly changing as nutrients are added and removed. In this "soup" of ever-varying inorganic and organic components, many interactions among ions and soil colloids occur. For example, when ammonium sulfate is regularly used as the source of nitrogen and sulfur, the soil pH may fall dangerously low. This acidifying of the soil solution occurs for several reasons. First, ammonium ions undergo nitrification with the release of hydrogen ions, H^+. The hydrogen ions combine with sulfur from the fertilizer, forming sulfuric acid. Acidification occurs in the same way when ammonium ions compete in cation exchange, displacing hydrogen and other cations into the soil solution, again forming sulfuric acid and further lowering pH. Leaching makes the problem worse, since the displaced basic cations are washed out of the root zone entirely and cannot compete with hydrogen in cation exchange. As the soil becomes more and more acidic, phosphorus uptake by plants is reduced, and in severe cases availability of aluminum or manganese, or both, is increased so much that these elements become toxic to plants (see Figure 1-5). Thus an already bad problem becomes worse. The pH tolerances of several grasses are shown in Table 2-5.

NUTRIENT DEFICIENCIES

Deficiencies of the essential mineral elements can be detected by the characteristic symptoms that appear on plants. These symptoms and the functions of the nutrient elements are shown in Table 2-6.

Nitrogen deficiency is by far the most common problem, resulting in a pale green to yellow turf. The purplish cast of phosphorus deficiency can be noted occasionally, most often in cold weather. However, it is easy to confuse this deficiency with the normal discoloration of turf that occurs as winter approaches. As in the case of autumn coloration of trees, chlorophyll content decreases and red leaf pigments are no longer masked by the dark green chlorophyll. If in doubt, and particularly if the lawn is a new sod or seeding, recommend that the next fertilizer application include an extra amount of phosphorus along with the nitrogen and potassium. Potassium deficiency can be recognized by the yellow streaking of the leaves. Yellowing and finally scorching occur from the leaf tips down toward the bases, with midribs usually remaining green.

Deficiencies of nutrients can occur in the plant even when high levels of the elements are present in the soil. For example, on highly alkaline soils micronutrients are

TABLE 2-5. Approximate pH Tolerances of Some Grasses on Mineral Soils. Adapted from Roy H. Follett, Larry S. Murphy, and Ray L. Donahue, *Fertilizers and Soil Amendments*, © 1981, pp. 397–399. Reprinted by permission of Prentice-Hall, Inc., Englewood Cliffs, New Jersey.

Grass Species	pH Range			
	4.0–5.5	5.5–6.5	6.5–7.5	7.5–8.5
Bermudagrass	x	x	x	
Dallisgrass		x	x	
Fescues		x		
Kentucky bluegrass			x	x
Orchardgrass		x	x	
Redtop	x	x	x	
Ryegrasses		x		
Smooth bromegrass		x		
Sudangrass		x	x	
Timothy		x	x	
Weeping lovegrass	x			

TABLE 2-6.   Some Important Nutrient Functions and Symptoms of Nutrient Deficiencies on Leaves.

Functions	Deficiences on Leaves
Macronutrients	
Nitrogen—constituent of proteins, amino acids, and chlorophyll.	Pale green to yellow, leaf tip dies first, appears on older leaves first.
Phosphorus—constituent of nucleic acids, or adenosine triphosphate (ATP), the energy carrier in all living systems. Important in seed germination, seedling growth, ripening of seeds and fruits, development of roots.	Purplish cast, especially in cool weather.
Potassium—possible role in protein and carbohydrate formation, water relations, enzyme actions, and photosynthesis. Known to play role in winter survival, drought tolerance, disease resistance, general turfgrass hardiness.	Leaves have yellow streaks; tips and margins become brown.
Calcium—important in plant structure; constituent of cell walls and middle lamella (calcium pectate), the glue that holds plant cells together (plants don't have a skeletal system).	Reddish brown between veins fading to a rose red; symptoms first appear in younger upper leaves
Magnesium—the center constituent of the chlorophyll molecule; also important in phosphorus metabolism and in several enzyme systems.	Much the same as calcium but appearing first in older lower leaves; coloring is also more banded than in calcium.
Sulfur—constituent of certain acids such as cystine and methionine; plays role in conversion of N fixed by legume root nodules into protein nitrogen. Deficiency increases powdery mildew susceptibility in Kentucky bluegrass.	Margins and tip of leaf appear "scorched" or red. Leaf sometimes appears striped yellow.
Micronutrients	
Iron—chlorophyll synthesis and important constituent of respiratory enzymes.	Yellowing between the veins with eventual loss of most chlorophyll. Easy to confuse with nitrogen deficiency, but appears first on younger leaves.
Manganese—important in enzyme systems and chlorophyll synthesis; closely related to iron. High concentration of iron reduces manganese deficiency and vice versa.	Same as iron.
Copper—component of several enzyme systems and in the synthesis of certain plant hormones.	Bluish discoloration at tips of young leaves followed by general yellowing.
Zinc—like copper.	Leaves darker, become dessicated; a white crystalline material appears on leaves of bermudagrass.
Molybdenum—cofactor in enzymes; involved in nitrate metabolism, thus affecting protein synthesis; essential for nitrogen fixation.	Mottled yellowing that occurs first in older leaves.
Boron—specific functions not well known; may play role in translocation of sugars and in water relations, affects the solubility of calcium and the metabolism of nitrogen to proteins.	Growth is impaired, leaf tips become pale green to yellow or have bronze tint.
Chlorine—function not known, possibly involved in the regulation of osmotic pressure.	No visual symptoms have been established.

changed into insoluble compounds and become unavailable for absorption by plant roots. Similarly, under drought conditions even macroelement deficiencies can develop because the flow of the soil water solution past plant roots is insufficient.

READING THE FERTILIZER LABEL

When the time comes to buy fertilizer and apply it to a turf area, your knowledge of fertilizers gained from reading will be put to the test. You will have to understand the information given on the label of the fertilizer bag.

You will first need to understand the NPK content, and it goes without saying that thinking in terms of NPK rates per acre or per 1000 sq ft will become an important part of your turf language. For example, a bag of 10-6-4 contains 10% nitrogen, 6% phosphorus, and 4% potassium. Note that N, P, and K together do not add up nearly to 100%: Most of the remainder of the weight of the bag consists of inert ingredients. Note also that the percentage of phosphorus given is actually percentage of P_2O_5 and the percentage of potassium is actually K_2O—only nitrogen is expressed in the elemental form. If the bag of 10-6-4 weighs 50 lb, you can calculate its N, P, and K content as shown here:

Calculation 1. How much N, P, and K are contained in a 50-lb bag of 10-6-4?

$$10\% \times 50 = 5 \text{ lb N}$$
$$6\% \times 50 = 3 \text{ lb P}$$
$$4\% \times 50 = 2 \text{ lb K}$$

(To multiply by a percent, first convert it to a decimal: 10% = 0.10, 6% = 0.06, 4% = 0.04)

Having found that this bag of fertilizer contains 5 lb of nitrogen, one must next determine how much area it will cover and therefore how many bags are needed for a given turf area of, for example, 10,000 sq ft. Remember that the normal spreading rate for a bluegrass lawn is 1 lb N per 1000 sq ft.

Calculation 2. How much turf area will this bag of 10-6-4 cover if applied at a rate of 1 lb N per 1000 sq ft?

$$5 \text{ lb N per bag} \div 1 \text{ lb N per 1000 sq ft} = 5$$
The 50-lb bag of 10-6-4 will cover $5 \times 1000 = 5000$ sq ft

Calculation 3. How many bags are needed for a lawn of 10,000 sq ft?

10,000 sq ft total $\div$ 5000 sq ft per bag = 2 bags

In the case of larger turf areas, the calculations should be made on an acre basis. To do this, one first needs to know that an acre contains 43,560 sq ft.

Calculation 4. How many 50-lb bags of 10-6-4 are needed to cover 1 acre of bluegrass turf?

1 acre = 43,560 sq ft
43,560 $\div$ 1000 sq ft coverage per lb = 43.5 lbs needed
43.5 lbs needed $\div$ 5 lb per bag = 8.7 bags needed

The above fertilizer, with its simple analysis of 10–6–4 and with the nitrogen from a soluble source such as ammonium nitrate or urea, is spoken of in the trade as a "farm" or "commercial" grade fertilizer. Because of their quick release of nitrogen and hence fast but short-lived green-up effect and their tendency to burn if over-applied, such fertilizers are usually avoided by many turf managers. Specialty turf fertilizers, that is, nutrient mixes that are designed specifically for turf, are preferred.

Let us examine the label on a popular specialty turf fertilizer, namely, O. M. Scott & Sons' "Super Fairway Fertilizer," in order to gain an understanding of a fertilizer analysis. The label reads as follows:

Net weight 43½ lb
Proturf Super Fairway Fertilizer 34–3–7 guaranteed analysis
Total Nitrogen (N) 34%

7% Ammoniacal nitrogen from ammoniated phosphate
28.1% Water soluble nitrogen from urea and methylene ureas
5.2% Water insoluble nitrogen from methylene ureas

Available phosphoric acid (P_2O_5) from ammoniated phosphate   3%
Soluble potash (K_2O) from potassium sulfate   7%
Sulfur as S from potassium sulfate   3%
Potential acidity equivalent to 1200 lb calcium carbonate per ton

Note that the nitrogen is from several sources, some of it from the ammoniated phosphate ($NH_4H_2PO_4$) used to supply phosphorus. The nitrogen from urea is water soluble and hence a fast-release type, whereas methylene urea, which requires some microbial decomposition for its breakdown, provides some slow release, water-insoluble nitrogen (WIN). Thus the fertilizer combines fast- and slow-release nitrogen sources. This fertilizer is relatively low in phosphorus, thus it is suitable for established turf but would not be the recommended formulation for a new seeding. It contains 7% potassium from potassium sulfate, which also provides 3% sulfur.

Since the fertilizer contains potassium sulfate, it will be acidic in reaction (the sulfate will combine in the soil with hydrogen, forming sulfuric acid). The label indicates that the acidity is equal to about 1200 lb of calcium carbonate per ton of fertilizer. Thus you will need to determine the amount of lime required to counteract the acidifying effect on a given turf area. One method of performing these calculations is given below:

Calculation 5.   What is the potential acidity equivalent of this bag of fertilizer?

1 ton = 2000 lb and requires 1200 lb lime
Bag weight = 43.5 lb
2000 ÷ 43.5 = 46 bags per ton
1200 ÷ 46 = 26.1 lb lime per bag required

Calculation 6.   How much turf area will this bag cover?

43.5 lb × 34% N = 14.79 lb N
14.79 lb N ÷ 1 lb N per 1000 sq ft = 14.79
The bag will cover 14.79 × 1000 = 14,790 sq ft

Calculation 7.   How much lime is required per 1000 sq ft to counteract the acidifying effect of this fertilizer?

26.6 lb lime required per bag
Bag covers 14,790 sq ft
14,790 ÷ 1000 sq ft = 14.79
26.6 lb ÷ 14.79 = 1.8 lb lime per 1000 sq ft

According to the calculations, then, the application of 1.8 lb lime per 1000 sq ft of turf area would neutralize the applied fertilizer. Note that this is not a great quantity of lime (normal spreading rate for lime is 50 lb per 1000 sq ft to raise the pH $1/2$ point). Note also, however, that Scotts recommends that this bag be used to cover only 11,000 sq ft of turf area. This means that at their recommended spreading rate (setting K on a Scotts rotary spreader at 3 mph) each 1000 sq ft of turf is receiving 1.34 lb of N (14.79 ÷ 11).

READING THE RESULTS OF A SOIL TEST

The best way to get an accurate determination of the fertility of a particular soil is to dig up a small amount and send it to a laboratory for analysis. When you send off a soil sample to be tested (for example, to the Ohio State Soil Testing Laboratory), the results will be returned to you in the manner indicated in Figure 2-5.

Soil pH.   As indicated in Chapter 1, the soil pH is a measure of the hydrogen ion concentration of the soil solution and hence its acidity or alkalinity. Turfgrasses grow best in the range of pH 5 to 7. It takes approximately 50 lb of lime per 1000 sq ft to raise the pH $1/2$ point and 10 to 20 lb of sulfur to lower the pH $1/2$ point.

Lime test index.   The amount of lime that a soil requires is sometimes given in another way, the lime test index. This is a measure of both the soluble (active) and exchangeable hydrogen in the soil—that is, the total potential acidity, rather than just the pH of the soil solution (active acidity). As a result, the lime test index is a more accurate measure of the soil acidity. If the soil pH is greater than 6.5, the lime test index is not calculated, because applications of lime are not usually needed for most crops. The highest number given would be 70 (neutral).

In our example the lime test index is 67, and from looking at prepared tables, the soil analyst will recommend a quantity of lime—in this case 1.5 tons per acre (T/A).

Phosphorus (P).   Best results are obtained when the phosphorus level ranges from 30 to 130 lb per acre. Phosphorus does not leach readily from the soil and normally is not lost unless erosion occurs. In the example shown, the reading of 7 lb per acre is very low, and the recommendation will be given to apply phosphorus at the rate of 230 lb per acre.

Green Grass Sod Farm
Columbus, Ohio 43210
COUNTY Franklin

RECEIVED SAMPLE 5/3/86   DATE PRINTED 5/10/86   PLAN

SAMPLE INFORMATION

PLOW DEPTH INCHES	LIME APPLIED IN LAST 2 YRS. T/A
8	1.0

STANDARD TEST RESULTS

pH	LIME TEST INDEX	PHOSPHORUS P lb/A	POTASSIUM K lb/A	CALCIUM Ca lb/A	MAGNESIUM Mg lb/A	CATION EXCHANGE CAPACITY
5.7	67	7	143	1870	252	10

BASE SATURATION

% Ca	% Mg	% K
49	11	1.9

SPECIAL TESTS RESULTS

MANGANESE Mn lb/A	IRON Fe lb/A	ZINC Zn lb/A	COPPER Cu lb/A	BORON B lb/A	NITRATES NO_3-N lb/A	ORGANIC MATTER %	SOLUBLE SALTS Mhos $\times 10^5$
	180	72	45	22		10	

GROWER COPY

Figure 2-5 The results of a typical soil test.

Potassium (K).   This should range between 200 and 400 lb per acre. The test result is again low, and depending on the crop to be grown, the analyst will recommend that potash be applied.

Calcium (Ca).   This nutrient has a very wide range of acceptable levels, from 800 to 2000 lb per acre.

Magnesium (Mg).   For most plants this should range from 150 to 2000 lb per acre.

Cation exchange capacity (CEC).   As indicated in Chapter 1, this is a measure (in milliequivalents per 100 g) of a soil's capacity to hold exchangeable cations such as H^+, Ca^{2+}, Mg^{2+}, and K^+. The reading depends in great part on the kinds and the amounts of clay, silt, sand, and organic matter in the soil being tested. CEC values generally range from 4 to 10 for sandy soils, 10 to 25 for silt loams, 25 to 50 for clays, and greater than 50 for organic soils. The values are relatively fixed for specific soils, changing only over long intervals of 25 years or more unless there is extensive erosion or heavy incorporation of organic matter. In soils under turf the CEC improves slowly by the continual accumulation of organic matter from decaying and dying grass roots, stems, and leaves.

Percent base saturation.   This is simply a measure of the percentage of each exchangeable cation (base) present in the soil. That is, it is the amount of space out of the total available for exchange that each cation occupies. In the soil test example in Figure 2-5, calcium occupies 49% of the space, over four times as much as magnesium. Potassium occupies only 1.9% of the space. The optimum ranges for some cations are indicated in Table 2-7. Boron, sulfur, and much of the soil reserve of nitrogen are held on the organic soil particles and hence are not tested.

Generally, the nutrients in the soil should be balanced. Although most plants grow well over a wide range of ratios, if the levels of calcium becomes 10 times greater than those for magnesium, one is usually advised to add magnesium (in the form of high magnesium-low calcium limestone—that is, a dolomitic limestone). If the amount of calcium drops to less than the amount of magnesium, then one is advised to

TABLE 2-7.   Percent Base Saturation Which Is Optimum for Plant Growth.

Cation	Percent Base Saturation
Calcium (Ca^{2+})	60–70
Magnesium (Mg^{2+})	12–20
Hydrogen (H^+)	10–15
Potassium (K^+)	2–5
Iron (Fe^{2+})	2–4
Manganese (Mn^{2+})	2–4
Copper (Cu^{2+})	2–4
Zinc (Zn^{2+})	2–4
Sodium (Na^+)	2–4

TABLE 2-8. The Minimum Amounts of Micronutrients Necessary for Optimum Growth of Plants and the Amounts Reported from Various Soils (lb per acre).

Element	Amount Needed for Growth (Lb/A)	Amount Reported in Soils (Lb/A)
Manganese (Mn)	20–40	100–10,000
Iron (Fe)	15–40	10,000–200,000
Copper (Cu)	0.5	20–400
Boron (B)	0.5	20–200
Molybdenum (Mo)	0.5	1–7

consider adding calcium (usually in the form of a low magnesium–high calcium limestone). The ratio of magnesium to potassium is also important and should be greater than 2:1. High amounts of potassium will reduce the uptake of magnesium, and the soil should be adjusted accordingly.

Available trace elements. Although the total soil content of micronutrients does not necessarily indicate the amounts available for plant growth during a single season, it does give a broad approximation of the abundance of a particular nutrient and the potential for a soil to supply it. Table 2-8 shows the amounts of trace elements necessary for good plant growth and indicates the range of amounts found in soils.

Nitrates. Nitrate (NO_3) is the form of nitrogen most readily used by turfgrasses and other plants. Nitrate nitrogen, however, has a negative charge and hence is not readily held by the particles of clay or organic matter in the soil, which also have negative charges. Nitrate is highly soluble in the soil solution and easily leached. As a result, special precautions have to be taken to get an accurate soil test. A moderate nitrate level in the soil is considered to be 20 to 40 lb per acre, whereas 80 lb or more is characteristic of a highly fertile soil.

Percent organic matter. Mineral soils typically contain from 1% to 10% organic matter, expressed as percent by weight. The higher the percentage, the more fertile the soil. Organic soils such as those in Michigan may contain over 90% organic matter. The nitrogen content of organic matter is usually about 5%.

Soluble salts. The problem of a too-high soluble salt content in the soil solution arises when an area is overfertilized or when there has been a fertilizer spill. When soluble salt readings rise above 200, turfgrasses will begin to discolor and suffer injury. If you should accidentally spill fertilizer on a turf area, clean up as much as possible, try to spread the rest out with a rake or broom, and water the area thoroughly. If a homeowner should discolor his lawn with an over-application of fertilizer, tell him to water heavily for several days. If the over-application has not been too heavy, the grass will survive.

3

Grasses

THE MEEK THAT INHERIT THE EARTH

The grass family, or Gramineae, is the third largest family of flowering plants. It consists of over 500 genera and 8000 species, and only the sunflower family (Compositae) and the orchid family (Orchidaceae) are larger. If we consider the usefulness of grasses as well as their worldwide geographic extent, they are surely the most important group of plants on earth. They cover about one fourth of the world's land area, stabilizing vast areas against soil erosion; they serve as essential habitats for wildlife; and they constitute the main pasture forage for the world's cattle. Just eight of them (wheat, rice, corn, barley, oats, rye, sorghum, and millet), known as cereals, provide 50% of the protein consumed by humans. In many tropical countries bamboos, which are among the largest of grasses, provide food and shelter and literally hundreds of other useful products.

The major grasses used for turf number only a handful—barely a dozen genera. Yet these cover large acreages, serving useful and aesthetic functions. On playing fields and golf courses they provide a base for recreational activities. They lend beauty to our home lawns and parks, thus contributing to our emotional and physical well-being. If the value of turfgrasses can be judged by the time, effort, and money spent on them, it is evident that these small plants are an exceedingly important part of our environment. They have been called "the meek that inherit the earth."

Grasses are so important to us and have such a distinctive structure that they have come to form the subject of a special science called *agrostology*. One who specializes in the identification and classification of grasses is an agrostologist. The Smithsonian Institution in Washington, D.C., houses the U.S. National Herbarium, where a large collection of dried grass specimens is maintained and where much of this research is conducted.

WHAT MAKES A TURFGRASS?

The paucity of turfgrasses in such a giant family as the Gramineae is due largely to the stringent requirements a grass must meet in order to be useful as a turfgrass. These requirements greatly limit the number of grasses that would be suitable for turf areas. Though wheat and corn are grasses, they would never do.

Most turfgrasses have several features in common: the ability to grow under the stress of a dense population; a relative tolerance to wear and tear and to frequent mowing; a reasonable degree of resistance to insects, diseases, and extremes of temperature; a low growth habit; and the ability to close over a bare area quickly and to knit tightly, especially after being torn (as in the case of a golf divot). Most turfgrasses produce *rhizomes* (underground stems) or *stolons* (lateral stems that grow across the soil surface), or both, which are important in knitting the plants into a tight sod.

There may be species of grasses suitable for turf culture that are as yet undiscovered, unselected, or undeveloped by plant breeders. By and large, breeding and development is currently limited to just a few species, from which useful varieties are selected or bred. Outstanding contributions to grass breeding have been made by Dr. Glenn W. Burton with bermudagrasses at the USDA Agricultural Research Service laboratories at Tifton, Georgia, and by Dr. Reed Funk with bluegrasses at Rutgers University.

PLANT NAMES

Before we look at the general and specific characteristics of turfgrasses, it is important to understand how they are named and classified. Since the great Swedish botanist Carolus Linnaeus established rules for naming plants in his book *Species Plantarum* in 1753, every plant has been designated by two names. The names are in Latin and recognized the world over, so that the confusion of common names in different regions and in various languages can be avoided. In this *binomial system* of nomenclature each plant has a *genus* and a *species* name and is followed by the name, usually abbreviated, of the person (or persons) who described it (the *author citation*). The genus name is written first, capitalized and underlined; it can be used alone. The species name is underlined also but uncapitalized. Thus *Poa* is the genus of the bluegrasses. *Poa pratensis* L. is Kentucky bluegrass, and *Poa annua* L. is annual bluegrass. Both species were named by Linnaeus himself. Note that Latin names are often informative, telling us something about the plant. Thus *pratensis* means growing in meadows, and *annua* means annual.

A species, then, consists of a group of individuals that closely resemble each other. The similarity extends to reproductive features and processes, so that members of a species are capable of interbreeding with each other. The members of a genus (such as all of the bluegrasses, for example) resemble each other less closely though still share a number of characteristics. They are, however, not normally capable of interbreeding. In the classification of plants, different genera are grouped into *families* (family names are distinguished by ending in -*aceae* or -*ae*), families are grouped into *orders*, orders into *classes*, and classes into *divisions*. All of these ranks are different for a simple moss, a pine tree, and a grass, but all three organisms belong to the great Kingdom Plantae.

In some species all members are not quite the same, but distinct groups of individuals or populations can be identified. This is frequently true of cultivated plants, in which small but highly desirable differences have often been noted and selected for. Such plants are referred to as cultivated varieties, or *cultivars*. Thus Merion, Fylking, and Park are all cultivars of Kentucky bluegrass.

GRASS CLASSIFICATION

Grasses are classified in the Division Anthophyta, or *flowering plants*. These plants reproduce by means of flowers, fruits, and seeds rather than by the simple spores characteristic of the more primitive bacteria, algae, fungi, mosses, and ferns. The flowering plants are divided into two classes, the dicotyledons and the *monocotyledons*. Grasses belong to the latter group because they possess the following distinctive characteristics:

First, when a grass seed germinates, only one "seed leaf," or *cotyledon* develops—hence the name, monocot. (Dicots have two cotyledons.) This leaf functions in photosynthesis until the true foliage leaves develop slightly later. The cotyledons of monocots and dicots are shown in Figure 3-1.

Second, monocot leaves are usually long and slender, with parallel veins running the length of the leaves. (Dicot leaves have broad nets of veins.) The veins consist of tissues that conduct water, dissolved minerals, foods, hormones, and other important substances in the plant. Monocot and dicot leaves are shown in Figure 3-2.

Third, if one cuts across the stem of a monocot and places a thin section under a microscope, it can be seen that the *vascular bundles*, or strands of conducting tissue, are either scattered throughout the stem or arranged in concentric circles. (The conducting tissue in dicot stems is usually arranged in a single ring.) Stem cross sections of monocots and dicots are shown in Figure 3-3.

Panicoid vs. Festucoid Grasses

Although many agrostologists recognize six groups, or subfamilies, of grasses, most turfgrasses belong to either the *festucoid* or the *panicoid* subfamily. Bluegrasses, bentgrasses, ryegrasses, and fescues are all festucoid grasses, whereas bahiagrass, centipedegrass, St. Augustinegrass, bermudagrass, and zoysiagrass are panicoid or related grasses (with the last two actually classified in the closely related eragrostoid subfamily).

CORN, A MONOCOT   BEAN, A DICOT

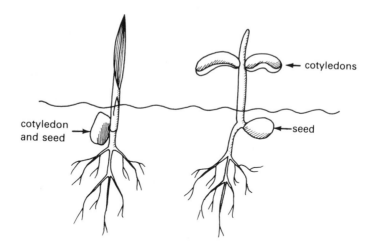

Figure 3-1   Germination of a monocot seed (*left*) and a dicot seed (*right*). The single cotyledon of the monocot remains in the seed below ground, whereas the two cotyledons of the dicot are elevated on the stem above ground.

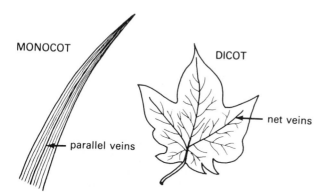

Figure 3-2   A typical monocot leaf with parallel veins (*left*) and a typical dicot leaf with net venation (*right*).

The festucoid and panicoid subfamilies are distinguishable in a number of ways. Most obvious, perhaps, is the geographical distribution of these grasses. As shown in Figure 3-4, festucoid grasses are all northern or temperate, whereas panicoid grasses are southern and tropical. The region where cool-season or temperate grasses grade into or coexist with warm-season or tropical grasses is known as the *transition zone*. A few panicoid grasses have migrated north past even the transition zone, where in the

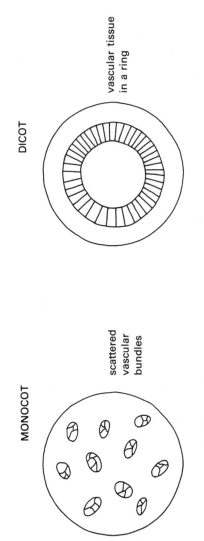

Figure 3-3   Cross-sectional views of monocot (*left*) and dicot (*right*) stems, showing the arrangement of conducting tissue.

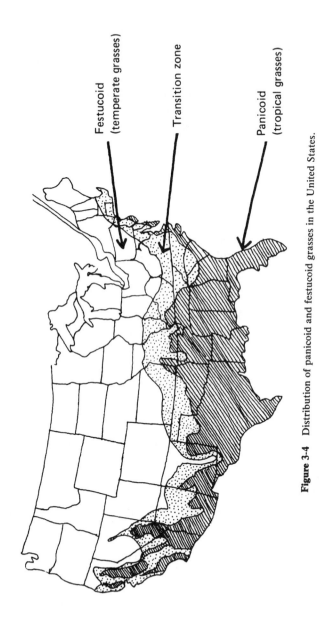

Festucoid (temperate grasses)

Transition zone

Panicoid (tropical grasses)

Figure 3-4 Distribution of panicoid and festucoid grasses in the United States.

summer they live as annuals. One of the more troublesome monocot weeds in northern turf, namely crabgrass, is included in this group.

It has recently been realized that the difference in geographical distribution between panicoid and festucoid grasses is correlated with physiological differences. Panicoid grasses are typically C_4 plants, whereas festucoid grasses are C_3 plants. These designations refer to the number of carbon atoms in the compound that is the first product of the photosynthesis reaction. However, the significant difference is the fact that the panicoid C_4 grasses are much more efficient in making, translocating, and assimilating food materials under high temperature and light conditions. Thus panicoid grasses are physiologically adapted to subtropical and tropical climates in which festucoid species would fail to thrive. Some of them, like crabgrass, are bad weeds in northern turf in midsummer, when they have a competitive advantage over the cool-season turfgrasses.

THE GRASS PLANT

Grasses have several unusual and distinctive modifications that distinguish them from other plants. These can be noted in Figure 3-5, which shows a typical grass plant.

The stem.   The most widely used turfgrasses develop both horizontal and upright stems. The erect stem of a grass is referred to as the *culm*. The prostrate stems are either *stolons,* which grow along the soil surface, or *rhizomes,* which grow underground. The development of stolons and rhizomes is important in obtaining a dense turf and in overgrowth of bare spots. The creeping bentgrasses, red fescues, bluegrasses, bermudagrasses, zoysias, St. Augustines, centipedegrasses, and carpetgrasses all reproduce by stolons or rhizomes, often more effectively than by seed. The panicoid grasses, in fact, are often so aggressive vegetatively that they are planted by plugs or runners, a cheaper method than use of seed.

Significant in the same way as stolons and rhizomes are the *tillers:* They are shoots that form from buds at the leaf bases and develop into new rooted plantlets. Grasses that lack rhizomes and stolons and spread vegetatively only by tillers are called *bunchgrasses* because of their tufted growth habit. Tillers form at the *crown* of the plant, the area where the shoot and root systems join. The point on a stem where a leaf originates is called a *node,* and the portion of stem between two adjacent nodes is an *internode.*

The leaf.   A grass leaf is divided into two parts: The *sheath* tightly encloses the stem of the plant, and the *blade* projects out at an angle. Both parts are green and photosynthetic. The area where they join, often lighter green in color, is called the *collar.* A small flap of tissue called the *ligule* is frequently found on the inner surface of the leaf at the junction of sheath and blade. It can take many shapes, but in panicoid grasses the ligule is often a row of hairs; in the festucoid grasses it is usually membranous. Some grasses have extensions at the base of the blade that project around the

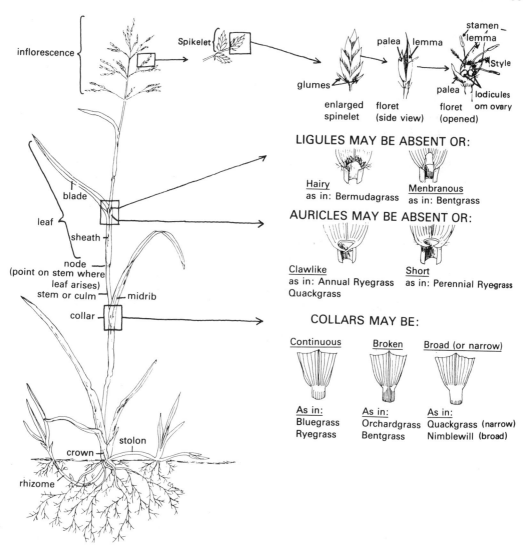

Figure 3-5 The grass plant.

stem. These ear-like protrusions are called, appropriately, *auricles*. Like ligules, they vary enough in form to be useful in the identification of grasses.

The flower and inflorescence. Like other flowering plants, grasses have distinct *flowers*. But because these are much less showy and brightly colored than most flowers, they are overlooked by most people. (Furthermore, in most turf areas they are eliminated by constant mowing.) A typical flower consists of green *sepals*, bright and showy *petals,* pollen-producing *stamens,* and a *pistil* containing ovules. The pistil at maturity develops into a *fruit* containing *seeds.*

Grass flowers are modified from this general plan in several ways, which appear to be adaptations to *wind pollination.* Insects are the vectors that carry pollen from one flower to another in most of the flowering plants, but in grasses and some other plants pollen is borne by air currents. Several adaptations for wind pollination can be noted in the flowers, shown in Figure 3-5. Each flower, called a *floret,* contains three stamens with long *anthers,* which hang out of the flower and shed pollen at maturity. The pistil consists of an *ovary* containing *ovules* with eggs, two hollow *styles,* and feathery *stigmas,* which filter pollen from other flowers out of the air. At the base of the flower are found two *lodicules,* which may represent highly reduced *petals* or *sepals.*

The floret is partially enclosed at its base by two small *bracts,* or modified leaves, called the *lemma* and the *palea.* Florets do not occur singly but are grouped in *spikelets.* The spikelets, similarly provided with two basal bracts called *glumes,* are grouped into a large flower cluster known as the *inflorescence.* There are three principal types of inflorescences in grasses: In a *raceme* the spikelets arise individually from the main axis of the inflorescence on small stalks, in a *spike* the stalks are lacking, and in a *panicle* the inflorescence is compound and branched. These three types of inflorescences are shown in Figure 3-6.

A Lab Exercise

If it is possible for you to do so now, take a break from your reading and do a small practical exercise. Take a trowel or spade, go outdoors, and dig up a sample of soil and grass. Pick the sample apart and look for each of the structures listed below. (Some items in the list may not be present in your sample.) Look at the parts of each

GRASS INFLORESCENCES

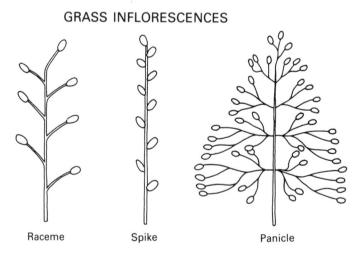

Raceme   Spike   Panicle

Figure 3-6 Three common types of grass inflorescences—the raceme (*left*), the spike (*center*), and the panicle (*right*).

structure, preferably with a magnifying glass or hand lens. Check off each item as you finish it. Refer to Figure 3-5 if necessary.

____crown	____leaf blade
____culm	____leaf sheath
____node	____collar
____tiller	____ligule
____rhizome	____auricle
____stolon	____inflorescence

Grasses vs. Sedges

Grasses, with their unique structure, are not difficult to distinguish from other monocots if one looks closely and carefully. However, there are two closely related families of monocots that are often mistaken for grasses by the amateur. The rushes (family Juncaceae) are small, sometimes wiry plants that somewhat resemble grasses. However, they have flowers that, although quite small and often greenish or brownish, contain all of the usual parts, namely sepals, petals, stamens, and pistil. Rushes are not commonly found in cultivated turf areas.

Sedges belong to the family Cyperaceae. These are frequently encountered as weeds in turf, especially in wet areas, where nutsedge can be a persistent nuisance. The most obvious distinction between grasses and these weedy sedges is that grasses usually have round stems and open leaf sheaths, whereas sedges have triangular stems and closed leaf sheaths, as shown in Figure 3-7. In addition, most grasses have a culm that is hollow between the nodes (most sedges have solid stems), and grasses have their leaves arranged in two rows (two-ranked) along the culm (sedges have three-ranked leaves). However, the principal distinction between grasses and other plants lies in the fruit. The pistil matures into a fruit called a *grain,* or *caryopsis,* a one-seeded fruit in which the seed inside is closely attached to the fruit wall. This small structure is usually called the grass "seed"; however, such terminology is botanically incorrect, since it is actually a whole fruit containing a seed.

GRASS GROWTH

Like other plants, grasses produce most of their growth in distinct regions called growing points, or *meristems.* These are patches of almost continuously dividing cells responsible for production of new stems, leaves, flowers, and roots. In most plants the principal meristems are located at the tips of all roots and stems, including branches (hence they are called *apical meristems*). Some meristematic activity can also occur in stem internodes and in leaves. However, grasses have pronounced and highly active meristems in the bases of the internodes and of the leaf sheaths. These are called *intercalary meristems* because they are interposed between adjacent areas of mature cells relatively inactive in division.

The practical significance of these intercalary meristems in the growth of turfgrasses should be immediately apparent: Turfgrasses can survive mowing, since re-

GRASSES VS. SEDGES

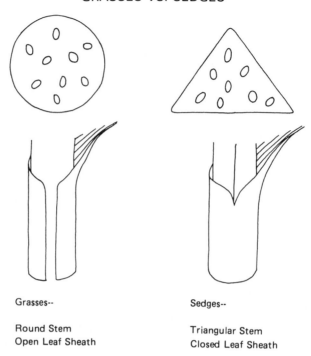

Grasses--

Round Stem
Open Leaf Sheath

Sedges--

Triangular Stem
Closed Leaf Sheath

Figure 3-7 Differences between grasses and sedges, showing the round stem and open leaf sheath typical of a grass (*left*) and the triangular stem and closed leaf sheath typical of a sedge (*right*).

growth can occur from the remaining stem and leaf bases. Other plants, which depend primarily on apical meristems for growth, would not regenerate stem and leaf tissues if the tips were removed. Of course, even grasses can be killed by mowing too closely (see Chapter 8); their tolerance to close mowing depends at least partly on the location of meristems.

Other growing points in a grass plant are found in the *buds* located at the nodes. Buds are of even greater significance in turf than are the basal intercalary meristems, since most of the growth and regrowth after mowing in a vigorous turf is due to development of dormant buds into tillers, culms, rhizomes, and stolons. In turfgrass species internodes tend to be short, which places many nodes close to the ground. Once again, turfgrasses can be mowed relatively closely without damage to buds.

We can see that grasses are special plants; their unusual structure makes them uniquely suited to their use in turf. With their many kinds and locations of growing points they can survive mowing and hard wear. If one type of growing point is destroyed, they can regrow from another. In the contest for survival that occurs in a turf area, grasses clearly have a competitive advantage over most other plants. If they are well managed, turfgrasses provide a dense green cover.

Apical Dominance

One botanical discovery that has had widespread practical application is the elucidation of the phenomenon known as *apical dominance.* It has long been observed that the apex, or shoot tip, of a plant "dominates" the regions lower down by suppressing branching. As long as the apex, with its apical meristem, is present on a stem, buds lower down on the branch remain dormant. (The degree of dominance varies from complete to, more typically, partial dominance, depending on the species.) However, as every nurseryman knows when pruning a shrub, when stem tips are cut off, the remaining buds come out of dormancy and grow into branches. Thus shearing of the tips of pines results in the bushy appearance desirable in Christmas trees.

It is now known that the biochemical basis of apical dominance resides in a plant growth hormone called *auxin* (indoleacetic acid). Auxin is synthesized in apical meristems and then moves down the stem in quantities great enough to inhibit development of buds. When a shoot tip is removed, the source of auxin is removed; buds are no longer inhibited, and they develop into branches.

Turfgrasses respond in much the same way as do Christmas trees, as shown in Figure 3-8. When some of the meristems are cut off by mowing, apical dominance is removed and buds remaining at the lower nodes are stimulated to develop into tillers, stolons, and rhizomes—the whole arsenal of grass-growing structures. As a result, the turf becomes more dense. Apical dominance is an important consideration in new seedings: They should be mowed as soon as possible so that the plants will spread and close in quickly. The mowing will encourage the production of stolons, rhizomes, till-

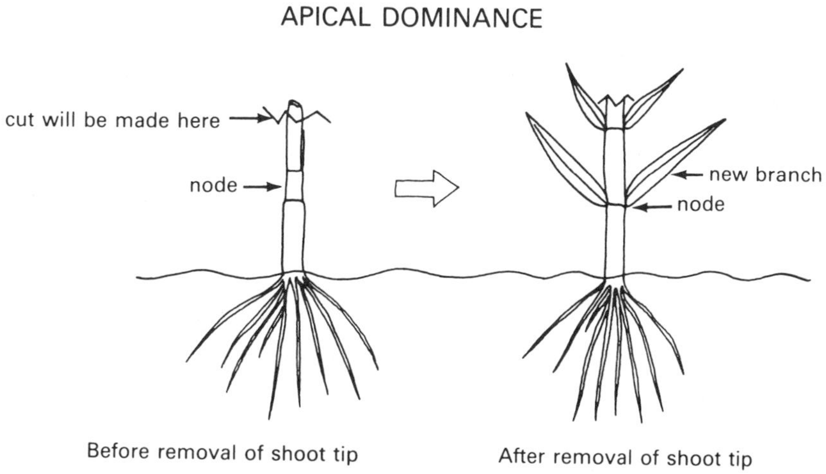

APICAL DOMINANCE

Before removal of shoot tip   After removal of shoot tip

Figure 3-8 Branching of a plant after its tip is removed. The shoot tip is cut off of the plant on the left. Branches then develop at the nodes, as shown in the plant on the right.

ers, and probably even roots. Thus an apparent paradox occurs in turf management: We cut off the plant and remove tissue in order to stimulate more growth and tissue development.

Apomixis

Turf areas are generally mowed so frequently that the grass plants never flower or produce seed. Thus the management of an established turf normally involves manipulating a plant that remains vegetative only. However, when establishing a new turf area, we do use seed, and it is important to understand some of the basic facts about seeds and their development.

The development of new grass plants from tillers or related structures is referred to as *vegetative reproduction,* because only vegetative parts are involved. This process is responsible for much of the spreading in a turf area, as well as for establishment of bentgrasses, bermudagrasses, and zoysiagrasses by plugging. Other crop plants, such as strawberries, and many house plants are most commonly propagated vegetatively as well. One of the important characteristics of vegetative propagation, or *cloning,* is that the new offspring are exactly identical to the parent organism. No variation occurs among them because all carry the same *genes,* or heredity factors. In every case the new organism developed from a group of cells of the parent.

The situation is the opposite, however, when *sexual reproduction* occurs. There, as in the case of humans, two parents are involved. The new organism develops by a combination of sex cells from both parents. The great difference between vegetative and sexual reproduction, then, is that the latter promotes variation. No two sexually produced individuals look exactly the same because of the shuffling and combining of different genes that occurs at their conception. Sex is the great mixer!

In grasses, we expect plants produced from stolons, rhizomes, and tillers to be uniform, whereas plants grown from seed will exhibit small differences in form, disease resistance, and other characteristics. One seed-produced turf species, however, does not conform to our expectation. Bluegrasses are unusual because they are able to produce seed without true sexual reproduction. The process is called *apomixis* (*apo,* without; *mixis,* mingling). Viable seeds containing embryos are formed even though fertilization has failed. (The embryo forms abnormally from some cell other than the fertilized egg.) Thus apomictic bluegrasses develop from seed but lack the variability of sexual species. If the plant is completely apomictic, the offspring are genetically uniform.

Needless to say, such a feature has had a widespread impact on the development of new bluegrass varieties. Unlike bermudagrass, bluegrass does not reproduce actively by stolons, hence seed has traditionally been the easiest and most economical method of propagation. If a superior strain of bluegrass is identified, the seed arising from it will give rise to plants identical to the superior parent or clone. Sex does not intervene to produce variation or to dilute the superior qualities. These desirable characteristics are exactly reproduced by seed over and over again: The process of apomixis "locks" them in.

Although the apomictic development of bluegrass seed is a great aid to the grass breeder and seed producer, there can be some problems with its use. The genetically uniform turf is known as a *monoculture*. All the plants will react in exactly the same manner to their environment. As long as no cultural problems arise, the turf may be of excellent quality. However, let us suppose that a fungal disease develops, to which the particular grass variety is susceptible. Since all the plants are identical, having arisen from seeds that were alike, they may well all be infected by the fungus and the entire turf area will be wiped out. There will be no partial resistance, no variant plants that are not susceptible, as there would be in a genetically variable line. Thus the turf manager has to question the establishment of turf from pure apomictic seed. A strong argument can be made for the use of seed blends or mixtures of different types (apomictic types can be included), rather than reliance on one so-called superior biotype.

KNOW THE GRASSES

The following sections are devoted to descriptions of selected turfgrasses that are important to and widely used in the turf industry. Overviews, or synopses, of some important cool-season and warm-season grasses, with their distinguishing characteristics, are presented in Figures 3-9 and 3-10. Get to know the names of those grasses prominent in your state by attending the field days and other meetings held by your state university or research center. Turfgrasses are tested in plots all over the country, and chances are great that some test plots are located near you. If in doubt, contact your county agricultural extension agent, who is listed in your telephone book.

You should acquire all the pamphlets and bulletins on turf issued by your state university or state agricultural experiment station. These centers have the technical knowledge and resources to identify those grass cultivars that will perform best in your specific locality. Your taxes are paying for this excellent service—take advantage of it.

Grass Cultivars

After the description of the turfgrass species, for example Kentucky bluegrass, you will see a listing of cultivars. A *cultivar* is a cultivated variety, a selection or hybrid for which seed or sprigging material is available commercially. Cultivars are thought to be superior in one way or another, hence they are often referred to as "premium" turfgrasses. Often the difference between cultivars, or premium grasses, is small or subtle and manifested physiologically rather than physically. This means that when you see two different cultivars side by side you may well not be able to tell them apart; but if they are subjected to stress—leaf spot disease or shade, for example—one grass may survive and flourish while the other weakens and declines. They may look physically alike initially, but their reaction to stress is quite different.

To complicate matters further, some cultivars react differently in different geographical areas. For example, the bluegrass cultivar Vantage is noted for its resistance to *Fusarium* blight in the mid-Atlantic states, whereas in California the grass is badly damaged by the same blight. The explanation for this different response in the West is not known, but it could be due to differences in weather or in races of the disease organism present, among other things. Thus it is important to remember that claims made on behalf of any new super cultivar, especially relating to disease resistance,

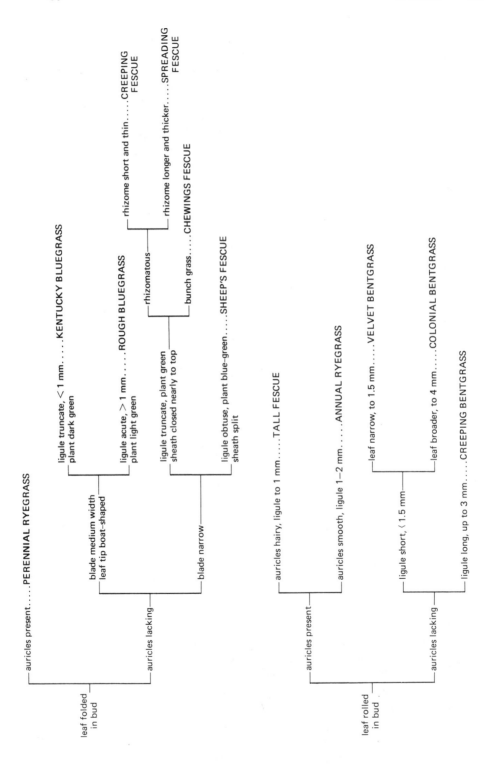

Figure 3-9   A synopsis of cool-season turfgrasses.

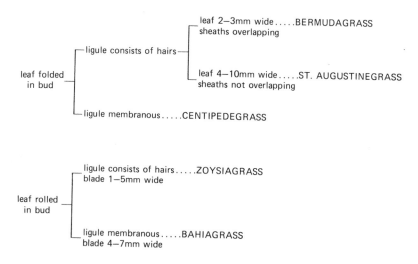

Figure 3-10   A synopsis of warm-season turfgrasses.

should always be regarded with caution. The best solution to choosing good cultivars for your area is to check state research plots at least yearly to see which cultivars are performing best under your exact environmental conditions.

Blends vs. Mixes

When speaking of seed, turf workers make a distinction between a blend and a mix. A *blend* consists of the seeds from two or more cultivars, whereas a *mixture* consists of the seeds of two or more species. Thus Glade, Nuggett, and Ram I together constitute a blend because they are all varieties of bluegrass, but Glade, Nugget (bluegrasses), Pennfine (a ryegrass), and Ruby (a fine fescue) make a mixture. Varieties of grasses are blended; different species are mixed.

Turfgrass Persistence in Mixes

A *monoculture* or monostand of a turfgrass consists of just one type of grass, whereas a *polyculture* or polystand is comprised of two or more cultivars or species. By and large stoloniferous grasses such as bentgrass, bermudagrass, and most other warm-season grasses are grown in monostands because of their aggressiveness. On the other hand, the majority of seeded grasses, such as bluegrass and most other cool-season grasses, are grown as polystands, since the seed is easy to blend or mix.

When a polyculture is subject to environmental pressures, one would expect a different response from each grass present. This in fact is what happens, and frequently the composition of the original blend or mix is changed. A knowledge of the changes likely to occur in a given turf over time can be very useful to a turf manager. In Table 3-1 are indicated some examples of changes in the composition of turf grown under various stressful conditions.

TABLE 3-1.   Changes in Composition of Turfgrass Mixtures When Grown under Various
Environmental Conditions.

An Original Mixture Consisting of These Grasses:	Grown Under These Conditions:	Eventually Results in this Grass Becoming Dominant:
Bermudagrass + St. Augustinegrass	Shade	St. Augustinegrass
Bermudagrass + St. Augustinegrass	Mowing at less than 1 in.	Bermudagrass
Bermudagrass + Centipedegrass	Shade	Centipedegrass
Centipedegrass + Zoysiagrass	Excessive wear	Zoysiagrass
Fine fescue + Kentucky bluegrass	Shade	Fine fescue
Fine fescue + Kentucky bluegrass	High nitrogen levels	Bluegrass
Kentucky bluegrass + Tall fescue	Mowing at less than 1½ in.	Bluegrass

Kentucky Bluegrass *Poa pratensis* L. (Figure 3-11)

This great grass was introduced from Europe some time during the colonial period. Romantics have it that Daniel Boone carried it across the Alleghenies into Kentucky, where the grass found a natural home on the limestone soils. Whether this story is true or not, the lush pastures rich in bone-building calcium make the bluegrass region of Kentucky an environment prized by horsemen.

Bluegrass is a long-lived perennial grass, a cool-season species that grows best when the temperature is between 60 and 75°F and the precipitation is between 20 and 50 in. per year. It spreads by tillers and rhizomes and produces an extremely dense sod with roots penetrating as deep as 1½ ft. These characteristics make it the premier lawn grass in the North, and though it is found in most states, it thrives particularly on fertile northern soils of limestone origin. Bluegrass is able to withstand hot, dry periods, usually going into dormancy and losing its green color, but it recovers when adequate water is supplied. It is not as well adapted to the sandy coastal plains as are fescues and zoysiagrass. In warmer climates bluegrass tends to prefer the shade; in cooler climates, the full sun.

The most effective time to fertilize is from September through the late fall, since tiller production and root growth are stimulated by the shorter days and cooler temperatures then. There is less leaf elongation in the fall, hence less mowing per pound of nitrogen applied. In comparison to spring application of nitrogen, fall fertilization is less likely to stimulate lush growth that is subject to disease and stress, and fall application yields greater turf density, winter color, and spring green-up. However, overfertilization in late fall should be avoided because the grass may fail to harden off before winter and the turf may be easily damaged.

Seed of common Kentucky bluegrass develops mostly (about 95%) by apomixis. Since it germinates slowly, seed of other faster-sprouting grasses is often mixed in with bluegrass. Bluegrass seed is harvested from fields in Kentucky, Missouri, and Kansas northward to Canada. Some is also imported into the United States from northern Europe, especially Denmark and Holland. Most seed of premium cultivars is grown and harvested in the Northwest. These superior varieties have been developed principally by simple selection, but several outstanding bluegrass strains have been produced through hybridization.

BLUEGRASS

- Short leaves with boat or keel shaped tips
- Rhizomes

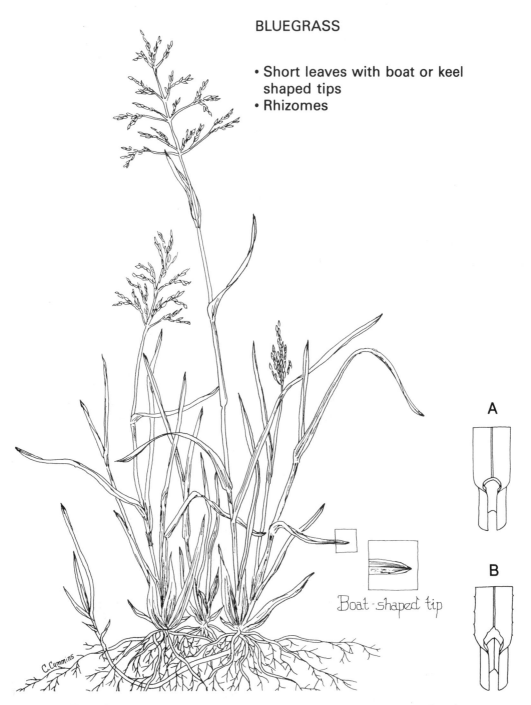

Boat-shaped tip

A

B

C.Cummins

Figure 3-11 Bluegrass *Poa* L. Inset *A*, Ligule of Kentucky bluegrass; *B*, ligule of rough bluegrass.

    Short leaves with boat-shaped tips.
    Rhizomatous.

Distinguishing features. Rhizomatous perennial; ligule short and membranous (to 0.6 mm); auricles lacking; leaf sheath compressed and smooth; leaf short with a boat-shaped tip; inflorescence, an open panicle. Mowing height: $3/4$ to 3 in. Fertilization: 2 to 6 lb nitrogen per 1000 sq ft per year.

Cultivars of Kentucky bluegrass

A-34 (Bensun): This older cultivar is noted for its tolerance of shade and close mowing. It grows dense, though it has a rather light green color. It has shown resistance to leaf spot, dollar spot, powdery mildew, and smut.

Adelphi: A popular variety bred at Rutgers University, Adelphi is low growing, dark green, and fine-leafed. In various trials it has exhibited resistance to a wide range of diseases that attack bluegrasses: leaf spot, stripe smut, *Fusarium* blight, dollar spot, and rust. It is also fairly tolerant to heat and has a good appearance even under low maintenance.

America: Also developed at Rutgers, this is a dwarf type, dense, fine-textured, and dark green. It exhibits resistance to leaf spot, rusts, and stripe smut. It is tolerant of low and high temperatures and of drought.

Banff: This is a low-growing Canadian selection of medium texture and medium dark green color. It is noted for its early spring green-up. It has moderate resistance to dollar spot and stripe smut.

Baron: This import from Holland has broad leaves, moderately low growth habit, and a medium dark green color. It shows moderate resistance to the various turf diseases and good seedling vigor, making it popular for bluegrass seed blends.

Birka: This grass has a medium fine texture, moderately low growth habit, and a medium dark green color. Imported from Sweden, it has good resistance to leaf spot, stripe smut, and powdery mildew, making it shade tolerant. However, it is susceptible to stem rust and is slow to green up in the fall. It is satisfactory for low-maintenance areas.

Bonnieblue: An offspring of the old favorite, Pennstar, Bonnieblue is moderately low growing and medium dark green. It has exhibited resistance to leaf spot, rusts, stripe smut, and dollar spot, but it is susceptible to powdery mildew.

Bristol: Another highly regarded Rutgers hybrid, Bristol has a rich, dark green color, wide leaves, and low growth habit. It has shown resistance to all the major turf diseases, including *Fusarium* blight and red thread. It is resistant to powdery mildew and hence is one of the better shade-tolerant bluegrasses.

Challenger: This grass is moderately low growing, medium fine in texture, fairly dense, and dark green. It is noted for its excellent early spring color and its ability to stay green later into the fall. It is tolerant of high temperatures and of close mowing. It has good resistance to leaf spot, melting out, rusts, stripe smut, and dollar spot.

Cheri: This Swedish import has medium broad leaves, moderately low growth, and medium dark green color. It has good resistance to leaf spot and melting out but only moderate resistance to rusts, dollar spot, and powdery mildew. It is moderately slow to green up in the spring but has good seedling vigor.

Columbia: A selection from Frederick, Maryland, Columbia has moderately low growth, medium texture, good density, and medium dark green color. Very cold hardy, it exhibits good spring green-up and late fall color. In protected areas it maintains a good winter color. It has good resistance to leaf spot, stripe smut, *Fusarium* blight, dollar spot, and rusts. It has also exhibited heat and drought tolerance. It has only average resistance to powdery mildew.

Eclipse: As the name implies, this new variety is noted for its shade tolerance and resistance to powdery mildew, as well as to leaf spot, leaf rust, stripe smut, red thread, and dollar spot. It is low growing, medium textured, and dark green. It has good density and vigor and establishes quickly. Tests around the country have given it high ratings.

Enmundi: Developed in Holland, this grass has moderately low growth and good resistance to leaf spot, stripe smut, and *Fusarium* blight. Its seed yields have been low, making it less attractive to produce commercially. It is somewhat shade tolerant.

Enoble: A low-growing introduction from Holland, this grass is reported to have excellent cold hardiness and good heat and drought tolerance. It is of medium shade tolerance, spring green-up rate, leaf texture, density, and green color. It has low water-consumption rate. It shows good resistance to *Fusarium* blight and stripe smut and moderately good resistance to leaf spot.

Fylking: This older beauty from Sweden is moderately low growing, dense, dark green, and fine-leafed, with good resistance to leaf spot and melting out. It can be mowed fairly low, down to 1 1/4 in.; and in May and June it maintains a leafy appearance when many other bluegrasses become stemmy (as they begin to flower, set seed, and complete the reproductive cycle). Unfortunately, Fylking is not very resistant to *Fusarium* blight or powdery mildew, shows little shade tolerance, and does not thrive in the heat of summer.

Georgetown: An Oregon selection, Georgetown is moderately low in growth, of medium texture, and medium dark green color. It shows excellent early spring green-up, good resistance to leaf spot and rusts, and moderate resistance to dollar spot and stripe smut.

Geronimo: This bluegrass is of medium texture and density, medium dark green color, and moderately low growth habit. It shows excellent cold hardiness and is tolerant also of heat and shade. It is susceptible to *Fusarium* blight but very resistant to *Fusarium* patch and rust. It is moderately tolerant of close mowing.

Glade: This cultivar is a selection from an old lawn in Albany, New York. It is noted for its moderate shade tolerance and seedling vigor. It has a high degree of resistance to stripe smut, rusts, *Fusarium* blight, and powdery mildew. It has moderate resistance to leaf spot and dollar spot.

Haga: This grass from Sweden is considered to be of medium texture, density, green color, and aggressiveness. It is reported to have excellent color retention in cool temperatures and good spring green-up. It tends to be stemmy in late spring. Good resistance to leaf spot and rusts and above-average resistance to dollar spot and stripe smut have been reported.

Kenblue: Developed in 1967, this cultivar is actually a blend of seed harvested from several different bluegrass fields in central Kentucky over a period of several years. The main attribute of such a variety is its wide genetic diversity.

Majestic: This grass is moderately low growing and dark green in color, with excellent spring and fall color. It has good resistance to leaf spot and leaf rust, and moderate resistance to dollar spot, stem rust, and stripe smut. It is not resistant to powdery mildew and hence is not recommended for shady lawns.

Merion: The first and probably still the most famous improved cultivar of Kentucky bluegrass, Merion was discovered in 1936 by Joseph Valentine at the Merion Golf Club near Ardmore, Pennsylvania. The grass had wider leaves, a lower growth habit, was darker green, and could be mowed closer than common Kentucky bluegrass. In addition it showed greater resistance to leaf spot disease and melting out, which often appeared in 80% of a stand of common bluegrass. The grass became widely acclaimed and was essentially the only commercially available variety until the 1970s. It eventually became obvious, particularly in older stands that had received excessive nitrogen, that although Merion is resistant to leaf spot and melting out, it is particularly susceptible to stem rust, stripe smut, and *Fusarium* blight. It is also susceptible to powdery mildew, which reduces its density in shady areas. In the 1970s Merion began to be replaced by a wide range of newer varieties bred or selected for even better disease resistance and superior physical characteristics.

Merit: This grass is moderately low growing, of medium coarse texture and medium density, with moderate spring and fall color retention. It exhibits moderate resistance to leaf spot and melting out and above-average seedling vigor.

Midnight: This heat tolerant, very dark green cultivar was selected from an old lawn near the Museum of Natural History in Washington, D.C. It is low growing and dense, a semidwarf type, with medium fine texture. It appears to have good resistance to leaf spot, stem rust, stripe smut, dollar spot, and powdery mildew.

Monopoly: This Dutch import is noted for its relatively rapid germination and excellent resistance to wear. It is vigorous, with medium texture, density, and green color. It has good resistance to leaf spot and dollar spot.

Mystic: This cultivar was selected from a country club fairway in Westfield, New Jersey. It is low growing, fine-textured, medium green, dense, and aggressive. It has excellent tolerance to close mowing. It competes well with annual bluegrass, making it suitable for use on golf courses. It has good resistance to powdery mildew and stripe smut and moderate resistance to leaf spot and melting out. It is susceptible to dollar spot.

Nassau: Moderately low growing, of medium texture and density and medium dark green in color, Nassau shows good early spring color. However, it tends to become stemmy in late spring. It has good resistance to leaf spot and above average resistance to dollar spot, red thread, pink snow mold, and rusts. It is recommended for a mixture with tall fescue.

Nugget: This grass was found in Hope, Alaska, and is good in the northern part of the bluegrass range or where turf is subject to severe winter damage. It exhibits moderate shade and smog tolerance but poor heat tolerance. It is low growing, dense, and it has good resistance to leaf spot, powdery mildew, and leaf rust but is susceptible to stem rust, stripe smut, dollar spot, *Fusarium* blight, and aphids.

Parade: An introduction from Holland, Parade is moderately low growing, of medium texture, and dark green. It has good resistance to leaf spot and rusts and above average resistance to dollar spot, *Fusarium* blight, and stripe smut. It shows good heat tolerance and early spring green-up.

Park: This is a blend of 15 selected strains released by the Minnesota Agricultural Experiment Station in 1957. It is similar to common Kentucky bluegrass. It has a relatively short germination time and good seedling vigor, making it a popular, inexpensive ingredient in bluegrass seed blends. It is moderately resistant to rusts, stripe smut, and powdery mildew, but like common Kentucky bluegrass, it is susceptible to leaf spot.

Plush: Selected from a New Jersey lawn, Plush is low growing, of medium-high density and medium texture and green color. It is aggressive, with good vigor, and is noted for good heat and drought tolerance. It is resistant to stripe smut and rusts but only moderately resistant to leaf spot. It is suitable for low-maintenance turfs.

Ram I: Discovered on a putting green in Kennebunk Beach, Maine, this grass is moderately low growing, of medium texture, and dark green. It has good early spring green-up, moderate resistance to leaf spot and stem rust, and good resistance to stripe smut and powdery mildew.

Rugby: This is a new, moderately low growing grass with medium texture, dark green color and good density. It has good color in late fall, winter, and early spring, but it tends to be stemmy in late spring. It exhibits good resistance to leaf spot, rusts, dollar spot, stripe smut, and *Fusarium* blight.

Sydsport: This import from Sweden has good tolerance to wear on athletic fields and forms a tight, dense sod. It has medium texture and medium green leaves and shows good resistance to leaf spot and stripe smut, but it is susceptible to dollar spot.

Touchdown: Noted for its aggressiveness, this grass tends to dominate in seed mixes. Like Mystic and A-34, it competes well against annual bluegrass. It is moderately tolerant of shade but develops more thatch under such conditions. It has excellent resistance to leaf spot, stripe smut, leaf rust, and powdery mildew but is susceptible to stem rust and dollar spot.

Vantage: This cultivar is low growing, with a wide leaf and medium dark green color. It is vigorous, with good heat and drought tolerance. It reportedly has good resistance to *Fusarium* blight in the mid-Atlantic states but is badly damaged in California. It shows good resistance to stripe smut and dollar spot and moderate resistance to leaf spot. It is susceptible to leaf and stem rust.

Victa: This grass has medium broad leaves, moderately low growth habit, and medium dark green color. It shows moderate resistance to leaf spots, rusts, dollar spot, and powdery mildew. It is slow to green up in the spring.

Wabash: This vigorous bluegrass from Purdue University is noted both for its ability to recover from stress and its cold hardiness. It has good fall color retention and medium density, leaf width, and green color. It is resistant to *Fusarium* but susceptible to leaf spot and melting out, especially if mowed too short, though it has good recovery.

Rough Bluegrass *Poa trivialis* L. (Figure 3-11)

The main features of "Poa triv," as it is often called, are that it will grow in areas too shady and moist for Kentucky bluegrass and that it can be mowed short once established. The grass has a shallow root system, so in sunny areas that become dry, it thins out and turns brown. Ranging from Newfoundland as far south as North Carolina in moist shady areas and from Alaska to California, the grass has good cold tolerance, winter color retention, and seedling vigor. It is sometimes mixed (10% to 15% rough bluegrass) with perennial ryegrass for winter overseeding in the South.

Once established in shady areas, *Poa trivialis* can be mowed as short as $1/2$ in., though higher is better in deep shade. It should be fertilized with a complete fertilizer, such as 20-5-5, once in the spring before the trees leaf out and again in the autumn after the leaves fall (and are removed from the turf), at the rate of 2 to 3 lb nitrogen per 1000 sq ft per year. As with any grass in the shade, herbicides should be applied sparingly, carefully, and never when the temperature is above 85°F.

For establishing a permanent turf in cool-season areas, seeding rates of 2 lb per 1000 sq ft are recommended. If used in a shade mixture, seed at the rate of 3 lb per 1000 sq ft. When used in overseeding mixes, as much as 15 to 20 lb per 1000 sq ft are used with perennial ryegrass or Chewings fescue. The new seeding should be irrigated 3 to 4 times per day and when it is established, soluble nitrogen should be applied at the rate of $1/2$ lb per 1000 sq ft every 2 to 3 weeks. When well established, the grass can tolerate mowing heights down to $3/16$ in.; however, in mixtures it is usually mowed at a height suitable for the other grasses.

Distinguishing features. Stoloniferous perennial; ligule long (2 to 6 mm), membranous, and pointed; auricles lacking; leaf sheath compressed, keeled, and rough to the touch; blade also rough on the edges near the tip, with a boat-shaped tip like that of Kentucky bluegrass; inflorescence, an open panicle. Mowing height: $1/2$ to 1 in. Fertilization: 2 to 3 lb nitrogen per 1000 sq ft per year.

Cultivar of rough bluegrass

Sabre: This grass was developed at Rutgers and released in 1977. It has a darker green color and grows lower and slightly more dense than common *Poa trivialis,* however, it still fails to thrive in heat and drought. It is susceptible to dollar spot and brown patch disease.

Creeping Bentgrass *Agrostis palustris* Huds. (Figure 3-12)

This species of bentgrass is a fine-leafed, low-growing, cool-season grass that has come to be considered the preeminent grass of the turf world. It was introduced from Europe during the 1700s, and its extensive use on the surface of putting greens has made it the standard to which all other turfgrasses are compared. It competes well with the weedy annual bluegrass, and its use on golf course fairways as well as on greens is increasing. Few turf workers have been spared conversations with typical homeowners who think that all grasses are the same and that a home bluegrass lawn can be mowed as short as the bentgrass greens at a golf course. In addition to expecting their home lawns to look like golf greens, most homeowners are unwilling to spend more than a fraction of the money actually required to maintain bentgrass.

Thus the principal difficulty with bentgrass lies in its high maintenance requirements. Although it forms a beautiful green carpet under optimum conditions, only an experienced and knowledgeable person can keep it that way. Bentgrass must be pampered, otherwise it is subject to insect damage, diseases, weeds, and thatch accumulation. These problems soon discourage all but the most affluent homeowners from wanting to maintain bentgrass lawns.

In general, bentgrass requires regular watering (almost daily on golf courses), is tolerant of acidic soils, and is moderately tolerant of shade. It is mowed as low as $1/4$ in., which on greens is repeated every 1 to 2 days. A high nitrogen level of 6 to 12 lb per 1000 sq ft per year is recommended. The extensive production of stolons soon results in a thick mat of thatch, which has to be continuously cut, sliced, plugged, dethatched, or topdressed. If these procedures are omitted, the thatch layer becomes excessive and retards the penetration of water and nutrients.

However, several turf experts feel that golf course bentgrasses are "overgrown," that is, too much water and fertilizer are applied to the grass and it is over-stimulated. More modest fertilizing has reduced the water requirement, thatch buildup, number of mowings necessary, and amount of *Poa annua* and has also improved the general hardiness of the grass.

Bentgrasses are adapted to cool, humid regions of the northern United States, but with careful management practices the range is being extended into the South, especially to golf greens in the Carolinas. Greens are established either by seed or by sprigging, the planting of vegetative pieces of the desired cultivar. The seed is quite small; one pound contains 6 to 8 million seeds. Because of this, seeding rates are comparatively low: $1/2$ to 1 lb per 1000 sq ft.

Distinguishing features. Stoloniferous perennial; ligule membranous, to 3 mm long, and pointed; auricles lacking; blade short and pointed; inflorescence, a tight panicle. Mowing height: $1/4$ to $1/2$ in. Fertilization: 4 to 12 lb nitrogen per 1000 sq ft per year.

Cultivars of creeping bentgrass

The U.S. Golf Association Green Section began segregating bentgrass cultivars in the 1920s, giving rise to the so-called C-series, of which some of the more prominent

BENTGRASS

- Tight, low growing with short pointed leaves
- Can withstand close mowing

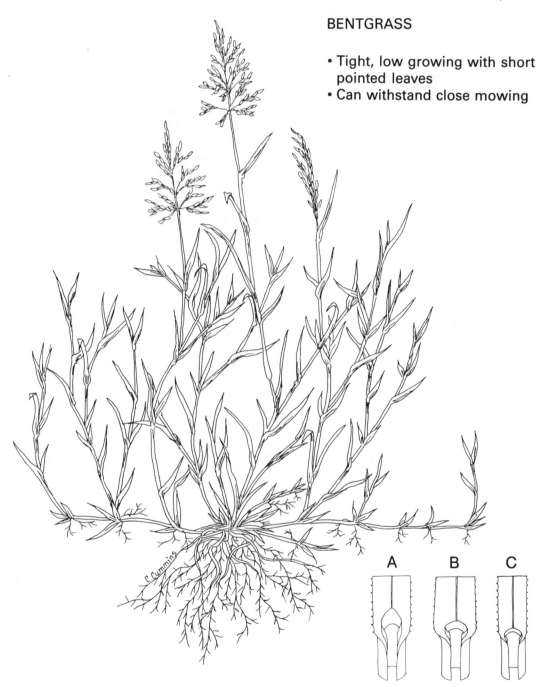

Figure 3-12 Bentgrass *Agrostis* L. Inset *A*, Ligule of creeping bentgrass; *B*, ligule of colonial bentgrass; *C*, ligule of velvet bentgrass.
   Tight, low growing with short, pointed leaves.
   Stoloniferous.

are described here. They are all propagated vegetatively, but Penncross, Penneagle, and Seaside are seed-produced bentgrasses.

Arlington (C-1): This slow-growing blue-green bentgrass requires a high level of fertility and close mowing. It is well adapted to the mid-Atlantic states but is susceptible to brown patch disease.

Cohansey (C-7): Selected at the Pine Valley Golf Club in Clementon, New Jersey, for its aggressiveness, this bentgrass is tolerant of frequent watering and high temperatures. It shows some resistance to brown patch and melting out diseases but is susceptible to dollar spot.

Congressional (C-19): This grass was selected at the Congressional Country Club, Rockwell, Maryland, and is adapted for use in the mid-Atlantic region. It has dark green color and good texture, hardiness, and early spring growth. It is susceptible to brown patch.

Old Orchard (C-52): This bentgrass was selected at the Old Orchard Grass Nursery in Madison, Wisconsin, in 1934. It has some degree of disease tolerance but tends to thin out during hot weather. It is adapted to the upper Midwest.

Penncross: This seeded variety was released by the Pennsylvania Agricultural Experiment Station in 1954. It was produced by the random crossing of three vegetatively propagated clones selected for their density, disease tolerance, and rate of recovery from damage. It has become a popular bentgrass owing to its ease of establishment (by seed), its competitiveness with *Poa annua,* and its fairly good performance over a wide area of the country. It is estimated that this grass has been used in over 90% of the golf courses constructed after the mid-1950s.

Penneagle: Developed in 1978 from Washington and Seaside, this grass was bred for upright growth and enhanced putting-green quality. It is less competitive than Penncross with *Poa annua.* A seed-propagated cultivar, its use is increasing on northern fairways.

Seaside: Established by seed, this bentgrass was selected from tidal pastures near Coos Bay, Oregon, in the 1920s. It was the only seeded bentgrass available until development of Penncross in 1954. It is rated below average in disease resistance, turf quality, and uniformity, though it develops less thatch than some other bents.

Velvet Bentgrass *Agrostis canina* L. (Figure 3-12)

Velvet bentgrass thrives in cool and moist areas, where it is very aggressive and forms dense patches. It is best adapted to the coastal areas of the Northeast and the warmer parts of the Pacific Northwest. It grows in shade and on acid soils but lacks tolerance to heat, drought, and poor drainage; like other bentgrasses it is susceptible to fungal damage. Very fine-textured, it is considered by many to be the most beautiful of all turfgrasses. Establishment is by seed or stolons.

Distinguishing features. Stoloniferous perennial; ligule membranous, pointed, to 1 mm; auricles lacking; leaf blade short and narrow, giving a very fine texture; inflorescence, a panicle, looser and more spreading than in creeping bent-grass. Mowing height: $1/4$ to $1/2$ in. Fertilization: 1 to 4 lb nitrogen per 1000 sq ft per year, less than creeping bent in order to avoid thatch.

Cultivar of velvet bentgrass

Kingston: This grass was released from the Rhode Island Agricultural Experiment Station in 1963. It was selected for its color, vigor, and disease resistance, especially to dollar spot. It can be propagated either vegetatively or by seed.

Colonial Bentgrass *Agrostis tenuis* Sibth. (Figure 3-12)

Colonial bentgrass is considered inferior to velvet and creeping bents for putting, but it is used on irrigated fairways and sometimes appears as a lawn grass in the Pacific Northwest, New England, and northern Europe. It grows more upright than velvet or creeping bentgrasses and has a tufted appearance, spreading by short stolons or rhizomes. It is more tolerant of acidic soils than is bluegrass, and it can be mowed to less than 1 in.; however, it is intolerant of heat and drought. It is subject to many fungal diseases, and it is often invaded by annual bluegrass. At one time colonial bent was frequently included in general-purpose lawn seed mixes, but it tends to dominate other grasses in the mix, forming a dense, close-knitted turf. Remnant patches of colonial bent from these seed mixes can still be seen on occasion in older northern lawns.

Distinguishing features. Stoloniferous or rhizomatous perennial; ligule membranous and short (1 to 2 mm); auricles lacking; inflorescence, an open panicle. Mowing height: $1/2$ to 1 in., slightly higher than creeping bentgrass. Fertilization: 1 to 4 lb nitrogen per 1000 sq ft per year.

Cultivars of colonial bentgrass

Astoria: Developed at the Oregon Agricultural Experiment Station in 1936, this grass has little to distinguish it from common colonial bent.

Exeter: This grass is a 1963 release from the Rhode Island Agricultural Experiment Station. It is composed of selections made from Rhode Island, Connecticut, and Massachusetts. A noncreeping type with very fine texture and good winter hardiness, Exeter is thought to have better spring and summer color and disease resistance than Astoria.

Highland: Released from the Oregon Agricultural Experiment Station in 1934, Highland exceeds all other bentgrasses in seed production. It has a distinctive bluish-green color, is erect, and is possibly more vigorous than the other colonial bentgrass cultivars.

Holfior: This variety was developed in Holland in 1940 and has a dark green color and upright growth habit. It does not mat as much as other colonial bentgrasses.

Annual (Italian) Ryegrass *Lolium multiflorum* Lam. (Figure 3-13)

The main features of annual ryegrass are its quick germination (less than a week), rapid growth, and low price. It is a coarse, annual, cool season bunch grass, which is killed by the cold winters in the upper northern states and by the hot summers in the South. This is a useful feature in the southern states: There the grass is used at heavy seeding rates to provide a green winter cover over southern grasses, which brown off in the fall. The ryegrass winter cover starts to die in the spring just as the southern grass begins to green up.

Prior to the development of turf-type perennial ryegrasses, which have supplanted it to a wide extent, annual ryegrass was frequently included in bluegrass and fescue turf seed mixtures. It functioned there to initiate a quick green cover and to act as a "nurse crop," providing some shade and retarding evaporation from the soil surface for the slower-growing bluegrasses and fescues. One has to be careful to keep the percentage of ryegrass low (less than 10%) in such a mixture, otherwise it may dominate or smother the other grasses. A good turf management practice to keep the annual ryegrass from quickly dominating a new seeding is to mow the new seeding at 1 in. in the first 2 to 3 weeks to allow the other slower grasses, especially bluegrass, a chance to become established and competitive.

Another danger in using annual ryegrass as a nurse crop in a fine-turf seeding is that seed lots may be contaminated with common perennial ryegrass, which is also a coarse bunch type. The two seeds are essentially indistinguishable and difficult to separate in the seed-cleaning process. The coarse perennial ryegrass may persist for a few years in the new bluegrass and fescue seeding and give it an uneven appearance.

Distinguishing features. Annual or short-lived perennial bunchgrass; ligule membranous and rounded, 1/2 to 2 mm long; auricles long, pointed, clasping, and prominent; young stem base green to yellow; blade rolled in the bud; spikelet awned, usually with 10 to 20 flowers; more robust than perennial ryegrass. Mowing height: 1 to 2 in. Fertilization: 3 to 4 lb nitrogen per 1000 sq ft per year.

Cultivars of annual ryegrass

Astor (Oregon AES, 1964), **Gulf** (Texas AES, 1958), **Magnolia** (Mississippi AES, 1965), and **Wimmera** (California AES, 1962) are all cultivars of annual ryegrass. Wimmera is thought to be a hybrid between annual ryegrass and *Lolium rigidum*. These cultivars are primarily forage grasses and used now only incidentally as turf types. The intermediate and perennial ryegrasses described below have been developed primarily for turf purposes.

Intermediate Ryegrasses

Intermediate ryegrasses, such as **Oregreen**, **3CN**, and **Agree**, are hybrids between annual and perennial ryegrass. Agree, for example, is a cross between annual ryegrass and Palmer, a turf-type perennial ryegrass. The intermediates are like annual ryegrass in that they germinate quickly yet lack heat tolerance. Their finer texture, deeper green color, and reduced shoot growth make them similar to perennial ryegrass. The lack of heat tolerance in these hybrids is an advantage in the winter overseeding of dormant warm-season grasses: the intermediates will disappear as the warm-season grass, such as bermudagrass, begins to grow in the spring. They do not shade and retard the bermudagrass as much as the more heat-tolerant, persistent turf-type perennial ryegrasses.

Perennial Ryegrass *Lolium perenne* L. (Figure 3-13)

Perennial ryegrass has long been used in Europe and the United States as a pasture grass, for which it was recommended by Thomas Jefferson as early as 1782. Like its annual relative, perennial ryegrass is a cool-season bunch-type grass that is also a quick germinator (although slightly slower than annual ryegrass). It is a short-lived perennial, usually persisting 2 to 5 years. In the past two decades many fine-leafed, or turf-type, perennial ryegrasses have been developed, starting with Northrup King 100 in the mid-1960s. This was followed by a Dutch cultivar, Pelo, which was blended with NK 100 to form Medalist 2, a combination that became popular in the South for winter overseeding. The next important cultivar was Manhattan, developed at Rutgers University from material selected in Central Park, New York City, and this was followed by Pennfine from Pennsylvania State University. Both these grasses were successful, widely used, and instrumental in changing almost overnight the reputation of perennial ryegrasses from coarse weeds to turf beauties. Aside from retaining the useful quality of quick germination, the fine-leaf appearance and dark color allow these grasses to blend with bluegrass into a more uniform turf. The new perennial ryegrasses have also retained the wear resistance for which ryegrasses are noted and hence are used alone or in seed mixtures designed for northern athletic fields. They spread by tillers and form a reasonably tight turf, and because of their quick growth they are frequently and routinely overseeded into damaged playing fields. These grasses flourish in cool, moist weather, but not in severe winters and summers. Many of the new cultivars, however, are winter-hardy into Canada and heat-tolerant into the South.

Although the new fine-leafed perennial ryegrasses blend well with bluegrass, and are indistinguishable by most people, the turf professional can spot them in a lawn rather easily: The leaves are glossy or shining, especially in sunshine, and have prominent, rigid veins. This latter feature makes them a little more difficult to mow, since mower blades must be sharp to avoid tearing or shredding the leaves.

The mix of bluegrass and perennial ryegrass also has a better response to disease than either grass has alone. The ryegrass is seldom damaged severely by leaf spot, *Fusarium* blight, or stripe smut, all of which have serious effects on bluegrass. On the other hand, bluegrass is more resistant to brown patch, red thread, and *Pythium* blight, which are serious problems on the ryegrass. Thus the mixture becomes a complementary combination that does not show severe damage to these diseases.

When a mixture of bluegrass and ryegrass is used for a seeding, the ryegrass germinates more quickly and vigorously than the bluegrass. To prevent it from dominating, and even smothering, the bluegrass or other slower turfgrass, a turf trick is to begin mowing the seeding at 1 in. as soon as the ryegrass is high enough. This is done

RYEGRASS

- **Leaves shiny with prominent mid-rib**
- **Prominent auricles, often clasping**
- **Spike type inflorescence**

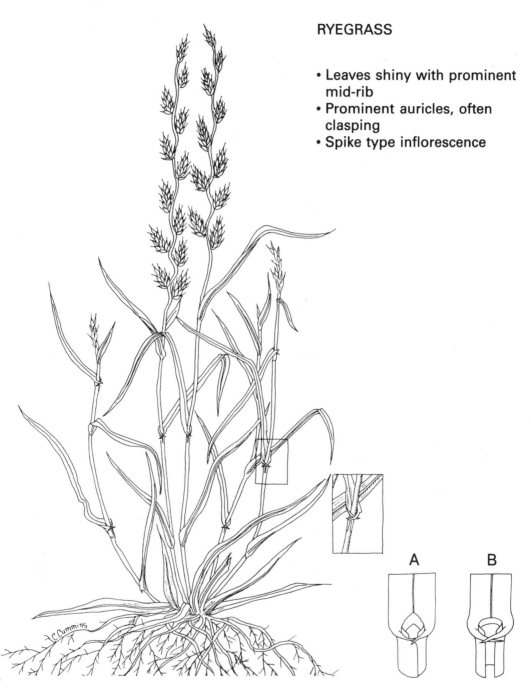

Figure 3-13   Ryegrass *Lolium* L. Inset *A*, Ligule of perennial ryegrass; *B*, ligule of annual ryegrass.

    Leaves shiny with prominent midrib.
    Conspicuous auricles, often clasping.
    Spike-like inflorescence.

for the first 2 to 3 weeks, allowing the bluegrass to develop more fully and to become more competitive.

An interesting recent development has been the release of perennial ryegrass cultivars resistant to chewing insects, such as the sod webworm or billbug adult. It has been determined that the resistance is related to the presence in the grass of a fungus *endophyte,* which lives within the plant. The fungus lives in a mutually beneficial association with the grass and causes no outward physical manifestations in its host. It is thought that the fungus produces a chemical toxin that repels the insects. The endophyte is transmitted by seed or vegetative propagation, and those ryegrass plants possessing it, aside from insect resistance, also appear to be more vigorous during summer heat and drought. These grasses thus have an "Endophyte Enhanced Performance," which may be indicated on seed bags of cultivars that contain at harvest at least 80% live endophyte.

Distinguishing features.   Perennial bunchgrass; ligule rounded, 0.5 to 2 mm; auricles pointed, reduced and not clasping, not as prominent as in annual ryegrass; base of leaf sheath usually reddish; blade folded in the bud, lower surface shiny or glossy, midrib prominent; spikelet awnless, usually with 6 to 10 flowers. The leaf blade folded in the bud (not rolled), the short and nonclasping auricles, the rounded (not pointed) ligule, the reddened leaf bases, and the awnless and few-flowered spikelet of perennial ryegrass distinguish it from annual ryegrass. Mowing height: $1/2$ to 2 in. Fertilization: 2 to 4 lb nitrogen per 1000 sq ft per year.

Cultivars of perennial ryegrass

All Star: This cultivar was selected from old lawns in Baltimore and College Park, Maryland. It shows good heat, drought, cold, and disease tolerance. It has a moderately dark green color.

Barry: This variety has a dark green color that is maintained into late fall. It is fine textured, dense, and late maturing. It has good resistance to brown patch and brown blight and above average mowing quality.

Belle: Belle has good winter hardiness and drought tolerance and survives hard wear. It tolerates close mowing and has good resistance to diseases. It is persistent and somewhat early maturing.

Birdie: This grass is moderately dark green in color and has good disease resistance except to winter brown blight. It has medium heat and cold tolerance but becomes stemmy in the late spring.

Birdie II: An offspring of Birdie, this grass is noted for its excellent seedling vigor and improved resistance to winter brown blight, brown patch, and stem rust. It has a lower growth habit than its parent and greater heat tolerance. It has a high endophyte level and good resistance to insects. It is rated one of the best perennial ryegrasses for overseeding into bermudagrass.

Blazer: This cultivar is considered to be of high quality, showing good disease resistance and mowing quality. Noted for its winter hardiness, it is persistent, medium-late maturing, and moderately dark green.

Caravelle: Considered one of the darkest green perennial ryegrasses, Caravelle is, however, rated low in density, winter hardiness, mowing quality, and heat tolerance. It is considered susceptible to *Rhizoctonia* brown patch disease. Its principal use is for winter overseeding in the South.

Citation: This grass is rated high for its dark green color and good mowing quality. It has good tolerance of heat and resistance to several diseases but is susceptible to winter brown blight disease. It is early maturing.

Citation II: This cultivar exhibits excellent seedling vigor and heat and cold tolerance and improved disease resistance and mowing quality. It is lower growing and tolerates closer mowing. It has one of the highest endophyte levels (94%), making it resistant to insects feeding above ground. It is good for overseeding in the South.

Cowboy: This variety was developed at Rutgers as a stem rust–resistant ryegrass with good resistance to winter brown blight, dollar spot, and other diseases. It tolerates high and low temperatures well. It is lower growing than other early maturing varieties.

Dasher: This low-growing type has shown good heat tolerance and moderate cold tolerance, with a medium-low growth habit and medium dark green color. It has good resistance to winter brown blight.

Delray: This variety tolerates winter temperatures and low fertilization. It is early maturing and moderately resistant to *Rhizoctonia* brown patch but highly susceptible to winter brown blight.

Derby: This moderately fine textured grass is tolerant of heat, cold, and wear. It matures early and has medium density and green color. Although susceptible to winter brown blight, it is moderately resistant to *Rhizoctonia* brown patch and dollar spot.

Diplomat: This cultivar is noted for its density, fine texture, and slow growth in height. It shows good tolerance to high and low temperatures, and it is moderately resistant to *Rhizoctonia* brown patch and winter brown blight.

Elka: With moderately good tolerance of cold temperatures and shade and excellent tolerance of close mowing, Elka produces a dense, light-green turf with slow growth rate. It is late maturing and has been rated excellent in spring but below average in summer. It is resistant to crown rust but moderately susceptible to *Rhizoctonia* brown patch, dollar spot, and winter brown blight.

Fiesta: This grass has good tolerance of high and low temperatures. It is of medium texture, density, and dark green color. It is a popular variety with good resistance to *Rhizoctonia* brown patch and moderately good resistance to winter brown blight.

Game: This early-maturing variety exhibits rapid growth of shoots and an erect growth habit. It is not very dense and lacks heat and cold tolerance. It has poor leaf appearance after mowing and is susceptible to *Rhizoctonia* brown patch.

Gator: Noted for its tolerance of low mowing height and other mowing qualities, Gator is low growing, fine textured, and of medium density and color. It is tolerant of heat and cold and resistant to *Rhizoctonia* brown patch, winter brown blight, and to many races of crown rust. It has very low endophyte content.

Jackpot: Jackpot has a fine-textured leaf and produces a moderately dark green and slow growing, highly dense turf. It has medium tolerance to cold, heat, drought, and shade. Although susceptible to leaf spot, it is resistant to snow mold.

Linn: This older ryegrass was released by the Oregon Agricultural Experiment Station in 1961. It lacks the winter hardiness, disease resistance, and other desirable characteristics of the newer cultivars.

Loretta: This variety is of medium green color, medium texture, and medium heat and cold tolerance. It is resistant to crown rust, *Rhizoctonia* brown patch, and winter blight but is susceptible to dollar spot.

Manhattan: Manhattan was the first modern turf-type perennial ryegrass. It is of moderate density, fine texture, slow shoot growth, and dark green color. It tolerates close mowing as well as high and low temperatures. It has good resistance to winter brown blight and moderate resistance to *Rhizoctonia* brown patch.

Manhattan II: An improvement over Manhattan, this grass has a fine texture, good density, and dark green color. It tolerates close mowing well and has very good tolerance of heat and cold. It is also more resistant to *Rhizoctonia* brown patch, winter brown blight, stem rust, and red thread than is Manhattan.

NK200:   This late-maturing variety has medium texture and dark green color. It has good cold tolerance but is less tolerant of heat. It is susceptible to *Rhizoctonia* brown patch and crown rust.

Omega: This grass shows good tolerance to heat, cold, and wear. Of medium density and with slow growth rate, it is resistant to *Rhizoctonia* brown patch and winter brown blight.

Omega II: This improved variety has better heat tolerance and disease resistance than Omega. It is of dark green color and has a more dwarf growth habit than most perennial ryegrasses. The endophyte level is 55%.

Palmer: Palmer produces a turf of dark green color, good density, and fine texture. It has good winter and summer hardiness and good tolerance of wear. It has good resistance to *Rhizoctonia* brown patch, winter brown blight, and many races of crown rust. It has moderate resistance to some species of sod webworms.

Pennant: This grass has good tolerance of heat, cold, drought, and close mowing. It is of medium-fine texture and medium-high density. It has good adaptation to shade and resistance to *Rhizoctonia* brown patch. It also has moderately good resistance to other fungal diseases and to billbug and some species of sod webworm. It has a reduced requirement for nitrogen.

Pennfine: This has been the most widely used cultivar of perennial ryegrass. It is of medium color, texture, and density and has low growth. It has good heat tolerance and medium cold hardiness. It has moderately good resistance to *Rhizoctonia* brown patch, *Typhula* blight, and some races of dollar spot, but it is susceptible to winter brown blight.

Prelude: This variety exhibits better mowing qualities than most others and good tolerance to heat, cold, drought, close mowing, and shade. It is of medium color, texture, density, and low growth habit. It has good resistance to *Rhizoctonia* brown patch and other diseases and to some species of sod webworm.

Premier: Premier has good tolerance of cold, heat, drought, shade, and close mowing. It is low growing, of dark green color and medium-fine texture. It has excellent seedling vigor and tolerance of many soil types. Considered one of the best ryegrasses, it has good resistance to *Rhizoctonia* brown patch and crown rust, with moderate resistance to brown blight and some types of sod webworm.

Regal: This cultivar is dark green in color and of medium texture, density, and cold hardiness. It has good tolerance to summer temperatures and good resistance to *Rhizoctonia* brown patch, dollar spot, and billbugs. However, it is susceptible to brown blight and crown rust.

Repell: Low growing and of dark green color, Repell is shade tolerant and dense. It has good resistance to *Rhizoctonia* brown patch, winter leaf spot, many races of crown rust, and sod webworms and billbugs.

Tara: This grass is tolerant of heat and cold. It is moderately dense, low growing, and dark green. It has good resistance to *Rhizoctonia* brown patch, crown rust, and other diseases. It was the highest rated cultivar in 1983 tests.

Yorktown II: This variety is dark green, fine textured, dense, and low growing. It is tolerant of heat and cold. It has good resistance to *Rhizoctonia* brown patch and moderately good resistance to some other diseases.

Fine Fescues *Festuca* spp. (Figure 3-14)

In contrast to the relatively broad-leafed tall fescues, there are several fescues used extensively in turf that have delicate, fine, and wiry leaves. As a group these are called *fine fescues*, and they are distributed throughout the temperate areas of the United States. Collectively they are noted for their shade tolerance and ability to compete with tree roots, their winter hardiness, their ability to survive on much drier and more infertile soils, and their compatibility with bluegrass in seed mixtures. They are, however, intolerant of wet soils. They germinate almost as quickly as perennial ryegrass, but their thin, delicate texture does not overwhelm the slower-growing bluegrass. They do not require as much fertilizer as bluegrass, ryegrass, or tall fescue, and fertilization should be avoided during the heat of summer.

The fine fescues are quick germinating and quick rooting. These characteristics, plus their wide tolerances, make them beneficial for seed or sod mixtures. They are often mixed with bluegrass, perennial ryegrass, or bentgrass or with perennial ryegrass alone for winter overseeding of bermudagrass.

There are four fine fescues that are much used in the turf industry: creeping fescue, spreading fescue, Chewings fescue, and hard fescue. Creeping and spreading

FINE FESCUE

- Thin, wiry leaves
- Short rhizomes

Figure 3-14   Fine fescue *Festuca* L. Inset *A*, Ligule of creeping red fescue; *B*, ligule of hard fescue.

Thin, wiry leaves.
Short rhizomes.

fescues are rhizomatous and of somewhat coarse texture, whereas Chewings and hard fescue are nonrhizomatous and finer textured. A fifth fescue, sheep fescue, is very widespread but occurs only sporadically as a turfgrass, particularly on sandy soils.

Distinguishing features.   Rhizomatous or bunch grass; ligule membranous, short; auricles lacking; inflorescence, a tight panicle. Mowing height: 1 to 3 in. Fertilization: 2 lb nitrogen per 1000 sq ft per year.

Creeping Fescue *Festuca rubra* L. subsp. *tricophylla* Gaud.

This is a major cool-season, winter-hardy turfgrass. It is a sod-forming perennial with short rhizomes, a delicate texture, and fine leaves. It is well adapted to cool, humid regions of the United States and grows on a wide range of soil types. It tolerates moderate shade better than most bluegrasses and hence is included in many all-purpose seed mixtures. However, it does not tolerate wet soils or excess nitrogen. It tends to discolor in hot and dry weather, and it is susceptible to fungal damage in the southern parts of its range.

Cultivars of creeping fescue

Dawson: This cultivar has a medium green color and good shade tolerance.

Pennlawn: Developed at Penn State in 1954, this grass was selected for its density, disease tolerance, rate of spread, and tolerance to close mowing. It has fair disease resistance and has performed well in tests around the country.

Wintergreen: Released in 1968 from the Michigan AES, Wintergreen has been rated in Michigan as superior to Pennlawn in color and density. It is comparable in disease resistance, but it can be maintained with less water and nitrogen.

Spreading Fescue *Festuca rubra* L. subsp. *rubra* Hack.

This fescue differs from creeping fescue in its longer and thicker rhizomes, which give it a more spreading habit, and its slightly wider leaves. Spreading fescue does not grow as dense as creeping or Chewings fescues, and it is more easily damaged by close mowing. It has good seedling vigor.

Cultivars of spreading fescue

Boreal: This fine fescue has a dark green color. Though susceptible to leaf spot, it shows moderate resistance to dollar spot.

Ensylva: Of medium texture, density, color, and low growth habit, Ensylva has excellent drought resistance and moderate tolerance to high temperatures. It is well adapted to shade and to acidic soils. It exhibits resistance to leaf spot but susceptibility to dollar spot. It persists even under close mowing.

Ruby: This spreading type from Holland has a dark green color and grows moderately tall. It is used mostly in mixtures.

Chewings Fescue *Festuca rubra* var. *commutata* Gaud.

This grass resembles creeping fescue except that it is more erect and lacks rhizomes, giving it a bunch-type, noncreeping habit. It has a very fine leaf texture, and many turf experts feel that it is more suitable for shady sites than creeping fescue. It is denser than that fescue, especially if mowed at less than 2 in. The density has been improved through cultivars that produce numerous tillers.

Cultivars of chewings fescue

Agram: This dark green and low-growing variety from Holland has fine texture and high density. It has a low growth rate and tolerates close mowing. It has moderately good resistance to leaf spot, powdery mildew, and red thread.

Banner: This cultivar is of medium green color and low growth habit. It is the result of a polycross. Banner is adapted to coastal areas.

Checker: This grass from the Oregon Agricultural Experiment Station is very fine textured, dense, and low growing. It has good tolerance of heat and drought. It is moderately resistant to leaf spot, red thread, and *Fusarium* patch.

Highlight: This cultivar from Holland is low growing and light green in color.

Jamestown: This dark green grass is low growing and dense. It tillers abundantly even on poor sites and in shade. Summer color is good.

Shadow: As its name implies, this fescue is noted for its adaptation to shade. It has good tolerance of close mowing, a low growth habit, fine texture, and moderately dark green color. It exhibits very good resistance to powdery mildew and moderately good resistance to leaf spot, dollar spot, and red thread.

Waldorf: This cultivar is noted for its very good tolerance of close mowing. It grows prostrate and has fine texture and good density. It has good heat and drought tolerance and good resistance to leaf spot, powdery mildew, and sod webworm.

Hard Fescue *Festuca longifolia* Thuill. or *Festuca ovina* var. *duriuscula* (L.) Koch (Figure 3-14)

This cool-season, perennial bunchgrass does not form rhizomes or a sod, as does creeping fescue. It has thin, firm leaves and is similar in appearance to Chewings fescue, but it is considered slower growing and more persistent. Some botanists consider this grass a variety of sheep fescue with wider, more firm leaves.

Improved varieties of hard fescue have been developed that show greater disease resistance, particularly to red thread, anthracnose, leaf spot, and pink snow mold. They also maintain a better green color over the summer, even during extended dry periods, and due to powdery mildew resistance, they have better shade tolerance. They are also salt tolerant. They should be mowed at 1 in. or higher. Hard fescue is frequently mixed with bluegrasses, turf type perennial ryegrasses, and other fine fescues. Some workers feel that the quality of a tall fescue turf is improved by including 10% hard fescue.

Cultivars of hard fescue

Aurora: This slow-growing cultivar has a fine texture, excellent density, and grows very low. It is very well adapted to shade and moderately adapted to close mowing. It exhibits good resistance to leaf spot, powdery mildew, red thread, and billbugs.

Reliant: This cultivar is noted for its ability to thrive under low-maintenance conditions. It is fine textured, low growing, and tolerant of heat and drought. It has good resistance to leaf spot, powdery mildew, red thread, and anthracnose.

Spartan: A recent release from Rutgers, this cultivar has a dark green color, good density, and excellent shade tolerance. It is more resistant to heat and drought than Chewings or creeping red fescues. It has been used in mixes with wildflowers.

Tournament: This hard fescue is a dark green color, with high density and low growth habit. It is slow growing and has a medium tolerance of close mowing. It has good resistance to leaf spot and red thread.

Waldina: This variety is recommended for use in mixtures with bluegrass and ryegrass. It has a dark green color and very low growth habit. It is fine textured, of excellent density, and has excellent resistance to red thread. It also exhibits resistance to leaf spot, powdery mildew, dollar spot, and billbugs.

Sheep Fescue *Festuca ovina* L. (Figure 3-14)

This is a cool-season perennial bunchgrass with fine, wiry, blue-green leaves. More clumpy and less attractive in color than the other fescues, it is grown to a limited extent as a turfgrass. However, it is useful particularly on dry, sandy, or rocky soils that are well drained. These tolerances make its genetic potential of more than just cursory interest to grass breeders. It is more tolerant of drought and infertile acid soils than is hard fescue.

Extremely winter hardy, sheep fescue is also very widespread. It ranges from Alaska down through the western United States to Arizona and New Mexico, throughout the upper Midwest to the Northeast and down the Atlantic coastal states to South Carolina.

Cultivar of sheep fescue

Aries: This cultivar is useful principally for areas receiving very low maintenance. It has a variable bluish-green color, fine texture, good density, and low growth habit. It has moderate tolerance of close mowing and good resistance to leaf spot.

Tall (Coarse) Fescue *Festuca arundinacea* Schreb. (See Figure 5-6)

This is a coarse textured and rather deeply rooted perennial bunchgrass that occasionally forms a few short, thick rhizomes. It has a large root system that penetrates as deep as 4 ft, and thus tall fescue has exhibited more drought resistance than fine fescues, perennial ryegrasses, or Kentucky bluegrasses. It takes traffic better than most grasses, and if planted at a heavy rate (6 to 10 lb per 1000 sq ft) makes a good turf for playing fields and lawns. In thin stands the grass becomes prostrate and objectionable. It often appears as an annoying, clumping weed in finer bluegrass turf and is treated to the same invectives by northern homeowners as crabgrass. Solid stands of tall fescue may thin out after several years and require overseeding to maintain their density and turf qualities.

Tall fescue has a relatively high degree of disease resistance and heat and drought tolerance, and it is too coarse for most insects if more succulent grasses, such as bluegrass, are readily available. These features make it suitable for lawns in the mid-South. In the upper northern United States it survives the very cold winters with difficulty. It has often been used in utility turf areas under low maintenance.

For thirty years, starting in the 1940s the best known tall fescue was Kentucky 31, a cultivar produced by the Kentucky Agricultural Experiment Station and representing a collection from a farm in Menifee County. A multipurpose grass, it was used largely as a forage grass for livestock but was also recommended for roadsides and around farm ponds, for erosion control, and, to a limited extent but especially in Tennessee and other transition zone states, as a turfgrass. About the same time another strain, Alta, was developed at the Oregon Agricultural Experiment Station for its improved cold tolerance. For turf purposes Alta was considered in the West to be equal to or slightly superior to Kentucky 31, whereas in the Southeast Kentucky 31 is typically rated higher in density and persistence.

In the 1970s a breeding program at Rutgers University was initiated to segregate tall fescue cultivars for turf. Rebel was the first "turf-type" tall fescue, followed by Falcon and Olympic. Then a virtual explosion of turf-type tall fescues occurred, with more than two dozen now available commercially, as indicated later.

Typically, the new turf types have finer leaves, more dense tillering, and frequently a darker green color than Kentucky 31. They are widely adapted north and south; are more shade tolerant; require less water, fertilizer, and fewer pesticides; and wear well. They may be the answer to the turf industry's increasing concern with energy and water, and it may be wise to get to know them well.

Distinguishing features.   Bunchgrass, with occasional rhizomes; ligule membranous, $1/2$ to $1^1/2$ mm long, rounded; auricles short and hairy; blade 5 to 10 mm wide, with prominent veins and rough margins; inflorescence, a tight panicle. Mowing height: $1^1/2$ to 3 in.; mowing at 4 in. every 2 weeks has been recommended for low-maintenance areas. Fertilization: 2 lb nitrogen per 1000 sq ft per year, applied in spring or fall, preferably after June to avoid excessive growth.

Cultivars of tall fescue

Adventure: This cultivar tolerates both full sun and partial shade well. It has good vigor and color at low levels of fertilization, and it has a medium-fine texture and good density. It exhibits good resistance to *Rhizoctonia* brown patch and moderate resistance to net blotch.

Alta: Released by the Oregon Agricultural Experiment Station in 1940, this old variety has low density, coarse texture, and rapid growth. It is heat and cold tolerant, but is susceptible to several diseases.

Apache: Apache is noted for its darker bluish-green color. It is of medium-fine texture, slow growth rate, and tolerates heat, drought, and wear. It has very good resistance to crown rust and moderately good resistance to net blotch and brown patch.

Astro: This tall fescue is rated good in tolerance to heat, cold, and drought. It has medium dark green color, texture, and density. It is moderately resistant to brown patch, crown rust, and net blotch.

Arriva: This cold-tolerant cultivar is of medium color, texture, density, and growth rate. It has good tolerance to close mowing and very good resistance to net blotch.

Bonanza: This variety is noted for its dark bluish-green color, even at low fertilization rates, its dwarf growth habit, and slow growth rate. It has very good tolerance of heat, cold, drought, and traffic. It shows very good resistance to crown rust, net blotch, and brown patch.

Brookston: Brookston is of medium color, low growth habit, texture, and density. It is cold tolerant and very resistant to crown rust and net blotch. However, it does not thrive under summer heat and drought stress.

Clemfine: This cultivar has a coarse texture and rather low density and does not stand close mowing well. It is similar to Kentucky 31. However, it is more persistent and more tolerant of heat and drought. It has moderately good resistance to *Rhizoctonia* brown patch and fair resistance to net blotch.

Falcon: This grass is of medium texture and density and low growth habit. It tolerates heat well and is moderately well adapted to shade. It has improved resistance to brown patch, net blotch, and crown rust.

Fawn: This is an older variety, released in 1964, that has more vigor than Alta and Kentucky 31. It is coarse textured and fast growing. It is also susceptible to brown patch, net blotch, and crown rust, and it lacks winter and summer hardiness.

Finelawn I: This variety is recommended for its heat, cold, and drought tolerance. It is moderately low growing and is moderately resistant to brown patch, net blotch, and crown rust.

Galway: Galway is adapted to shade and has good drought and cold tolerance. It is of medium texture, density, and dark green color. It is moderately resistant to brown patch and net blotch. It is intermediate between Kentucky 31 and the new turf-type cultivars in its growth characteristics.

Goar: An older variety released in 1946, Goar is coarse textured, vigorous, and suited to heavy alkaline soils. It is susceptible to brown patch, crown rust, and *Helminthosporium* blight.

Houndog: This cultivar is of medium texture, density, and dark green color; it grows semiprostrate. It tolerates heat and drought well and is moderately resistant to brown patch, net blotch, and crown rust.

Jaguar: This variety is noted for its fall color retention and its tolerance of heat, drought, and shade. It retains good color and density at low nitrogen levels, and it has very good resistance to brown patch, net blotch, and crown rust.

Kenhy: Released in 1976 by the Kentucky Agricultural Experiment Station, Kenhy was derived from selected annual ryegrass × tall fescue hybrids. It is rather coarse and fast-growing, with improved heat and drought tolerance.

Kenwell: Of medium dark green color, this slow-growing cultivar is well adapted to shade. It has low density and is susceptible to net blotch, but its lack of aggressiveness makes it suitable for use in mixtures.

Kentucky 31: Released in 1934, this variety is widely adapted to a range of soil types and extremes of climate. It is coarse and fast growing, with moderate tolerance of brown patch, net blotch, and crown rust.

Marathon: This cultivar is of medium texture, density, and low growth habit. It has good heat and drought tolerance and good resistance to crown rust, with moderately good resistance to brown patch and net blotch.

Maverick: This variety surpasses most in its heat tolerance and is also adapted to shade. It is moderately fine textured, of dark green color, and is low growing.

Mustang: Mustang has good tolerance of close mowing and a low rate of thatch accumulation. It has dark green color, medium texture, density, and low growth habit. It is well adapted to shade and high temperatures. It has very good resistance to net blotch and moderately good resistance to brown patch.

Olympic: This variety has a dark green color, medium texture and density, and low growth habit. The color is maintained well even into the fall and even under low nitrogen fertilization. Olympic is well adapted to shade, with good resistance to net blotch and crown rust and moderate resistance to brown patch.

Rebel: This variety has three-species crosses of tall fescue, meadow fescue, and perennial ryegrass in its ancestry. It has a medium dark green color, with finer texture and slower growth rate than most types. It persists well when mowed closely and does not produce much thatch. It has good adaptation to shade and good heat tolerance. It has shown moderate resistance to brown patch and net blotch.

Tempo: Tempo has medium color, texture, and density. It has improved drought tolerance and slow growth rate. It is moderately resistant to net blotch.

Willamette: This cultivar is of medium dark green color, texture, and density. It has improved tolerance to heat, cold, and drought, with improved resistance to brown patch and crown rust and moderate resistance to net blotch.

Bermudagrass *Cynodon dactylon* (L.) Pers. (Figure 3-15)

Bermudagrass has the same prominence in the turf industry of the South as bluegrass has in the North. In the South, improved strains of common bermudagrass, such as Coastal and Suwanee, make an excellent forage. The grass was introduced into the South from Africa, possibly by slave ship, sometime in the mid-1700s. From the common forage type or from hybrids produced by crossing *C. dactylon* with another African species, *C. transvaalensis,* have come a number of superior turf types. Many of these were developed by Dr. Glenn Burton of the USDA, Agricultural Research Ser-

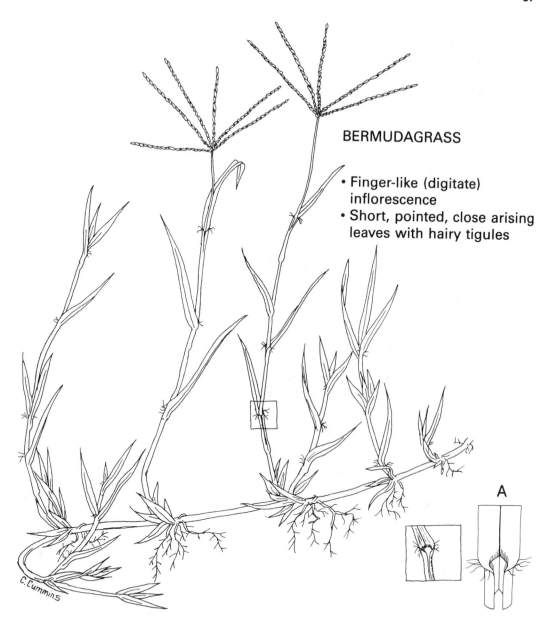

BERMUDAGRASS

- Finger-like (digitate)
  inflorescence
- Short, pointed, close arising
  leaves with hairy tigules

Figure 3-15 Bermudagrass *Cynodon dactylon* L. Inset *A*, Leaf blade-sheath junction showing hairy ligule and hairs around leaf collar.

Short, pointed, close-arising leaves with compressed sheaths and hairy ligules.

Rhizomes and stolons.

Digitate inflorescence.

vice, working at the Coastal Plains Experiment Station in Tifton, Georgia. Their place of origin is reflected in the names of the improved strains: Tifdwarf, Tiffine, Tifgreen, Tiflawn, and Tifway.

Bermudagrass occurs into the transition zone and in sporadic plantings in the North, where it is at times a difficult weed in bluegrass lawns. Its northern range has been extended by selection of winter-hardy varieties such as Midiron and Midway, and the grass can be found on favorable sites in southern New England and the southern portions of some of the midwestern states. It grows on a wide range of soils and, with its root system penetrating as deep as 8 ft, is tolerant to drought. However, it lacks shade tolerance, requiring full sun (more than 6 hours per day in summer). It spreads aggressively by stolons and rhizomes, forming a tight sod. It is a high-maintenance grass, and many of the improved varieties during their peak season require mowing two to three times per week, limiting their use in great part to golf courses. One of the problem weeds in this turf is bermudagrass itself—the common type looks weedy in a turf composed of an improved cultivar and vice versa.

With cool weather, bermudagrass goes off color. It becomes dormant when the soil temperature stays below 60°F, and it turns brown after frost. In some cases it is sprayed with a green vegetable dye for the winter season. More commonly, however, it is overseeded with annual or perennial ryegrass, which dies in the heat of the next summer at about the time when the bermudagrass is beginning to grow vigorously again. In the transition zone winter damage to bermudagrass occurs when temperatures are excessively low, especially during an unusually long winter. Tests indicate that the survival rate in these areas can be improved by limiting traffic on the turf during winter, using high potassium fertilization, and reducing preemergent herbicide levels, especially immediately before dormancy is broken.

Seed is available for common bermudagrass, but the improved varieties are all propagated vegetatively.

Distinguishing features.   Rhizomatous and stoloniferous perennial; ligule 2 to 5 mm long with fringe of white hairs; auricles lacking; leaf sharp-pointed and stiff; inflorescence, digitate. Mowing height: 3/4 to 1 1/2 in. Fertilization: 4 to 8 lb nitrogen per 1000 sq ft per year. Maintaining high potassium levels is important for cold tolerance.

Cultivars of bermudagrass

Midiron: An old variety released in 1966, Midiron is noted for its cold hardiness and resistance to winter wear during dormancy. Thus it is often used in high-traffic turf areas. It is of medium coarse texture and medium density. It has a semiprostrate growth habit and low nitrogen requirement. It shows good resistance to spring dead spot and bermudagrass mite and moderately good resistance to rust and leaf spot.

Midmo: Of gray-green color, this bermudagrass is noted for its excellent tolerance to drought and cold. However, it does maintain its color well in low temperatures or leafhopper infestations. It has medium texture and density and is adapted for low maintenance. It is recommended for the transition zone.

Midway: Midway exhibits excellent cold hardiness and minimum thatching. It has medium texture and density and good resistance to leafspot and bermudagrass mite. It is susceptible to billbugs, however. It is well adapted to the transition zone, especially in areas of alkaline soils.

Ormond: Of medium texture and dark green color, this cultivar is used mostly in Florida. It has good low-temperture color retention. It is, however, susceptible to disease and insect damage.

Pee Dee: A mutant of Tifgreen, Pee Dee is adapted for high maintenance regimes in the Carolinas. It has a dark green color, fine texture, and high density. It grows vigorously in a prostrate manner and accumulates thatch. It lacks cold hardiness and low-temperature color retention. It is somewhat resistant to spring dead spot.

Santa Ana: This variety is noted for its tolerance to wear, salt, and smog and its color retention in cold. It is of dark blue-green color and medium texture and density. It grows prostrate and vigorously, with a tendency to accumulate thatch. It has shown good resistance to bermudagrass mites. With only moderate cold hardiness, it is used mostly in coastal and warm winter areas such as Arizona and southern California.

Sunturf: This older variety has fine texture, low growth habit, a dark green color, and very high density. It has excellent drought, salt, and wear tolerance but only medium tolerance to low temperatures. It is susceptible to dollar spot and rust.

Texturf: Released in 1957, this grass has high density with heavy thatch accumulation. It is dark green, medium textured, and low growing. It exhibits excellent tolerance to traffic but is susceptible to *Helminthosporium*. It is recommended mostly for arid regions of the Southwest.

Tifdwarf: This grass exhibits superior tolerance to close mowing, suiting it to use on greens, where it is mowed two or three times a week. It is adapted to shade but not to low temperatures or smog. It has dark green color, very fine texture, very high density, and is low growing. It is susceptible to spring dead spot and sod webworms.

Tifgreen: Tifgreen has a dark green color and very fine texture. It is tolerant of cold temperatures, drought, and traffic. It is low growing, with good resistance to leaf spot and bermudagrass mites. However, it is susceptible to scale, sod webworms, and army worms and suffers damage from smog and 2,4-D. It has been largely replaced by Tifdwarf and other varieties on greens. Like them, it requires several mowings per week.

Tifgreen II: This cultivar is lighter green than Tifgreen but more resistant to nematodes and mole crickets. It has better spring recovery under low-maintenance conditions.

Tifway: This widely adapted grass has a dark green color, medium fine texture, and high density. It grows vigorously, with good cold hardiness. It has a tendency to accumulate thatch and performs best under medium to high maintenance with frequent mowing. It is tolerant of bermudagrass mites but susceptible to mole crickets and sod webworms.

Tifway II: Noted for its very good tolerance of close mowing and immunity to rust, this new bermudagrass is dark green and of medium texture and density. It exhibits excellent resistance to leaf spot and excellent color retention under low temperatures.

Tufcote: This variety is tolerant of traffic, salt, and cold temperatures. It has medium color, texture, and density but is susceptible to bermudagrass mites and spring dead spot. It is recommended for the Middle Atlantic states.

U-3:   An older cultivar, U-3 has a dark gray-green color, medium fine texture, and medium high density. It is noted for its tolerance to wear, drought, and cold, although it does not retain its color well under low temperatures. It is susceptible to spring dead spot. It was once widely used in the transition zone.

Vamont: This is a new variety of light green color, medium coarse texture, and medium high density. It has an intermediate growth habit and tends to accumulate thatch. It tolerates close mowing and has good cold hardiness.

Westwood: Released in 1970, Westwood has shown good spring green-up and cold hardiness. It is blue-green in color, of medium coarse texture, and grows vigorously.

Zoysiagrass *Zoysia* spp. (Figure 3-16)

Zoysia is a grass of subtropical and tropical regions of the Orient. In Korea it is called the "golden grass" because of its golden dormant color in winter. Like bermudagrass it turns brown with the first frost in cooler regions and is a slow starter in the spring. It is also slow to establish by rhizomes and stolons, but once it begins to grow vigorously, it can form a thick turf. It has been sold widely throughout the North, mostly by growers advertising zoysiagrass plugs in national periodicals. Many northern homeowners become disenchanted with it, however, when it turns brown and dead-looking in the fall or when it begins to spread into a neighbor's bluegrass lawn.

  Zoysia grows on nearly all soils. Compared with bermudagrass, it is more shade tolerant and cold hardy, it wears better, it requires less mowing, and it has fewer disease and insect problems. It is also tolerant to salt. However, it is not as drought tolerant as bermudagrass, and it has a serious thatch problem.

  Zoysiagrass is difficult to get established and is slower growing than bermudagrass, St. Augustinegrass, or bahiagrass. Golf course fairways are planted by first removing all vegetation, then spreading (typically with a manure spreader) as much as 300 bushels per acre of sprigs or stolons, lightly disk harrowing, and watering immediately. With continued regular watering it may take 2 to 3 years for the grass to close in. As much as 8 to 10 lb of nitrogen per 1000 sq ft is applied in the first few years, with applications made during the warm months. Fertilizer should not be aplied after mid-August to allow the grass to harden for the winter. After the grass is established the fertilizer rate is dropped to 2 lb nitrogen per 1000 sq ft per year.

  Some seed of Korean common zoysiagrass is available. The seed requires high temperatures to germinate, and spring plantings are often covered with 4-mm plastic sheeting for thermal gain.

  There are three main species of *Zoysia*. Japanese lawngrass (*Z. japonica* Steud.) grows widely throughout the Far East. The main grass used on Korean and Japanese

ZOYSIAGRASS

- Tight growth with short, pointed, close arising leaves
- Hairy ligules

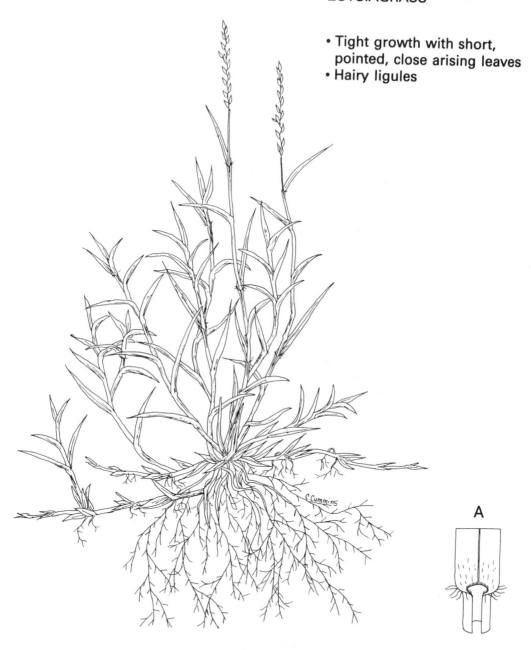

A

Figure 3-16 Zoysiagrass *Zoysia* Willd. Inset *A*, Leaf blade-sheath junction showing hairy ligule, hairs around collar, and pubescence at base of leaf blade.

Dense plants with short, pointed, close-arising leaves.
Ligules hairy.
Creeping rhizomes.

golf course fairways, it is coarse textured and more vigorous and cold hardy than the other two species. A second species, called Manilagrass (*Z. matrella* [L.] Merr.), is more dominant in southern Japan and the Philippines and is estimated to have been used on 60% of the putting greens in Japan (30% are creeping fescue and 10% are planted to hybrid bermudagrasses). Manilagrass is finer textured but less cold hardy than Japanese lawngrass. A third species, Korean velvetgrass (*Z. tenuifolia* Willd. ex Trin.), also more adapted to warm seasons than *Z. japonica,* is distinguished by its finer leaves and narrower spikelets. It is the least aggressive and least cold hardy of the three species.

Distinguishing features.   Rhizomatous and stoloniferous perennial; ligule a fringe of hairs; auricles lacking; blade short and pointed. Mowing height: $1/2$ to $1^1/2$ in. A reel mower is preferred. Fertilization: 1 to 3 lb nitrogen per 1000 sq ft per year on established turf.

Cultivars of zoysiagrass

Emerald: A hybrid of *Zoysia japonica* × *Z. tenuifolia,* Emerald has a fine texture, high density, and medium dark green color. It grows low and spreads rapidly and is tolerant of partial shade. However, it accumulates thatch and is susceptible to low temperatures and dollar spot. With increased winter hardiness, it is adapted into the transition zone.

FC 13521:   This *Zoysia matrella* was released by the Alabama Agricultural Experiment Station in the 1930s. It is well adapted to shade, with dark green color, fine texture, and high density. It grows low and slowly and is intolerant of cold and drought. It is susceptible to dollar spot, rust, and billbugs. It has been largely superseded by Emerald.

Meyer: This cultivar is a *Zoysia japonica* of medium color, texture, and growth rate. It is tolerant of low temperatures, drought, and wear, but not of shade. Coarser than Emerald, it establishes slowly and is susceptible to rust and billbugs. It grows dense, however, and so tends to resist invasion by weeds. It is used in the upper transition zone.

Midwest: This *Zoysia japonica* has a dark green color, medium coarse texture, and medium low density. It spreads faster than Meyer and accumulates less thatch. It retains its color well under cold temperatures but is very susceptible to rust and billbugs.

St. Augustinegrass *Stenotaphrum secundatum* (Walt.) Kuntze (Figure 3-17)

A native of the West Indies, this warm-season grass is limited by its lack of cold tolerance to the Gulf Coast areas and milder parts of California and the Southwest. It does, however, keep its green color at temperatures even 10°F below those that discolor bermudagrass. It is a very coarse-textured stoloniferous perennial. It will grow well on moist, sandy, and slightly alkaline soils, and it is widely used in Florida. Though less

ST. AUGUSTINEGRASS

- Short, wide blades with boat-shaped tips
- Thickened seed-head with embedded spikelets

Figure 3-17 St. Augustinegrass *Stenotaphrum secundatum* (Walt.) Kuntze.
Coarse texture.
Short, wide blades with boat-shaped tips.
Flattened sheaths with prominent midvein.
Thickened seed-head with embedded spikelets.

drought tolerant than bermudagrass, St. Augustinegrass is one of the best shade-tolerant southern grasses. It is also tolerant of salt but not of low fertility or poor drainage. It is subject particularly to chinch bugs, nematodes, brown patch disease, and a virus disease called St. Augustine decline (SAD). All of these cause a yellowing, discoloration, or decline of the turf.

Yellowing of the turf may be caused as well by iron deficiency, which can occur on soils high in phosphorus. Therefore, fertilizers high in phosphorus should be applied only when indicated by a soil test. Iron deficiency can be corrected with application of iron sulphate, 3 oz per 1000 sq ft, or chelated iron according to label directions. If a soil test indicates a pH greater than 6.5, add sulfur (10 lb per 1000 sq ft) or fertilize with either ammonium nitrate (3 lb per 1000 sq ft) or ammonium sulfate (5 lb per 1000 sq ft) at intervals of 6 to 8 weeks, until the yellowing is corrected. The last fertilization should be done a month before hard frost is expected. Since potassium promotes winter hardiness, apply about 1 lb potassium per 1000 sq ft in a fall application.

Distinguishing features.   Stoloniferous perennial; ligule very short (to 0.4 mm), a fringe of hairs; auricles lacking; leaf sheath flat and compressed, with a prominent midrib; blade short, broad, and blunt with a boat-shaped tip as in bluegrass; inflorescence, a fleshy spike with one-seeded embedded spikelets. Mowing height: $1^1/_2$ to $2^1/_2$ in. Fertilization: 2 to 6 lb nitrogen per 1000 sq ft per year.

Cultivars of St. Augustinegrass

Bitter Blue: Of blue-green color and medium texture, density, and growth habit, this grass is well adapted to shade and has improved color retention under cold temperatures. It is used mostly in Florida, where it has proven susceptible to SAD virus, chinch bug, and gray leaf spot.

Floratam: Used throughout the lower South, this variety has coarse texture and does not tolerate well shade, cold, or wear. However, it is resistant to SAD virus and moderately resistant to chinch bugs. It has improved resistance to triazine herbicides.

Floratine: This variety released in 1957 is of blue-green color and medium texture and density. It is low growing with branched stolons and has improved tolerance to close mowing and shade. Used mostly in Florida, it is not cold hardy, and it is susceptible to SAD virus, chinch bugs, and gray leaf spot.

Raleigh: Raleigh is moderately tolerant of shade, cold, and close mowing. It is medium green, with medium coarse texture and density. It spreads rapidly. It is resistant to SAD virus but susceptible to gray leaf spot, downy mildew, and brown patch.

Seville: Released in 1981, Seville has improved cold hardiness and low temperature color retention. It is of medium dark green color, texture, and density. It is resistant to SAD virus but susceptible to chinch bugs and gray leaf spot.

Texas Common: This grass has a medium color, texture, and tolerance to cold and wear. It exhibits good adaptation to shade and is tolerant of phenoxy herbicides. It is susceptible to SAD virus, chinch bugs, and gray leaf spot.

CENTIPEDEGRASS

- Leafy stolons
- Inflorescence a spike-like raceme

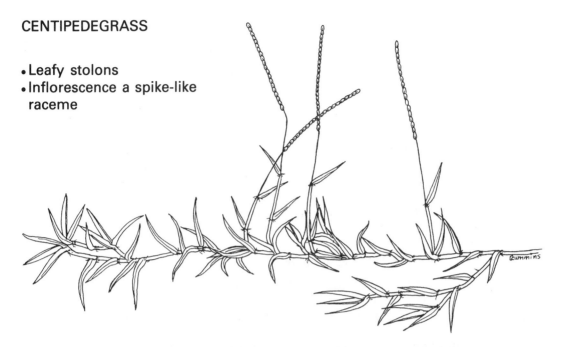

Figure 3-18 Centipedegrass *Eremochloa ophiuroides* (Munro) Hack.
Compressed leaves and blades with prominent midvein.
Ligule a short membrane with hairy margin.
Leafy stolons.
Inflorescence a spike-like raceme.

Centipedegrass *Eremochloa ophiuroides* (Munro) Hack. (Figure 3-18)

Like zoysiagrass, centipedegrass was introduced from Asia, reportedly from seed found in the baggage of Frank Meyer, a USDA plant explorer who disappeared on an expedition to China in 1916. Centipedegrass, adapted to the humid climate of the southern United States, has a shallow root system that makes it less drought tolerant than bermudagrass, St. Augustinegrass, or bahiagrass. It is a coarse-textured, slow-growing plant that is low and creeping with leafy stolons. It grows well on moderately acid soils (pH 5.0 to 5.5) and under the shade of pine trees, but it does not thrive if drainage is poor. Its cold tolerance, particularly on sandy soils, is reported to be improved by an application of potassium (1 lb per 1000 sq ft) in September.

An important feature of the grass is its ease of culture: It requires less mowing than other turfgrasses and little or no fertilizer (1 to 2 lb nitrogen per 1000 sq ft, maximum) to keep it green. It should not be fertilized more than once a year. Like St. Augustinegrass, it may require application of iron to correct yellowing not attributable to poor drainage, insects, or disease. Centipedegrass is very competitive and may require no chemical weed controls. Herbicides that are safe on other grasses may injure it, so study labels carefully for exclusions.

Three to six years after establishment, the grass may become subject to centipedegrass decline, not exactly understood but seemingly related to overfertilization or high phosphorus levels in the soil, or both. Phosphorus is typically omitted from fertilizer applications. Overfertilization also seems to encourage spittlebugs, ground pearls, and *Rhizoctonia* brown patch, all of which are major pests of the grass.

Distinguishing features. Stoloniferous perennial; ligule a short purplish membrane fringed with hairs; auricles lacking; blade hairy toward the base, compressed or flattened, 3 to 5 mm wide; leaf sheath compressed with overlapping margins and tufts of hair at its throat; inflorescence, a digitate, solitary spike-like raceme. Mowing height: 1 to 2 in. Fertilization: 1 to 2 lb nitrogen per 1000 sq ft per year, maximum. If addition of iron is indicated to correct yellowing, see methods of application listed for St. Augustinegrass. Do not use herbicides unless they are specifically listed for centipedegrass.

Cultivars of centipedegrass

Two cultivars of centipedegrass, Oaklawn and Tennessee Hardy, are available, but their advantages over the common type have not been well established. They are established from sprigs, although common centipedegrass can be planted from seed.

Carpetgrass *Axonopus affinis* Chase (Figure 3-19)

This low-maintenance southern grass grows well on sandy or sandy loam soils from Virginia south to Florida and west to Texas. It is a low-growing perennial with wide, light green, blunt-tipped leaves, and it spreads by stolons as well as seed. Like centipedegrass, it tolerates moderate shade and tends to yellow on alkaline soils. It is less cold tolerant than bermudagrass, St. Augustinegrass, or centipedegrass and less drought resistant than bermudagrass. It can be established by seed, and its rate of spread and density can be improved with fertilizer. In summer it tends to form unsightly seed stalks.

No cultivars of carpetgrass exist at this time. However, another species of the grass, tropical carpetgrass *Axonopus compressus* (Swartz) Beauv., is vegetatively similar but less winter hardy than *A. affinis*. It is found largely in Florida and southern Louisiana.

Distinguishing features. Stoloniferous perennial; ligule a short fringe of hairs; auricles lacking; leaf sheath compressed; blade 4 to 8 mm wide, often hairy at the base, blunt or obtuse at the ends; inflorescence digitate, with two or three spike-like racemes. Mowing height: 1 to 2 in. Fertilization: 1 to 2 lb nitrogen per 1000 sq ft per year.

Bahiagrass *Paspalum notatum* Flügge (Figure 3-20)

This is a coarse, aggressive, subtropical perennial that spreads by short rhizomes. Like carpetgrass and centipedegrass, it is adapted to infertile acid and sandy soils in coastal areas from North Carolina to Florida to Texas. Considered an aggressive weed in most areas, its use as a turf is confined largely to central and southwest Florida. It is

CARPETGRASS

- Short, wide blades with rounded tips
- Flattened leaf sheaths

Figure 3-19 Carpetgrass *Axonopus* Beauv.
Short, wide blades with rounded tips.
Leaf sheaths flattened.
Stoloniferous, with hairy nodes.
Digitate, spike-like racemes.

used mostly as a forage grass. Bahiagrass is a good seed (mostly apomictic) producer and has some shade and drought tolerance.

Distinguishing features.   Rhizomatous perennial; ligule short and membranous; auricles lacking; leaf sheath compressed and sparsely hairy; inflorescence, digitate, with two or three spike-like, one-sided racemes. Mowing height: $1^{1}/_{2}$ to $2^{1}/_{2}$ in. Fertilization: 1 to 4 lb nitrogen per 1000 sq ft per year.

Cultivars of bahiagrass

Argentine: Released in 1949 by the Florida Agricultural Experiment Station in conjunction with the USDA, mostly for forage use, this is the cultivar generally used for turf. It is reported to have better density, color, and disease resistance than common bahiagrass or Pensacola. Its texture is coarse and it produces abundant seed stalks.

Paraguay: This cultivar has a grayish color. Its leaves are short and narrow, and it exhibits poor tolerance to cold temperatures.

Pensacola: Developed mostly for forage purposes at the Florida Agricultural Experiment Station in 1944, this grass has narrow leaves and good tolerance to low temperature. It forms a dense sod with a deep root system and is used extensively along roadsides in Florida.

Wilmington: This bahiagrass is recommended for its fine texture and low seed-head production. It is dark green, with few seed stalks and good cold tolerance. It is susceptible to dollar spot.

Buffalograss *Buchloe dactyloides* (Nutt.) Engelm. (Figure 3-21)

Like gramagrass, buffalograss is above all an important range grass in the Great Plains. Native to Texas and only occasionally used as a turfgrass, it helps to stabilize millions of acres of land from western Minnesota to central Montana south to Texas and northern Mexico. It is not suitable for use in the Southeast.

It is a gray-green, stoloniferous sod-former with fine leaves. It is better adapted to clay soils than to sandy soils. It tolerates alkaline soils and intensive grazing, and it is very resistant to drought. It should not be given excessive water or fertilizer. Mowed and fertilized infrequently, buffalograss can be transformed into a tolerable turf.

Distinguishing features.   Stoloniferous perennial; ligule a fringe of hairs; auricles lacking; blade narrow and ridged with long hairs; inflorescence with separate male and female flowers; male spikelets held aloft in two or three short spikes, female spikelets arranged in a bur partially hidden by the leaves. Mowing height: $^{1}/_{2}$ to $1^{1}/_{2}$ in. Fertilization: 0.5 to 2 lb nitrogen per 1000 sq ft per year.

Blue Gramagrass *Bouteloua gracilis* (HBK) Lag.

This is an important range grass in the Great Plains that, like buffalograss, volunteers at times as a turfgrass. It has short rhizomes and stems that easily root at the nodes, forming dense gray-green tufts that are heat and drought resistant and adapted to

BAHIAGRASS

• Wide, pointed, sparsely hairy,
  blades

Figure 3-20 Bahiagrass *Paspalum notatum* Flügge.
Wide, sparsely hairy, pointed leaf blades.
Short, sturdy rhizomes.
Digitate inflorescence with rounded spikelets.

BUFFALOGRASS

- Separate male (*left*) and female (*right*) inflorescences
- Gray-green

Figure 3-21 Buffalograss *Buchloe dactyloides* (Nutt.) Engelm.
Short, thin, curly blades, gray-green and sparsely hairy.
Stoloniferous.
Separate male (*left*) and female (*right*) inflorescences.

alkaline soils. Blue gramagrass is used along roadsides and for a turf in unirrigated regions of the semi-arid West.

Distinguishing features. Rhizomatous perennial; ligule a dense fringe of hairs; auricles lacking; blade narrow with prominent veins tapering to a sharp point; inflorescence, a distinctive drooping, one-sided spike.

Kikuyugrass *Pennisetum clandestinum* Hochst ex Chiov.

Often a weed but sometimes used as a turfgrass in southern California, kikuyugrass is a coarse, aggressive, sod-forming perennial. It was introduced from Africa in the 1920s and is used extensively as a forage plant in Central America. There and in warm, moist, tropical regions of Central Africa it is best adapted to the higher elevations (above 6000 ft) and is weakened by disease at lower elevations.

Kikuyugrass produces vigorous rhizomes and stolons. It is established vegetatively by sprigs and forms a dense turf when mowed close.

Distinguishing features. Rhizomatous and stoloniferous perennial; ligule a fringe of hairs; auricles lacking; leaf sheath hairy; inflorescence, a dense spike-like panicle.

4

Pesticides

USE PESTICIDES WITH SKILL AND CAUTION

In the next three chapters we will discuss the effects of weeds, insects, and fungi in turf management. In limiting damage from these organisms, the turf manager often has to rely on pesticides. Because of the dangerous nature of these materials, it is extremely important that you understand their characteristics, their special properties, and their proper utilization. The pesticide laws in the state in which you operate should be understood fully. The exams that are given by state agencies should be regarded not as an imposition of bureaucratic regulations but as a distinct aid to the practice of intelligent turf management.

It is the era to approach pesticides with intelligence. Simply stated, the environment cannot tolerate people who are careless with poisons, and the government is out to prove it. Our position as accomplished turf managers should be one in which we use pesticides always with a high degree of professional skill—only to a limited extent and only when absolutely necessary. Except on golf greens, where there is usually no alternative, we believe that a so-called preventive program is usually unwarranted—a crutch, so to speak, for mediocre skill at turf management. Preventive use of pesticides is like taking an aspirin every day for fear of catching a cold one weekend of the year—the consequences may be worse.

SOME PROBLEMS WITH PESTICIDES

Since pesticides came into wide usage in the United States in the 1950s, these chemical compounds have become our major weapon in the continuing war against insects, fungi, and weeds. Use of pesticides has produced at least two major benefits for us all. First, human health has been greatly improved owing to eradication of disease-carrying organisms. One needs only to think of the great reduction worldwide in the incidence of malaria to understand the magnitude of this benefit: Literally hundreds of millions of human lives have been saved through the use of DDT against the *Anopheles* mosquito. A second benefit from the use of pesticides has been the increase in crop plant yield owing to reduction of agricultural pests. Insecticides, fungicides, and especially herbicides have contributed in a major way to the greatly increased yields of corn, wheat, rice, and other crops that have been attained in the last three decades.

However, the widespread use of pesticides has not brought only benefits. In her book *Silent Spring* (1962),* Rachel Carson brought some of the harmful effects of DDT to public attention. Use of DDT was subsequently banned in the United States in 1972, though reinstated later for a few uses and still used in other parts of the world. The banning of DDT in the United States caused a general reexamination of pesticide use, and several important objections have been raised. It has been shown clearly that with continued use of pesticides, resistant strains of target pests have actually increased. When an insecticide, for example, is widely used, only resistant strains can survive, so they come to constitute an ever-increasing proportion of the total insect population. Although the immediate problem may be solved, pesticides may result in much worse problems in the future.

Another problem with pesticides is that they are often lethal to beneficial and nontarget organisms as well as to harmful organisms. For example, fungicides may eliminate beneficial mycorrhizal fungi as well as disease-causing pathogens from the soil environment. Numerous cases have been documented in agriculture where an insecticide has eliminated more of the predators of a harmful pest than it has the target pest itself.

A third damaging effect of some pesticides is their persistence in the environment. This, together with the harmful effects on birds, fish, and other wildlife, was the primary reason for the banning of DDT. Many of the newer pesticides persist in soil for only a few days or weeks. This avoids long-term environmental damage and is sometimes also helpful, as for example with the herbicide glyphosate: A turf area can be seeded a few hours after the application without danger to the developing grass seedlings.

A fourth major concern with the use of pesticides is their effect on human health. Some are known to be highly toxic and should be handled with great care. Others are without demonstrated effect on mammalian systems and are considered safe. For example, several herbicides work by affecting photosynthesis, a reaction not present in animals. However, in many cases the long-term effects of these chemicals may not yet be known.

Biological Control and Integrated Pest Management

Even before biologists recognized the harmful effects of widespread use of pesticides, they understood that the numbers of a given organism in the world are kept in check by its natural predators. However, when some pesticides were banned, great impetus

*Rachel Carson, *Silent Spring* (Boston: Houghton Mifflin Co., 1962).

was given to research on *biological control* of insects and other pests. Biological control refers to the use of one biological organism to control another; broadly construed, it can include management of the environment to favor the growth of one organism such as a crop plant at the expense of a harmful organism. Thus proper management of the turf ecosystem takes on a new significance. When biological control is used as just one component of a carefully designed pest management system, often also including use of synthetic pesticides, the system is referred to as *integrated pest management*.

The turf industry still relies heavily on the use of chemical insecticides, fungicides, and herbicides, but the turf manager should be aware that alternative strategies are rapidly becoming available. One biological control already widely used is milky spore disease as a control for the Japanese beetle. This disease results from infection of the beetle larva by the bacterium *Bacillus popilliae.* The larva ingests bacterial spores, which germinate inside its body into rapidly reproducing bacterial cells. More spores are released into the blood of the larva, which eventually turns white and opaque. Metamorphosis is usually inhibited, and the larva dies, spreading spores into the soil. After this cycle has been repeated for several years, the soil may come to serve as an effective reservoir of milky disease spores, thus preventing future infestations of Japanese beetles.

In a similar way the fungus *Beauveria bassiana* has long been known to infect the chinch bug, causing a disease called muscardine. The white fungal threads may completely cover and fill the body cavity of the bug, causing death in about three days. Recent renewed interest in this biological control may soon make *Beauveria* a realistic choice for chinch bug control.

Turf managers are already using an additional biological control. As indicated in Chapter 3, perennial ryegrasses with an Endophyte Enhanced Performance rating are now available. These grasses are resistant to chewing insects because they carry certain fungi as *endophytes,* or organisms living within their cells. The fungi secrete substances that are toxic to the insect pests but harmless to the host grass plants. The fungi serve as a built-in biological control for chewing insects. The fungi live principally in the shoots of the grass plants, where they secrete chemical compounds such as nitrogen-containing alkaloids. These toxins kill or inhibit feeding of chewing insects. In the case of turf species used also as forage grasses, grazing livestock may also be harmed. The improved resistance to insects and to general environmental stress of endophyte-containing grasses has attracted great interest from turf managers. At present, endophyte-based insect resistance is best known in some perennial ryegrasses and tall fescues, but work is underway to introduce these beneficial fungi into additional grass species and cultivars.

There is a growing feeling among many turf managers that pesticides, and especially their routine use, are often more deleterious to turf than the original pests they were designed to control. It should be understood, for example, that a completely "selective" herbicide does not exist. That is, the turfgrass that is treated with a herbicide will also sustain some damage, albeit nearly imperceptible. The rate of growth will be affected, as will any new rooting. Obviously, if some herbicides are used continually, the turf in time will be significantly affected. The same is apparently true of some insecticides: Chlordane, for example, before it was banned completely, caused a progressive thinning of turf and was related to increased chinch bug activity.

In regard to control of insects and fungal diseases and especially weeds, the first line of defense on a lawn should be proper turf management, including a concern for the quality of the soil, choice of the right grasses, and proper fertilization, mowing, and watering. Many pests begin to damage turf only *after* the entire soil–grass ecosystem has begun to deteriorate and to show the ravages of poor management, which may include the unwise choice and use of pesticides. Our best advice for the incipient turf manager, then, is to approach pesticides with healthy skepticism, using them only after careful consideration but then with total accuracy and intelligent concern. As with any health practitioner, there is no substitute for an accurate diagnosis coupled with the choice of the right medicine.

PESTICIDE REGULATIONS FOR TURF MANAGERS

The information below is based on the amended Federal Insecticide, Fungicide, and Rodenticide Act: Public Law 95-396, September 30, 1978, and, as an example of state legislation, on the Ohio Pesticide Law of January 1, 1977. *Make sure that you check the pesticide laws for your own state!*

Pesticide registration.   All pesticides that are produced, distributed, or sold in the United States must be registered with the federal Environmental Protection Agency (EPA) and within each state in which they are used with the Director of Agriculture of that state.

Labeling.   In order to be issued a registration number, a pesticide must have a complete *label*. This is written, printed, or graphic material that is attached to the pesticide container. It may also include booklets or other literature that may accompany the pesticide. The label must be printed clearly, not be misleading in any way, and be expressed in "such terms as to render it likely to be read and understood by the ordinary individual under customary conditions of purchase and use." The label must contain the following information:

1. A registration number
2. A list of ingredients, including inert ingredients (materials that act as solvents or fillers) and particularly the active ingredient (a.i.), or material that acts as the pesticide
3. Clear directions for use of the product—rates to be used, timing of the application, special instructions
4. A warning and caution statement adequate to protect health and environment
5. The name and address of the producer
6. The name, brand, or trademark under which the pesticide is sold
7. The net weight or measure of the contents.

If the pesticide contains any substances highly toxic to humans, the following must be clearly printed on the label: (1) a skull and crossbones, (2) the word *POISON* prominently in red on a background of a distinctly contrasting color, and (3) a statement regarding an antidote or practical treatment in case of poisoning. It is against the law to use any pesticide except in accordance with the label.

Any pesticide product registration will be suspended, revoked, or refused if (1) it does not warrant the proposed claims for it, (2) its labeling does not comply with the requirements of the federal act, or (3) it will not perform its intended function without unreasonable adverse effects on the environment.

General and restricted use.   When pesticides are registered with the EPA, they are classified in one of two ways: for *general use* or for *restricted use*. (Some are classified in both categories, depending on each specific use.) If the EPA determines that the pesticide "when applied according to directions for use . . . will not generally cause unreasonable adverse effects in the environment" it is classified for general use. If, on the other hand, it is determined that the pesticide may cause adverse effects on the environment, including injury to the applicator by skin absorption or by direct inhalation, the pesticide is classified for restricted use only.

Certified applicator.   If a pesticide is classified for restricted use (which includes some turf pesticides), then it shall be applied only by or under the direct supervision of a *certified applicator*. This is one who is certified—that is, "determined to be competent with respect to the use and handling of pesticides." Normally the certification is accomplished by enrolling in a training program and taking an exam administered by a state agency and approved by the administration, the head of the federal EPA.

There are several levels of certified applicator:

1. *Private applicator*—a certified applicator who applies restricted-use pesticides only to his own property or to that of his principal employer.
2. *Commercial applicator*—one who applies pesticides for compensation to another's property. There are several categories of commercial applicator:
   A. *Custom applicator*—"a person who personally or by his agent owns or operates a custom application business that applies pesticides to the property of another" (e.g., a lawn service).
   B. *Custom operator*—an individual who is employed or directly supervised by a custom applicator (e.g., by a lawn service).
   C. *Limited commercial applicator*—an applicator who is certified as competent by the director to apply restricted-use pesticides in certain categories specified in his certification (e.g., sheep dipper or blacktopper).
   D. *Public operator*—a certified individual who is employed at any level of government.

Trained serviceman. This is an employee who is not certified but whom a certified applicator has instructed in the proper use of the equipment and materials with which the employee is to work. This employee must be a "competent person," that is, one who is "properly qualified to perform functions associated with pesticide application" and who is capable of performing "repetitive and routine ground operations."

Direct supervision. Noncertified applicators or trained servicemen may apply pesticides as long as they are under the *direct supervision* of a certified applicator. Direct supervision is interpreted loosely to mean that the certified applicator must be "within close geographic proximity to the work site, which, under ordinary circumstances shall not exceed *25 miles* and/or be available within a short period of time," which under ordinary circumstances shall not exceed *two hours*.

Or alternatively: "In the absence of the supervising certified applicator, clearly legible or otherwise verifiable instructions and/or directions for handling and applying the pesticide shall be readily available to the noncertified applicator at the work site and shall be made available for inspection by properly identified agents of the director upon request. (The pesticide label is part of such instructions and may suffice in those matters which it covers.) When required by the label, the actual physical presence of a certified applicator is required when application is made by a noncertified applicator."

No person shall employ as an aide or helper in pesticide operation any person who is mentally incompetent or for any reason is unable to satisfactorily communicate with or understand instructions given by the applicator of pesticides.

All aides or helpers employed or supervised by an applicator should be acquainted with the hazards involved in the handling of pesticides and with appropriate precautions to avoid these hazards.

Applying pesticides

1. No person shall operate equipment that draws water from surface waters or public water supplies unless the equipment has an effective antisiphon device to prevent backflow.

2. No person shall operate equipment in such condition or in such a manner as to create a hazard from leaking, spilling, dripping, backflow, vapors, or drift to the health and safety of the public or to animals or wildlife.

3. No person shall knowingly rent or loan faulty equipment that has not been thoroughly cleaned in a manner to prevent contamination of a pesticide solution or other formulation by previous use.

4. Any human illness requiring medical attention resulting from or allegedly resulting from pesticide use must be reported by an applicator to the state Director of Agriculture (see later) by telephone within 48 hours of learning of the incident.

5. Any property damage in excess of $250 allegedly resulting from the operation of an applicator must be reported *in writing within 10 days* of knowledge of the damage.

6. No person shall apply a pesticide at such time or under such conditions that the wind velocity will cause the pesticide to drift and cause damage.

7. No person shall apply herbicidal foliage sprays to woody vegetation by aircraft on rights of way when the wind velocity *exceeds seven miles per hour* at eye level.

8. No driver of a moving vehicle shall apply a herbicide to roadside vegetation within public right-of-way limits unless the spray is directed by a second person or unless a special permit has been obtained from the Director (see later).

9. Some restricted-use pesticides require that a notice be given to occupants or nearby properties or that the area to be treated be posted with reentry times. It is unlawful to apply the pesticide unless these conditions have been met.

10. If requested to do so, the applicator shall leave with each customer a clearly printed or written statement of the pesticide(s) applied, the date applied, and any pertinent information pertaining to possible residues and hazards.

It is also unlawful for any person to apply, use, supervise, or recommend the use of any pesticide inconsistent with its labeling or other restrictions imposed by the Director of Agriculture; to apply a restricted-use pesticide without being licensed or certified to do so; to represent the effect of pesticides or methods to be utilized falsely or fraudulently; to apply known ineffective or improper materials; to operate in a faulty, careless, or negligent manner or operate faulty or unsafe equipment; to impersonate any federal, state, county, or city official; to make false or fraudulent records, invoices, or reports; to use or supervise the use of a restricted pesticide on the property of another without having a certified applicator in direct supervision; to use fraud or misrepresentation in making application for a license or certificate or renewal of a license or certificate; to make a false or misleading statement in an inspection concerning any use of pesticides; to distribute restricted-use pesticides to the ultimate user at any time without a pesticide dealer's license; to use any pesticide that is under an experimental use permit contrary to the provisions of such permit; to engage in fraudulent business practices in the application of pesticides; to dispose of any pesticide product or container in such a manner as to have unreasonable adverse effects on the environment; and to display any pesticide in any manner to produce unreasonable adverse effects on the environment, or to contaminate adjacent food, feed, or other products.

State pesticide control authority. You should identify the person or agency responsible for controlling the use of pesticides in your state. Typically, this is the state Director of Agriculture, and within that agency there is someone designated Specialist in Charge of Pesticide Regulation. This is your contact for state pesticide laws, a list of restricted-use pesticides, special rulings, date of examinations, and other information pertaining to pesticides.

The state Director may have a pesticide *Advisory Council* consisting of such people as the Dean of the College of Agriculture of the state university, Dean of the College of Biological Science, the Director of the state Agricultural Experiment Station (AES), and others who are familiar with pesticide usage. A *Standards Committee* may also be appointed to assist the director in establishing standards of training, examination, and licensing of applicators.

Examinations. Each applicant for a license "shall be required to show by written examination that he possesses adequate knowledge concerning the proper use and application of pesticides in the categories for which he has applied.

"Applicants who fail to pass an exam . . . may apply for a reexam to be administered at a prearranged time and location but no sooner than five days after a previous examination, except by special permission of the Director.

"Reexamination will be required at *three-year intervals* except that a certified applicator may be exempt from such reexamination provided that he can document his participation in at least one approved training session during the two years prior to the date of his scheduled reexamination."

Restricted-use pesticides and special rulings. You should ask your state Director of Agriculture or Specialist in Charge of Pesticide Regulations for a list of pesticides in your state that are restricted in their use and for any *special rulings*. Certain special rulings, for example, may restrict the use of specific pesticides in areas where there are plant nurseries, bee and honey producers, or specialized horticultural crops. In some areas it may be necessary to post a site or notify the owner or caretaker before a pesticide is applied.

Applicator records. Records of all applications of pesticides made by commercial applicators and limited commercial applicators shall be held for a period of three years and be made available to the Director of Agriculture or his agent upon request. The following information shall be recorded when applicable to the operation being conducted:

1. Name and address of responsible certified applicator and name of operator (if not the certified applicator himself)
2. Name and address of person contracting for service
3. Date of application and reentry date when applicable
4. Type of plants, crop, or animals to be treated
5. Principal pests to be controlled
6. Acreage or number of plants or animals treated
7. Location of treatment area or owner or tenant of property (if different from Point 2, above)
8. Trade name (brand name) and lot number, if on container of pesticides used
9. Total amount of each pesticide product used
10. Rate of application and concentration of pesticide formulation applied
11. Type of equipment used
12. Time of day of application, including the time of starting the actual application and the time of completion of application or, if uncompleted, the time when operations ceased for the day
13. Wind direction, its estimated velocity, and weather conditions.

Right of entry.   The Director of Agriculture is authorized to enter any public or private premise or transport vehicle to inspect books and records kept pertaining to pesticides. The Director can inspect the storage and disposal of pesticides and the equipment or devices used to apply them and can collect samples of any pesticides being applied or sample any vegetation, animal life, water, soil, or other matter to which pesticides have been applied.

If the Director has reasonable cause to believe that pesticides are being applied improperly, or a piece of equipment used by an applicator requires calibration, adjustment, or repair, a *stop operation* can be issued.

The sale or use of any pesticide can be stopped and the pesticide can be seized or removed if it is felt that it causes unreasonable adverse effects on the environment, if the pesticide is adulterated or misbranded, or if it is not registered or labeled properly.

Suspension of license and seizures.   The Director can suspend or revoke a license or can modify any provision of a license if an applicant or holder of a license is found to be no longer qualified or has violated any provision of the law. The Director can obtain a permanent or temporary injunction or initiate a prosecution when a violation of the law has occurred.

The Director can seize any pesticide or device if there is reasonable cause to believe that it is being distributed, stored, transported, or used in violation of the law.

Pesticide dealers.   A pesticide dealer—that is, one who sells or distributes but does not apply pesticides—must also obtain a license from the state Director of Agriculture. A license is required for each location or outlet within the state from which pesticides are distributed or sold. He must sell restricted-use pesticides *only* to pesons who are certified.

No dealer shall sell a restricted-use pesticide except to a certified private applicator, licensed custom applicator, or limited commercial applicator; to a public agency that employs a public operator; or to a person who holds a valid "User's Permit."

The dealer shall retain a record of all sales of restricted-use pesticides and shall include the name and address of the purchase, the type and serial number of the license or permit, and the kind and quantity of the restricted-use pesticide sold. The dealer's copy of the user's permit and the records of sales shall be kept on file and be available during all reasonable hours for inspection upon request of the Director. The dealer shall retain such records for no less than two years.

The dealer shall submit to the State Pesticide Authority a copy of each such sales record within 15 days following the last day of each of the following months: May, August, November, and February.

Storage of pesticides.   Pesticides shall be stored in a manner that will not contaminate animal feeds or commercial fertilizers.

1. Pesticides shall not be stored in work areas where equipment is used for the production of animal feeds or for the storage of feed components or finished products that are approved for use in animal feeds.

2. Herbicides shall not be stored in work areas where equipment is used for the mixing of fertilizers for commercial crops or for the storage of fertilizer components or finished products.

3. Pesticides shall not be stored or loaded into application equipment within 100 yards of an airline passenger terminal.

4. In retail stores pesticides shall not be stored or shelved in close proximity to foodstuffs, pet foods, or children's toys and in no case stored or shelved above them.

5. Areas used for pesticide display shall be thoroughly cleaned before reusing for display of other products.

6. Restricted-use pesticides shall not be displayed in such manner as to be accessible to children.

Handling and loading.   Pesticides shall be handled and loaded in a manner that will assure the protection of crops, livestock, and the general public. Toxicity and volatility of pesticides shall be considered in the storage and handling practices.

DISPOSING OF PESTICIDES . . . HAZARDOUS WASTES

If you or your company generate more than 100 kg (220 lb) of hazardous waste *per month* (such as unrinsed pesticide containers or the rinsings from a 2,4-D can), which is equivalent to approximately half of a 55-gallon drum, you are considered by the federal government to be a big operator. You must follow a set of federal procedures for handling and disposing of that waste. If you have not done so, call your state Hazardous Waste Management Agency or the Waste Management Division of your regional EPA, or call the EPA Hotline, (800) 424-9346, for a list of procedures.

Many users of small amounts of pesticide avoid becoming "big operators" (that is, 100-kg operators) in the eyes of the government by simply planning their use of pesticides with care: Plan your applications to avoid leftovers, dispose of containers as promptly as possible so that they do not accumulate or carry over into the next month, triple-rinse all containers with a volume equal to 10% of the container's regular capacity, and spray the rinsings on a regular target site according to the label. (Containers that are triple-rinsed are no longer considered hazardous.) The best idea is to use the rinsings from the used pesticide container to form the basis for your next tankful of pesticide material. In this way you generate no hazardous waste.

EPA Hotline for questions about pesticide disposal: (800) 424-9346 (in Washington, D.C., 382-3000)
EPA Small Business Hotline: (800) 368-5888

PESTICIDE TOXICITY

Toxicity, or the property of a pesticide to cause adverse physiological effects, is expressed by the abbreviation LD_{50}. This expression—the *lethal dose*—indicates the amount of toxicant taken orally that will kill 50% of the animals (usually laboratory rats) being tested. It is expressed in weight (usually mg) of the chemical per unit of body weight (usually kg) of the rat. (1000 mg = 1 g; 1000 g = 1 kg; 454 g = 1 lb; 2.2 lb = 1 kg.)

For example, if pesticide X has an oral LD_{50} of 200, that means that 200 mg (1/5 g) of the pesticide is required to kill five out of 10 rats, each weighing 1 kg (2.2 lb). When this is extrapolated into human terms, 10 g (about 1/2 oz, or 1/2 teaspoonful) could kill a 100-lb person, making pesticide X a fairly toxic compound.

The lower the LD_{50}, the more dangerous the pesticide! Make sure you understand that a pesticide with an LD_{50} of 10 is more toxic than a pesticide with an LD_{50} of 1000, because in the former case only 10 mg/kg are sufficient to kill half the animals tested, whereas in the latter case it takes 1000 mg to have the same effect.

Most LD_{50} ratings are stated in regard to oral ingestion, and if not otherwise stated, it is presumed that the tests pertain to oral dosage and to rats. Dermal tests and inhalation tests are also performed. In the dermal test the LD_{50} is determined by placing the pesticide on the skin of the animal and covering it with a bandage for 24 hours.

Pesticides that give off gases, fumes, vapors, or dust are subjected to an inhalation test in which the animals are placed in an airtight container for 1 hour with a given quantity of pesticide in 1 L of air. The inhalation values are recorded as Lethal Concentration (LC_{50}) and expressed in micrograms (μg). Therefore, if a pesticide has an LC_{50} of 100, this means that it will take 100 g of the pesticide per liter of air to kill five out of 10 test animals. (1000 μg = 1 mg; 1000 mg = 1 g; 1 L = 1.06 qt.) Gas or vapor inhalation can also be expressed in parts per million (ppm).

Based on the LD_{50} and LC_{50} values, pesticides are classified according to the

TABLE 4-1. Toxicity Classes of Pesticides

Pesticide Class	Pesticide Label Signal Words	Oral LD_{50}	Dermal LC_{50}	Inhalation LC_{50}	Lethal Oral Dose for a 150-lb Man
I. Highly toxic	Danger—poison	0–50	0–200	0–2,000	Few drops to 1 teaspoon
II. Moderately toxic	Warning	50–500	200–2,000	2,000–20,000	1 teaspoon to 1 ounce
III. Slightly toxic	Caution	500–5,000	2,000–20,000	20,000+	1 ounce to 1 pint or pound
IV. Relatively nontoxic	Caution	5,000+	20,000+	—	Over 1 pint or pound

degree of their toxicity, as shown in Table 4-1. These values are indicated for some common turf pesticides in Table 4-2. Study these tables carefully.

WETTING AGENTS

Pesticides are sometimes applied more effectively and in lesser concentrations if they are mixed with a wetting agent, or surfactant. Surfactants include activators, dispersants, deflocculators, compatibility agents, emulsifiers, detergents, wetting agents,

TABLE 4-2.   The LD_{50} of Some Common Turf Pesticides

Pesticide	Acute Oral LD_{50} (mg/kg)[a]
Herbicides[b]	
Benefin (Balan)	10000
Bensulide (Betasan)	1082
DCPA (Dacthal)	3000[c]
Dicamba (Banvel)	2900
DSMA	1000
Glyphosate (Roundup)	4320
MCPP (Mecoprop)	930
Siduron (Tupersan)	7500
2,4-D (amine)	300–1200
Insecticides	
Baygon (Propoxur)[d]	95–104
Diazinon (Spectracide)	891–1700
Dursban (Chlorpyrifos)[d]	163
Dylox (Proxol)	450–500
Ethion	208
Malathion	1375
Oftanol (Isofenphos)	28–39
Fungicides[e]	
Anilazine (Dyrene)	2710
Benomyl (Tersan 1991)	10000
Chloroneb (Tersan SP)	11000
Chlorothalonil (Daconil)	10000[f]
Cycloheximide (Actidione)	2
PCNB (Terraclor)	12000
Thiram (Tersan 75)	780
Zineb (Dithane Z-78)	5280

[a]Dose given in milligrams of chemical per kilogram of body weight in rats unless otherwise specified.

[b]Note that the most commonly used herbicide, 2,4-D, has one of the lowest LD_{50} values. None of the herbicides listed here are classified as Highly Toxic (oral $LD_{50} = 50$).

[c]LD_{50} in rabbit.

[d]These insecticides are nearly toxic enough to be considered Highly Toxic.

[e]Note that except for cycloheximide, most fungicides are relatively harmless.

[f]Daconil was fed to rats and dogs with no ill effects after two years.

spreaders, stickers, drift suppressors, and probably more. They are molecules consisting of a hydrophobic (water-hating) and a hydrophilic (water-loving) part. These special properties decrease the surface tension of water, allowing it to spread out more, essentially to wet more surface and to infiltrate a soil or a leaf more rapidly. Phosphorus, for example, in a household detergent acts as a wetting agent, increasing the water's ability to infiltrate, wet, and dissolve dirt. There are surfactants that make it possible to mix even oil and water.

Typical surfactants used in agriculture are nonionic, that is, they do not possess either a positive or a negative charge. Nonionic wetting agents, as opposed to cationic or anionic ones, are thought to be longer lasting and less phytotoxic, or harmful to plants.

PESTICIDE LETTER DESIGNATIONS

Pesticide labels frequently have one or more letter designations that are useful in deciding how to mix and apply the chemical. For example, powdered pesticides that will readily absorb water are labeled W or WP for wettable powder or WPG for water-dispersible granules. L means flowable liquid, and E or EC means emulsifiable concentrate. Sometimes the letters are preceded by a number, such as 2WP, which is used to indicate a wettable powder with 2 lb of active ingredient.

MIXING PESTICIDES

In order to treat several problems in one application, it is common to mix pesticides with each other and with fertilizers. Although this procedure reduces labor and equipment costs and frequently gives good results, it must be approached with caution.

Listed are several precautions one should use when mixing various turf chemicals together:

1. Read the label of each pesticide—it may rule out specific mixtures.
2. If in doubt, mix the pesticides first in a jar and observe them for several minutes. If they tend to become gelatin-like or foam excessively or if some part of the mixture separates or "salts out" to the bottom of the jar, the chemicals are probably not compatible.
3. Do not mix pesticides in concentrated form. Place them in a tank already filled with water, preferably with an agitation system running.
4. Frequently when pesticides are mixed, the rate of each individual pesticide is reduced. A classic example is the herbicide mixture of MCPP, 2,4-D, and dicamba. Alone the recommended rate for MCPP is 1 to $1^1/2$ lb per acre; for 2,4-D it is 1 lb per acre; and for dicamba it is $^1/4$ to $^1/3$ lb per acre. When combined, the rate for MCPP drops to $^1/2$ lb per acre; for 2,4-D it drops to $^1/4$ lb per acre; and for dicamba it drops to $^1/8$ lb per acre.

5. Wettable powders or water-dispersible granules are mixed in water first and agitated, followed by liquid products, water-soluble powders, surfactants (wetting agents), if used, and finally emulsifiable concentrates.

6. Organic fungicides should not be mixed with any pesticides that contain xylene as a solvent.

7. High pH, or alkaline, reactions in the tank should generally be avoided. Alkaline reactions reduce the effectiveness of many pesticides.

PROTECT YOURSELF!

Great strides have been made in the last few years in the development of pesticides that are low in toxicity to warm-blooded animals and also relatively nonpersistent in the environment. The transition to these pesticides, however, is far from complete, and there are still plenty of so-called hard pesticides in common use.

Protect the various routes of entry into the body: oral, dermal, and respiratory. Studies on hundreds of pesticide applicators indicate that 97% of the pesticide to which the body is subjected during most exposure situations is deposited on the skin. The area of greatest absorption on man is the scrotum. The head and neck were found to be areas of greater absorption than the arms or hands. The ear canal is also relatively efficient at absorbing pesticides.

1. Clothing should be changed and laundered daily.

2. Wash your hands and face before eating; take a shower every evening.

3. Don't ever smoke while using pesticides and, of course, avoid breathing them.

4. If you should spill a pesticide on your skin or soak your clothing, wash thoroughly with soap and water and change your clothes at the first opportunity; then have your clothes washed.

5. Be conscious of how you dispose of empty bags and containers so that they impose no hazard to water, humans, animals, or plants.

6. Be extremely careful on windy days. If there is a chance of drift, *don't apply pesticides.* This is the so-called petunia factor—overspreading the material so that it kills the neighbor's shrubs and flowers. It is a common complaint with poorly trained personnel. If an applicator does not understand this danger and others, his employment should be terminated.

The best advice in using pesticides is simply, *Be cautious, be careful, and use your common sense.*

Protective Clothing

In the application of any pesticide labeled *Caution,* one should always wear long trousers, long-sleeved shirts, shoes, socks, and a hat. Only a very foolish person uses the occasion of a pesticide application to "get a tan." If the label signal word is *Warning,* add a wide-brimmed hat, gloves, and rubber boots. If the label says *Warning* or *Danger* and includes "do not breathe" or "poisonous if inhaled," add goggles and a respirator.

If the company you are working for objects to protective clothing for fear of alarming customers, look for another job. No amount of money is worth a serious health problem in the future.

Symptoms of Pesticide Poisoning

These symptoms of poisoning are listed in order from mild to severe poisoning:
Fatigue . . . headache . . . dizziness . . . blurred vision . . . weakness . . . muscle twitches . . . vomiting . . . diarrhea . . . change in heart rate . . . pupil constriction . . . lowered blood pressure . . . fever . . . respiratory failure . . . convulsions . . . coma . . . cardiac arrest . . . death.

DECONTAMINATING A SPRAYER

Use 1 pt of household ammonia in 10 gal of water or 2 to 3 tablespoons per gallon of water.

In lieu of ammonia, use 1 cup of household detergent per 10 gal of water or 1 to 2 tablespoon per gallon of water.

If possible, let stand for eight hours or more, but in any case agitate, drain, and rinse with clean water *three times.*

Many sprayer manufacturers recommend *Neutra-Sol,* which is produced by Thomas G. Kilfoif Co., P.O. Box 396, San Bruno, CA 94066.

The cleaning water, or rinsate, should be handled and disposed of in the same manner and with the same respect as the original pesticide formulation.

CONVERTING PARTS PER MILLION TO POUNDS PER ACRE

Concentrations of chemicals in solution are frequently expressed in parts per million (ppm), but applications are usually expressed in pounds per acre. The calculation of pounds per acre (lb/A) is based on an acre furrow slice, or the top 6 in. of soil, which when oven dried, yields a typical dry weight of 2,000,000 lb.

To convert from ppm to lb/A: This calculation is made by multiplying ppm by 2 (representing 2,000,000 lb/A). If for example, test results indicate a soil phosphorus concentration of 30 ppm and you want to know how many pounds per acre that is, multiply 30 ppm by 2 million lb, giving an answer of 60 lb/A of phosphorus. The calculation can be expressed in the following way:

Calculation: How many lb/A is 30 ppm?

$$\text{ppm} \div 1{,}000{,}000 = \text{lb/A} \div 2{,}000{,}000$$
$$30 \div 1{,}000{,}000 = x \div 2{,}000{,}000 = 60 \text{ lb/A}$$

TABLE 4-3. Area, Volume, and Concentration Equivalents

1 acre = 43,560 sq ft = 4840 sq yd
1 lb/1000 sq ft = 43.56 lb/A
1 pt/1000 sq ft = 5 gal/A
100 gal/A = 2.5 gal/1000 sq ft

3 t = 1 T
2 T = 1 fl oz
1 c = 8 fl oz
1 pt = 16 fl oz
2 pt = 1 qt
4 qt = 1 gal

1 ppm = 1 mg/L
= 0.0001%
= 0.013 oz in 100 gal

1% = 10,000 ppm
= 10 g/L
= 1.28 oz/gal
= 8 lb/100 gal

Useful Turf Measurements

You should memorize the equivalent measurements listed in Table 4-3.

REFERENCES FOR INFORMATION ON PESTICIDES

British Crop Protection Council. *The Pesticide Manual, A World Compendium* (7th ed.). Lavenham, Suffolk: The Lavenham Press, Ltd., 1983.

Royal Society of Chemistry, University of Nottingham. *The Agrochemical Handbook*. Old Woking, Surrey: Unwin Bros., Ltd., 1983.

Windholz, Martha, ed. *The Merck Index: An Encyclopedia of Chemicals, Drugs, and Biologicals* (10th ed.). Rahway, N.J.: Merck & Co., Inc., 1983.

5

Weeds and Herbicides

PLANTS OUT OF PLACE

Weeds have been called "plants that are out of place": They are simply plants growing where they are not wanted. We are all familiar with ugly thistles and persistent dandelions. But bentgrass growing in a patch in a bluegrass lawn is considered a weed too, although its presence is desirable in some other circumstances, such as in a bentgrass putting green.

Many weeds do have some special characteristics that account for their aggressiveness and their broad distribution. They have the ability to tolerate a wide range of growing conditions, and they grow thickly and rapidly. However, their most interesting characteristics have to do with reproduction and seeds. Weeds reproduce at prodigious rates: A study of 101 annual weeds gave an average seed production of 20,832 seeds per plant! A single plant of the common turf weed, purslane, may produce more than 2 million seeds in one season! Weed seeds are often small and easily dispersed by wind, animals, or humans (who have difficulty separating them out of crop seed lots). They may remain viable for decades in the soil. Studies in Minnesota have shown that topsoil sampled to a depth of 6 in. may contain more than 2000 seeds per cubic foot. An acre of farmland may contain over $1^{1}/_{2}$ tons of weed seeds. Many weed seeds germinate only in light, so they remain dormant in the soil until it is cultivated and the seeds are brought to the surface. Thus one method of reducing weed populations before a crop is planted is to plow or disk the soil, then leave it for several weeks, then repeat the cultivation. This technique first brings weed seeds to the surface, then allows them to grow into plants, then destroys the plants.

Weeds are particularly abundant in disturbed and cultivated areas, and along

118

with people, they have migrated around the world. It is to be expected that turf areas represent prime breeding grounds for these persistent, adaptable plants. *Annual* weeds are easiest to control, because they develop from seed, reach mature size, flower, set more seed, and die all within one growing season. In the colder parts of the United States most annuals are prominent during the spring, summer, and fall. These *summer annuals* include such turf weeds as crabgrass. However, in southern areas *winter annuals,* which begin their development in the fall, live through the winter and die with the warm weather of late spring; they are a severe problem in turf. Chickweed and shepherd's purse live as winter annuals. A few weeds, such as some thistles, are *biennials,* which live for two years only. They grow vegetatively during the first year, then flower, set seed, and die by the end of the second year.

Perennial weeds, which live for more than two growing seasons, are often hard to control because they have large, persistent root systems and other subsurface structures, such as rhizomes and bulbs. It is difficult to eradicate these underground propagative parts, as anyone who has tried to dig dandelions out of a lawn knows. The perennials often die back to the underground parts for the winter, but regrowth begins in early spring. Quackgrass, plantain, and dandelion are perennials.

GOOD TURF MANAGEMENT REDUCES WEED PROBLEMS

Fortunately, with proper management, keeping weeds out of a fine turf is a fairly simple matter. Weeds are not the cause of poor turf, but rather the result. Most turfgrasses have been selected over the years for their vigor and aggressiveness. If properly nourished and mowed at the right height, they can out-compete most weeds. For example, weedy quackgrass can be suppressed in a bluegrass lawn by fertilizing and irrigating the bluegrass as recommended and mowing to the proper height every five days. Quackgrass cannot compete successfully under those conditions. Weed control, then, starts by fertilizing, mowing, irrigating, and otherwise managing the existing turf intelligently. This *cultural weed control* is not difficult, but it requires a good knowledge of weeds, of turf species, and of environmental factors.

Before jumping to the arsenal of chemical weed controls in an established turf, you should try several common-sense cultural techniques that promote weed control:

1. Mow high.
2. Postpone dethatching and similar operations until the season when weed seed germination is at a minimum.
3. Avoid fertilizing when turf is dormant.
4. Apply phosphorus fertilizer when weed seed germination is at a minimum.
5. Avoid frequent but shallow irrigation.

Numerous studies have shown that one of the best ways to help control weeds in an established turf is to mow at the highest level recommended for the turf species. For bluegrasses, this would be $2\frac{1}{2}$ to 3 in. Mowing height is important for at least two reasons. If the grass plants are mowed too closely, light will reach the soil and cause germination of light-requiring weed seeds. In addition, the grass will thin out owing to damage to the crowns and growing points, once again allowing light to penetrate to the soil. If the turf is mowed high, however, its height and dense growth will shade out many weed seeds and small plants before they can become established. This shading effect explains why we don't see much crabgrass growing under the canopy of a large tree.

A recent study demonstrates the importance of proper mowing height. It was shown that when a turf area consisting of 85% weeds and 15% St. Augustinegrass was mowed at the correct height and fertilized properly over a period of two years, the turfgrass increased to 99% of the cover and the weeds were reduced to 1%.

Dethatching, raking, core aerating, and other cultural practices that open up the turf also promote germination of weed seeds by permitting light to reach them. These operations are particularly damaging when the turfgrasses are dormant, because grass regrowth will not occur rapidly. Dethatching should be scheduled for a time of year when weed seed germination is at a minimum. For northern turf areas, fall is preferred.

If weeds are a problem in a dormant turf area, as in the summer in the North, do not fertilize. The turfgrass plants do not benefit much from fertilizer at such a time, but weeds tolerant of summer heat will be stimulated to grow and spread. Postpone fertilization until the turf comes out of dormancy.

As indicated in Chapter 2, phosphorus promotes germination of seeds and is thus included at a high level in starter fertilizers. Of course, this stimulation of germination applies equally to turfgrass and to weed seed. Therefore, application of phosphorus, or at least of high levels of phosphorus, to turf should be avoided at the season when weed seeds germinate. Addition of high phosphorus levels to bluegrass in the spring promotes germination of crabgrass seeds and is not necessary for the mature turf; postpone it until fall.

The timing of irrigation can determine the weediness of a turf area. Frequent shallow waterings encourage germination of surface weed seeds and are not particularly beneficial to the often deeper-rooted turf. Shallow watering is especially undesirable when the turfgrass is dormant (summer for cool-season turf, winter for warm-season turf). Less frequent but heavier irrigation is preferred, with the soil surface allowed to dry out between waterings.

BIOLOGICAL CONTROL OF WEEDS

Although the appearance of disease-causing fungi on a lawn is usually bad news for the turf manager, there are a few cases in which these organisms may be welcomed. When fungal diseases attack and kill turf pests, they can be considered beneficial. A recent example of this biological control (see Chapter 4) of a weed is the infection of nutsedge, a difficult weed in turf, by certain rust fungi. The fungi significantly reduced the nutsedge population without harming the desirable species. Further study may bring to light more examples like this one, giving us more weapons in the fight against weeds and reducing our dependency on herbicides in turf management.

BASIC FACTS ABOUT HERBICIDES

When other methods have not been sufficient to control weeds, *herbicides,* or chemical weed killers, must be used. Occasionally a *soil sterilant,* which destroys all vegetation for a long period of time, or a *fumigant,* which eradicates all vegetation by production of a vapor, is chosen for a turf area. For example, fumigation is probably the best way to eradicate nutsedge or bermudagrass from a large area. But the difficulty of using these materials and their expense usually precludes their use, since many excellent herbicides are readily available and easily applied.

Herbicides can be classified in several ways, as on the basis of their chemical formula, their mode of action, or their target species. *Nonselective* herbicides affect all plants with which they come in contact, whereas *selective* herbicides affect only certain target plant species. Much of the research in herbicides over the past decades has been aimed at development of chemicals that function as selective herbicides, toxic to noxious weeds but nontoxic to the crops in which those commonly grow.

In turf management two types of herbicides, differing in their timing in regard to the weed life cycle, are frequently used. These are the preemergence and postemergence herbicides.

Preemergence herbicides prevent or retard the germination of weed seeds. They are watered into the soil, where they can be adsorbed onto clay and humus particles, so a higher concentration may be necessary in heavy clay soils than are needed in sandy soils. Most of these herbicides suppress young plants by inhibiting cell division, and therefore forming a barrier through which weed seedlings cannot grow.

Application of preemergence herbicides should be timed for 1 to 2 weeks before the weed seeds germinate. Hence it is necessary to know the weeds and their life cycles, and it is necessary to know the climate of your local area and its fluctuations. For control of summer annuals these herbicides are applied in spring, and for control of winter annuals fall application is appropriate. In southern zones turfgrasses may exhibit herbicide damage if the temperature during and after application is too high, so it is best to apply these materials earlier in spring or later in fall. Some preemergence materials used on warm-season turf areas can be applied only when the turfgrasses are completely dormant, so care must be taken to avoid unusually warm winter days when the grasses may temporarily break dormancy. Since preemergence herbicides have a relatively long life in the soil, often two years or more, good weed control may still be achieved if reduced amounts of material, or none at all, are applied in the second or third year. In most cases, because of the long residual period, new seedings cannot be established where the herbicide has been used until 2 to 3 months have elapsed.

Postemergence herbicides are used on actively growing weeds. Some kill only the plant part they touch (*contact herbicides*), but most are *systemic herbicides,* in which the material is absorbed by leaves or roots and translocated through the conducting system to all parts of the plant. Such materials are clearly the weed-killers of choice when one wants to eradicate a perennial weed with underground reproductive parts such as rhizomes and tubers.

Most postemergence herbicides are selective against various turf weeds, but some nonselective types such as glyphosate have an important use in turf renovation. They can be used to kill unsightly clumps of grassy weeds like nimblewill and coarse fescue or to totally eradicate vegetation in a particular area. Such systemic materials may be the only effective control for bentgrass, bermudagrass, kikuyugrass, and difficult perennials with underground reproductive parts.

Many postemergence herbicides have a short soil life of only a few weeks before they are destroyed by microbial action. Thus, viewed from this standpoint, they are reasonably safe. However, this short residual period means that repeated applications may be necessary in order to achieve good weed control, as in winter annual control in bermudagrass. Furthermore, postemergence herbicides tend to have acute toxicity, rather than the chronic toxicity associated with preemergence materials.

As with preemergence herbicides, the timing of the application of postemergence materials is crucial. The principal requirement is that the weed be growing actively when the herbicide is applied. This means that both time of day and time of year must be considered. In the bluegrass region, for example, warm and humid days of spring and fall are excellent times to apply herbicides because weeds are growing vigorously then. During the dry and hot "dog days" of midsummer, translocation of the chemical in the plant may be much slowed and good kill may not be achieved. In addition, the turfgrasses are under heat stress at those times and may be highly susceptible to herbicide damage themselves. It has been shown that 2,4-D, for example is most effective when the temperature is over 90°F and the relative humidity is over 70%. Below 60°F, during drought, or when for any reason weeds are not actively growing, the effectiveness of herbicides diminishes rapidly.

Early morning is particularly important with granular herbicides, which must stick to a wet leaf to be most effective. Although this timing is not quite so crucial with liquid herbicides, morning is still the preferred time of application. This is because in humid early morning conditions herbaceous plants, including most weeds, secrete some intercellular sap onto leaf surfaces. The process is called *guttation* (Figure 5-1), and the exudate is often confused with dew. As the morning becomes warmer and drier, the sap is withdrawn into the leaf interior in response to internal osmotic pressures. If a herbicide has been applied to the plant during guttation, the liquid herbicide will be drawn into the leaf also.

It should be understood that in addition to understanding the growing conditions of the weed, one should also consider the growing conditions of the turfgrass before applying a herbicide. This is because no herbicide is totally selective and without effect on the grass. All herbicides damage, albeit only slightly, the turfgrasses to which they are applied. The damage may not be easy to detect, but under exacting laboratory conditions reduction in growth and cell enlargement, increase in water absorption, and other physiological effects can be noted after a "selective" herbicide has been applied to a grass plant.

Whenever a living system is weakened in any manner, seemingly unrelated problems can arise. If turf has already been stressed by such problems as drought, excessively hot weather, lack of fertility, thatch buildup, or mowing damage, an untimely application of a herbicide may kill it. Fungal diseases, particularly, enjoy their greatest success on weakened turf systems. It is essential to use common sense when applying a herbicide: Think beyond the weeds and consider the entire turf ecosystem!

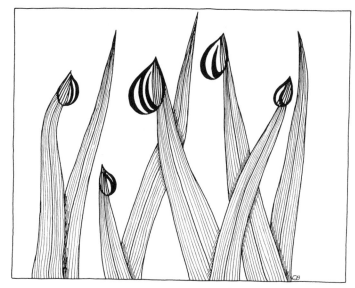

Figure 5-1 Guttation, showing droplets on the tips of grass leaves.

MAKING THE CHOICE

Many factors enter into the choice of an appropriate herbicide for each application. These include such factors as solubility, volatility, and type of formulation, as well as the target weed and the turf species present. Thus a preemergence herbicide should not be so soluble that it is washed away immediately but should remain in place on the soil surface for some time. Volatile herbicides may cause damage to desirable plants nearby, especially if used on a hot summer day when they evaporate readily into the air. The herbicide formulation chosen is often a matter of convenience. For example, granular materials can blow in the wind and may not be easy to apply evenly. However, liquid formulations may be difficult to mix properly and to wash out of spray tanks after use. Table 5-1 indicates the tolerances of various turfgrasses to commonly used herbicides. Table 5-2 lists the herbicides recommended for control of many weeds.

SYNERGISM

When two or more weed killers are applied together in a combination, the potency of the mixture is often greater than the potency of the herbicides applied separately. This phenomenon is known as a *synergism:* The combined effect of two or more ingredients is greater than the sum of the ingredients acting alone. For example, the effectiveness of 2,4-D when used in conjunction with dicamba or MCPP, or both, is much greater

TABLE 5-1.   Tolerance of Turfgrasses to Some Common Herbicides. (T = tolerant, C = caution. Any herbicide with neither T nor C for a given turfgrass species should not be used.)

Herbicides	Bahiagrass	Bentgrass	Bermudagrass	Bluegrass	Buffalograss	Centipedegrass	Fescue, Red	Fescue, Tall	Ryegrass	St. Augustinegrass	Zoysiagrass
Atrazine						T				T	C
Benefin (Balan)	T	C	T	T	T	T	T	T	T	T	T
Bensulide (Betasan)	T	T	T	T	T	T	T	T	T	T	T
Bentazone (Basagran)		C	T	T		T	T	T	T	T	T
Bromoxynil	T	T	T	T		T	T	T	T	T	T
DCPA (Dacthal)	T	C	C	T	T	T	C	T	T	T	T
DSMA, MSMA		C	T	T	T		T	C			C
Oxidiazon (Ronstar)	C		T	T		T		T	C		T
Pendimethalin	T		T	T				T		T	T
Pronamide		T									
Siduron		C	C	T			T	T	T		T
Trimec (2,4-D + MCPP + dicamba)	T	C	C	T	C	C	T	T	T	C	T
2,4-D	T	C	T	T	C	C	T	T	T	C*	T
MCPP	T	T	T	T			T	T	T		T
Dicamba	T	C	T	T			T	T	T		T

*St. Augustinegrass will tolerate up to 0.5 lb per acre of 2,4-D with no to minimal injury. However, both St. Augustinegrass and centipedegrass are tolerant of atrazine, which is used on these grasses instead of 2,4-D for broadleaf weed control.

and the necessary dose much less than when these herbicides are used alone. This principle is embodied in the popular weed control product know as Trimec, which combines the three herbicides.

TWO HERBICIDES SAFE FOR NEW SEEDINGS

Siduron (Tupersan) can be incorporated into the soil at the time of seeding bluegrass, fescues, perennial ryegrasses, and zoysiagrass without damage to those turfgrasses. Acting as a preemergence herbicide, it will prevent germination of crabgrass, foxtail, and barnyardgrass. Since it is sensitive to light, it should be worked into the soil.

Bromoxynil (Buctril) can be applied as a postemergence control for broadleaf weeds in most seeding turf.

THE SPECIAL PROBLEM OF ST. AUGUSTINEGRASS

St. Augustinegrass is sensitive to the phenoxy herbicides used for broadleaf weed control, such as 2,4-D and MCPP. As a result, many turf managers use atrazine, which is tolerated by both St. Augustinegrass and centipedegrass. However, St. Augustine-

TABLE 5-2. Herbicides Used to Control Various Weeds.

	Benefin (Balan)	Bensulide (Betasan)	DCPA (Dacthal)	DSMA, MSMA	Glyphosate (Roundup)	Oxadiazon (Ronstar)	Pendimethalin (Prowl)	Siduron (Tupersan)	2,4-D	MCPP	Dicamba	2,4-D + MCPP	2,4-D + MCPP + Dicamba (Trimec)
Grassy Weeds													
Bahiagrass					X								
Barnyardgrass	X	X	X		X	X	X	X					
Bentgrass					X								
Bermudagrass					X								
Bluegrass, annual[a]	X	X	X	X	X	X	X						
Crabgrass	X	X	X	X		X	X	X					
Dallisgrass				X	X								
Fescue, tall					X								
Foxtail, green	X	X	X			X	X						
Foxtail, yellow	X	X	X		X		X	X					
Goosegrass[b]	X	X	X			X	X						
Johnsongrass			X		X			X					
Kikuyugrass					X								
Lovegrass			X		X								
Nimblewill[c]					X								
Nutsedge[d]				X^2									
Orchardgrass					X								
Panicum, fall		X			X	X	X						
Quackgrass					X								
Sandbur			X										
Timothy					X								
Torpedograss					X								
Velvetgrass					X								
Witchgrass			X		X								
Broadleaf Weeds													
Bedstraw													X
Bindweed									X		X		X
Bittercress									X	X	X		X
Black medic												X	X
Burdock													X
Buttercup, creeping									X		X		X
Carpetweed			X			X			X		X		X
Carrot, wild									X		X		X
Chickweed, common	X	X					X			X	X	X	X
Chickweed, mouse-ear	X	X					X			X	X	X	X
Chicory									X		X		X
Clover, hop							X			X	X	X	X
Clover, red									X	X	X		X
Clover, white									X	X	X	X	X
Cranesbill									X	X	X	X	X
Daisy, English											X	X	X
Dandelion									X	X		X	X
Dichondra									X	X			X

(continued)

Note: X^2 = two or more applications may be needed
[a]Use pronamide in bermudagrass turf.
[b]Only marginal control with benefin, bensulide, and DCPA.
[c]May possibly be controlled by siduron.
[d]For yellow nutsedge, bentazone (Basagran) and Eptam are recommended.

TABLE 5-2. *(continued)*

	Benefin (Balan)	Bensulide (Betasan)	DCPA (Dacthal)	DSMA, MSMA	Glyphosate (Roundup)	Oxadiazon (Ronstar)	Pendimethalin (Prowl)	Siduron (Tupersan)	2,4-D	MCPP	Dicamba	2,4-D + MCPP	2,4-D + MCPP + Dicamba (Trimec)
Broadleaf Weeds (cont.)													
Dock, curly									X^2		X	X	X
Garlic, wild											X	X	X
Ground ivy										X	X	X	X
Hawkweed											X		X
Heal-all									X	X	X		X
Henbit	X						X				X		X
Knapweed											X		X
Knawel											X		X
Knotweed									X		X	X	X
Lambsquarters	X	X		X	X				X	X	X	X	X
Lespedeza									X	X			
Lettuce, wild									X				X
Mallow									X			X	X
Moneywort									X				X
Morning glory									X				X
Mugwort											X		X^2
Mustard, wild									X		X		X
Onion, wild											X	X	X
Parsley piert										X	X		X
Pearlwort										X	X		X
Pennycress									X		X		X
Pennywort									X	X			X
Peppergrass									X	X	X		X
Pigweed, prostrate									X	X	X	X	X
Pigweed, redroot	X	X				X			X	X	X	X	X
Plantain, buckhorn									X		X		X
Plantain, common									X		X		X
Puncturevine									X				X
Purslane		X				X			X		X	X	X
Ragweed									X	X			X
Shepherd's purse	X								X	X	X	X	X
Sorrel, sheep											X	X	X
Speedwell, annual													X^2
Speedwell, creeping[e]		X				X							
Spurge, prostrate		X				X	X				X		X^2
Spurge, spotted		X				X	X				X		X
Spurweed									X		X	X	X
Stitchwort												X	
Strawberry, wild											X		X
Thistle, bull									X^2		X		X
Thistle, Canadian									X^2		X		X
Thyme											X		X
Violet[f]													
Woodsorrel												X	X
Yarrow											X	X	X
Yellow rocket						X			X			X	X

[e]Dacthal 75WP is applied at 12 lb ai/A as a postemergence application in early spring or fall.
[f]No good control; two or more applications or Trimec may be effective.

grass will tolerate 2,4-D up to a level of 0.5 lb of active ingredient per acre (ai/A) with minimal injury. Low rates of 2,4-D in combination with MCPP and dicamba have given good weed control in this turf.

CORRECTING MISTAKES

It is hoped that you will never have a herbicide spill on turf or make a miscalculation of the necessary amount. However, if this should happen, it may be possible to correct the mistake. Activated charcoal applied at a rate of 7 lb per 1000 sq ft and watered into the soil will inactivate some chemical weed controls. Seeding can then be done on the same day, though some have recommended a one-week wait as a safety measure. The charcoal treatment has also been shown to be effective in inactivating herbicide residues before installation of new sod on a lawn.

SOME PREEMERGENCE HERBICIDES

Benefin (Balan)

Origin: Elanco Products Co., 1965. LD_{50}: 800 mg/kg. Controls crabgrass and other annual weedy grasses. Low water solubility, minimizing leaching. Has a residual of 3 to 4 months, so wait at least 2 months before seeding turfgrasses. Not safe for use on bentgrass turf.

Bensulide (Betasan)

Origin: Stauffer Chemical Co., 1962. LD_{50}: 770 mg/kg. Effective against crabgrass, annual bluegrass, goosegrass, purslane, and henbit. At slightly higher rates (10 lbs/A) will also control foxtail and other grassy weeds. Can be used on all cool-season turfgrasses, though may cause discoloration of bentgrass. Also used on bermudagrass, zoysiagrass, centipedegrass, St. Augustinegrass, and bahiagrass. An organophosphate that inhibits root cell division. Should be used only on mineral soils. Watering increases effectiveness. Has a residual of 6 to 8 months and may carry over even to the next year, so wait 4 months before seeding. Can be deactivated with charcoal applied at the rate of 7 lb per 1000 sq ft; seeding can be done 7 days after charcoal application.

DCPA (Dacthal)

Origin: Diamond Shamrock Co., 1960. LD_{50}: 3000 mg/kg. Effective against many annual weedy grasses, such as crabgrass, foxtail, annual bluegrass, goosegrass, and fall panicum. Also useful against several broadleaf weeds such as speedwell, spurge, chickweed, and purslane. Widely used on ornamentals and vegetable crops. Less effective if incorporated into the soil. Marked increase in activity if watered. Use only on mineral soils; do not disturb soil after application. May cause thinning of bentgrass and fine fescue. Do not seed for 3 months after use.

Oxadiazon (Ronstar)

Origin: Rhône-Poulenc. LD_{50}: 8000 mg/kg. Controls crabgrass, goosegrass, and a wide variety of annual grasses and broadleaf weeds in bluegrass and bermudagrass turf. Will injure bentgrasses. Toxic to fish and bees.

Pendimethalin (Prowl)

Source: American Cyanamid Co., 1973. LD_{50}: 1050 to 1250 mg/kg. At rates of 1.5 to 3.0 lb/A, controls crabgrass, foxtail, barnyardgrass, fall panicum, goosegrass, annual bluegrass, chickweed, oxalis, spurge, cudweed, hop clover, henbit, and evening primrose in both northern and southern turfgrasses. A relatively new herbicide for turf. Toxic to fish but not to bees. Compatible with 2,4-D and dicamba.

Siduron (Tupersan)

Origin: DuPont, 1964. LD_{50}: 750 mg/kg. Effective against crabgrass, foxtail, and nimbleweed but injures bermudagrass and some bentgrasses. Annual bluegrass is resistant. Useful because it is nontoxic to seedings of bluegrass, fescue, perennial ryegrass, and certain strains of bentgrass, thus eliminating the usual 2-month waiting period before seeding can be done. Can be used up to 2 months before weeds germinate. Must have 1/2 in. of water to activate.

SOME POSTEMERGENCE HERBICIDES

2,4-D (Weed-B-Gon)

Origin: Amchem Products, Inc., 1942. LD_{50}: 375 mg/kg. A systemic herbicide used successfully as early as 1944 to remove dandelion, plantain, and many other broadleaf weeds from bluegrass turf. Comparatively inexpensive and not highly toxic. Short-lived in moist fertile soil, remaining only a few weeks before being broken down by microbial action. Somewhat toxic to bentgrasses; proceed with caution if using near bentgrasses or St. Augustinegrass. Not safe for use on seedling turf. After studying the information in Chapter 4 on pesticides, precautions about their use, and LD_{50} values, one may be left with the impression that pesticide use almost inevitably leads to medical problems. A lot of studies on the effects of 2,4-D have indicated that this is not the case.

The USDA has studied urine samples from ground and aerial applicators who had applied 2,4-D for at least 30 days a year for 30 years. They found that in the average 175-lb worker less than 1 g (about half the weight of a dime) was absorbed and excreted over the applicator's lifetime. No ill effect was detected from this lifetime of 2,4-D exposure. The American Medical Association reported no conclusive evidence that 2,4-D or other phenoxy herbicides were mutagenic or carcinogenic or caused any reproductive difficulties. Studies by the Canadian Department of Agriculture found no detrimental effect after 35 years of 2,4-D use on the microbial processes that ensure soil fertility. As well, as 2,4-D is not fat soluble, hence not collected in the body's fatty tissue. It is not easily absorbed through the skin, and in humans it is rapidly excreted from the body in a matter of hours.

Nevertheless, the jury on 2,4-D and many other pesticides is still out. Other studies underway at this writing may have a very negative impact. Regardless, one should always approach pesticide use with mature intelligence, care, and caution.

Bromoxynil (Buctril)

Origin: May Baker, Ltd., 1960. LD_{50}: 245 mg/kg. A contact herbicide, selective, non-volatile. Controls several weeds not easily controlled by 2,4-D. Most effective on young plants prior to the three- and four-leaf stage. Can be applied to new turf without injury to the seedlings, eliminating the usual waiting period. Kills by inhibiting photosynthesis and respiration. Compatible with 2,4-D and MCPP. Increase application rate when temperature is below 65°F.

Dicamba (Banvel)

Origin: Velsicol Chemical Co., 1959. LD_{50}: 1040 mg/kg. Effective for control of chickweed, thistle, nutsedge, and crabgrass. A systemic benzoic acid herbicide compatible with and frequently combined with 2,4-D and MCPP, as in the product Trimec. Less popular than it used to be, owing to its persistence in the soil, though some claim that the amount of dicamba necessary to effect synergism in the mixture is so slight as to be insignificant. Use only outside the drip line of trees and shrubs, since uptake by their root systems may occur. Do not use under canopy of a tree. Not safe for seedling turf, and do not seed until 6 weeks after application.

DSMA

Origin: Ansul Chemical Co., 1956. LD_{50}: 600 mg/kg. Along with related materials CMA, AMA, MSMA, and MAMA, DSMA is an organic derivative of arsenic. Used as a postemergence control for nutsedge, goosegrass, barnyard grass, dallisgrass, foxtail, and crabgrass. Most effective when plants are small and young. On mature grassy weeds may be necessary to repeat the application at 7 to 10 day intervals. Fescue and bentgrass are more susceptible than other cool-season turfgrasses. Should not be used where St. Augustinegrass, carpetgrass, or centipedegrass is the primary turf species. Do not apply to dry turf, and keep turf moist after application. More effective at high temperature, so increase rate below 80°F.

MCPP (Mecoprop)

Origin: Boute Puse Drug Co., 1953. LD_{50}: 650 mg/kg (mice). A systemic phenoxy herbicide noted for effective control of surface creeping broadleaf weeds such as clover, chickweed, knotweed, and ground ivy. Tolerated by bentgrasses. A translocated, slow-acting herbicide that requires 3 to 4 weeks for full effect. Not safe for seedling turf.

SOME NONSELECTIVE HERBICIDES

Amitrole (Amitrol T)

Origin: Amchem Products Co. and American Cyanimid Co., 1956. LD_{50}: 5000 mg/kg. Commonly sold in garden stores in aerosol cans for poison ivy control. Effective against virtually all annual and perennial, broadleaf and grassy plants. Does not control morning glory. Has a 4- to 6-week residual under many conditions, but breaks down in 2 to 3 weeks in warm, moist soil. Thorough coverage is essential. Takes 10 to 20 days for control.

Dalapon (Dowpon)

Origin: Dow Chemical Co., 1950. LD_{50}: 7500 mg/kg. Effective against quackgrass, bermudagrass, and other annual and perennial grasses. Used as a preplanting treatment for these weeds on cropland. Acts like 2,4-D on broadleaf plants. More effective if split applications are made 5 to 20 days apart (see label). Leaches and washes off foliage easily. There is a 6- to 8-week residual before seeding can be done.

Glyphosate (Roundup)

Origin: Monsanto Co., 1971. LD_{50}: 4320 mg/kg. A nonresidual, postemergence herbicide particularly effective against deep-rooted perennials such as quackgrass. Used for control of winter annuals in completely dormant warm-season turf. Postpone application if rainfall is expected within 6 hours. Corrosive to iron and galvanized steel. Popular in turf renovation work because seeding can be done within a few days after its use. Relatively nontoxic to humans; affects amino acid synthesis in plants. Given its safety, the nonselective herbicide of choice for most uses. Wait at least 3 days for it to take effect before seeding.

KNOW YOUR WEEDS

There is no substitute for a good knowledge of turf weeds. Look at them closely and learn to recognize them by sight. The monocot weeds may be more difficult to identify than the broadleaf dicot weeds, especially since you may need to recognize and eradicate grassy weeds before they produce their characteristic inflorescences. However, practice will help, and such small features as ligules, hairy leaf sheaths, and blade texture can be seen with a hand lens of 20-power magnification. Some common weeds found in cool-season, transition zone, and warm-season turf are illustrated in Figures 5-3 to 5-40.

ONLY A FEW ARE SERIOUS PROBLEMS

By and large most weeds can't tolerate the close mowing and the competitiveness inherent in turf and are naturally excluded from such an area. The great bulk of those remaining can be removed by one or more herbicides, as indicated in the previous sections. The combination of 2,4-D, MCPP, and dicamba is effective against 95% of the broadleaf weeds that occur among turfgrasses tolerant to these herbicides. But this combination of herbicides can also damage bentgrasses, St. Augustinegrass, carpetgrass, dichondra, and possibly other grasses under certain conditions. Furthermore, dicamba, which damages roots, should not be applied to turf where there is danger of harming tree and shrub roots. (This danger can be circumvented to a large degree by simply avoiding any herbicide applications in shady areas.) There remain, then, that 5% of the weeds, a small group of persistent weeds that impress us with their vigor, hardiness, and tolerance of our attempts at eradication. If you find yourself frustrated at their persistence, you might consider the problems that turf managers would have if crabgrass were a perennial instead of an annual! In fact, some wild crabgrass species in other parts of the world do grow in this manner.

Following are described some of the difficult, problem weeds in turf:

Annual Bluegrass *Poa annua* L. (See Figure 5-3)

This stubborn annual grass can be a difficult weed, particularly where the turf is mowed short and irrigated frequently. Seeds can germinate both in spring and fall, so preemergence controls may need to be applied at both times. In hot weather it dies back, leaving objectionable brown areas. However, under cool, moist conditions it can live as a perennial. Annual bluegrass is one of the most widespread weeds in southern and transition zone turf, where it grows as a winter annual. Germination occurs about September, when night temperatures fall and rainfall increases, and the weed infests turf areas late in the growing season through the dormant period. It is a nonrhizomatous plant, of lighter green color than Kentucky bluegrass.

Controls include an application of bensulide in late summer before the seeds of the weed germinate. Excellent control has been reported in bermudagrass with pronamide (Kerb). On bermudagrass golf greens that have been overseeded with ryegrass, ethofumesate (Prograss) applied 15 to 30 days after overseeding has given good results. In winter before the turf has broken dormancy, glyphosate (Roundup) can be applied as a postemergence treatment for annual bluegrass and other annual weeds. Make sure that the turf is completely dormant, and for best results apply before seed heads have formed.

Crabgrass *Digitaria sanguinalis* (L.) Scop. and *Digitaria ischaemum* (Schreb.) Muhl. (See Figure 5-4)

This notorious weed is at the top of the list of difficult weeds in turf. Common throughout the United States, it is worst in cool-season turf. It is an annual grass, spreading rapidly as it roots at the nodes, and smothering other vegetation. Crabgrass can be recognized by its characteristic short, pointed, and broad blade, its yellowish-green color, and when in flower by its finger-like inflorescence.

Rather than trying to control it, it might be simpler to devote some of the money spent on control to collecting its African ancestors and breeding them to produce a super turfgrass. One species of crabgrass (*Digitaria didactyla*) is already used as a turfgrass in South Africa. In the meantime most controls center around application of a preemergence herbicide with good timing in the spring. Using the crabgrass germination chart shown in Figure 5-2, you can determine the appropriate time to apply controls in your area.

Preemergence herbicides from our list of commonly used materials that have given good control of crabgrass are benefin, bensulide, DCPA, oxydiazon, and pendimethalin. Of these, bensulide is probably the most widely used: It has a good safety record, is tolerated by all turfgrasses, and has a 3- to 4-month persistence. This is considered important, since in the northern United States crabgrass may germinate from April to August. It also makes the timing of the application in the spring less critical; that is, it can be made a few weeks before actual germination and still be effective. After the first season application at full rate, the application rate is typically cut in half in subsequent seasons.

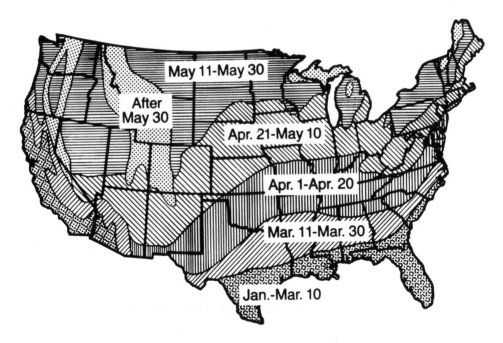

Figure 5-2 Approximate crabgrass germination dates in the continental United States. Reprinted by permission of the O. M. Scott & Sons Company, Marysville, OH.

Application of a preemergence herbicide should be omitted in shady areas. The lawn should not be raked or dethatched after the application. Timing is often considered appropriate when forsythia or lilac begin to bloom or when soil temperatures stabilize at 55°F, or air temperatures maintain a mean of 55 to 57°F or more for at least 10 days. This may be February to March in Atlanta but April to May in Cleveland.

DSMA and MSMA can be used for postemergence crabgrass control in bermudagrass and bluegrass. Only Asulan is labeled for St. Augustinegrass.

Dallisgrass *Paspalum dilatatum* Poir. (See Figure 5-5)

In the South this is a close second to crabgrass as an annoying weed. It has a coarse texture and tufted growth habit.

The controls are similar to those for crabgrass: largely benefin, bensulide, DCPA, pendimethalin, or oxydiazon applied as preemergence herbicides in the spring. DSMA or MSMA are applied as postemergence materials, and only Asulan is labelled for postemergence control of dallisgrass in St. Augustinegrass turf.

Tall (Coarse) Fescue *Festuca arundinacea* Schreb. (See Figure 5-6)

Tall fescue is a perennial bunchgrass, whose coarse texture and tall growth habit make it quite unsightly in bluegrass and other turf. It is, however, sometimes planted as a utility turf, and improved, turf-type cultivars are coming into wide usage (see Chapter 3). Its long leaves have prominent midveins.

It can be removed by treatment with glyphosate (Roundup) by the same method as indicated for quackgrass. It has been reported that tall fescue also can be mowed out: Fertilize it heavily in the fall and mow close. If the winter is a cold one, the fescue population may be significantly reduced. Selective herbicides for tall fescue may be available in the near future.

Goosegrass *Eleusine indica* (L.) Gaertn. (See Figure 5-8)

This is considered by many to be the most difficult grassy weed to control in the South. The plant is an annual, characteristically lying flat in the turf. It has a finger-like inflorescence and a silvery cast.

Timing of a herbicide application is crucial: It has been reported that goosegrass germinates at the same time as crabgrass (presumably in the lower South) and up to 6 weeks after crabgrass (in the upper South and North). Good control has been reported with oxydiazon, but check the label before use. DSMA, MSMA, and metribuzin (Sencor) are used for postemergence control.

Moss and Algae

These lower plants of various species often appear in a turf area that is too wet, shady, poorly drained, compacted, acidic, infertile, or all of these. Sometimes there is excessive thatch, and sometimes the turf is thin and weak. Mosses and algae are not always easy to distinguish from each other except under a magnifying lens. However, in general mosses form a loose, leafy growth, whereas algae produce a green to black "scum" that becomes crusty when dry.

Before resorting to chemical controls, which are only temporary, one should determine the underlying cause. Answer the following questions: Can the drainage be improved? Is the area too shady even for a shade-tolerant grass? Will some tree trimming be cost effective? Should the soil be aerated? Does the soil need lime or fertilizer?

For temporary control of mosses use 4 to 6 oz of ferrous sulfate or 10 oz of ferrous ammonium sulfate per 1000 sq ft. Algae are controlled with copper sulfate at a rate of 2 to 3 oz per 1000 sq ft or hydrated lime at a rate of 2 to 3 lb per 1000 sq ft.

Nimblewill *Muhlenbergia schreberi* Gmel. (See Figure 5-9)

Nimblewill is an eastern representative of a largely western group of grasses. It is found from the Atlantic coast to Nebraska and Texas. It is a stoloniferous perennial, recognized by its delicate texture and preference for damp, shady places.

It has been reported that an application of siduron (Tupersan) to bluegrass turf in the spring will inhibit nimblewill and give the bluegrass a competitive edge. Glyphosate (Roundup) can be applied after the nimblewill greens up in the early summer; reseeding or sodding will then be necessary.

Yellow Nutsedge *Cyperus esculentus* L.
(See Figure 5-10)

This sedge is a prime turf nuisance. It is perennial and of yellow-green color, recognizable as a true sedge by its triangular stems and three-ranked leaves. It is frequently found in wet spots.

Nutgrass spreads by rhizomes and then in late summer forms underground tubers, or nutlets, that confer a high degree of winter resistance. Each tuber can give rise to hundreds of new plants in only one season; hence it is desirable to treat the plant before it reaches this stage (usually at day lengths of 12 hours and decreasing night temperatures). If there are just a small number of plants in a lawn, pull them by hand carefully so that any nutlets come out with the plant. Where nutsedge is beyond hand control and the turfgrass is tolerant, apply bentazon (Basagran) or DSMA (two or more applications at weekly intervals). Some turfgrasses may discolor, particularly if the temperature is over 85°F and the soil is dry.

Since nutsedge grows faster than the turfgrass and hence is taller between mowings, it may be possible to brush the sedge with a wick applicator (commonly used in agriculture) filled with glyphosate. This wick is moved across the leaves of the sedge without touching the shorter leaves of the turfgrass. Remember that glyphosate is a nonselective herbicide and will kill both weeds and turf.

Quackgrass *Agropyron repens* (L.) Beauv. (See Figure 5-12)

This perennial grass with vigorous creeping rhizomes is a problem, particularly in bluegrass turf. The plant can be identified by its clasping auricles and spike inflorescence.

It can be killed with glyphosate (Roundup), after which the bare area must be reseeded or sodded. Quackgrass, like tall fescue, will grow higher than bluegrass; if not too extensive, it can be killed by brushing the leaves with a wick applicator filled with Roundup. Of course, great care must be taken to avoid touching the leaves of the bluegrass.

It is sometimes possible to mow quackgrass out of bluegrass turf. Fertilize and water regularly, and mow frequently and close, down to 1 in. The bluegrass over time will stand this stress slightly better than the quackgrass, which may weaken and disappear. However, this technique is not without danger, since bluegrass is also adversely affected by the procedure.

Spotted Spurge *Euphorbia maculata* L. and other species (See Figure 5-37)

Spotted spurge is a bothersome perennial that requires a little more attention than the typical broadleaf weed. It is a creeping plant characterized by opposite ovate leaves, often with a red spot in the center.

Two or more applications of the herbicide may be required, preferably including a nonionic surfactant. Always try to selectively spot-weed if possible when applying herbicides at higher than normal levels. Good preemergence control of both prostrate and spotted spurge has been obtained with application of pendimethalin. Spotted spurge has also been controlled in bermudagrass with DCPA applied before soil temperatures reach 55°F or with two applications of bromoxynil applied a month apart.

Woodsorrel *Oxalis stricta* L. (See Figure 5-39)

Like spurge, woodsorrel is a difficult perennial to control. It is recognized by its yellow flowers, each with five petals, and its three-parted leaves, each leaflet notched at the tip.

This weed is controlled in the same way as spurge, using multiple herbicide applications. Pendimethalin has been effective as a preemergence material.

Grassy Weeds

ANNUAL BLUEGRASS

- Low-growing annual with abundant, spreading seed heads
- Boat-shaped leaf tips

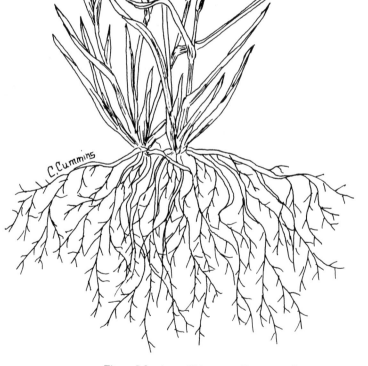

Figure 5-3   Annual bluegrass *Poa annua* L.
Low-growing with abundant, spreading seed heads.
Short, soft leaves with boat-shaped tips.
Vigorous in cool, moist weather but dyes when it's hot and dry.

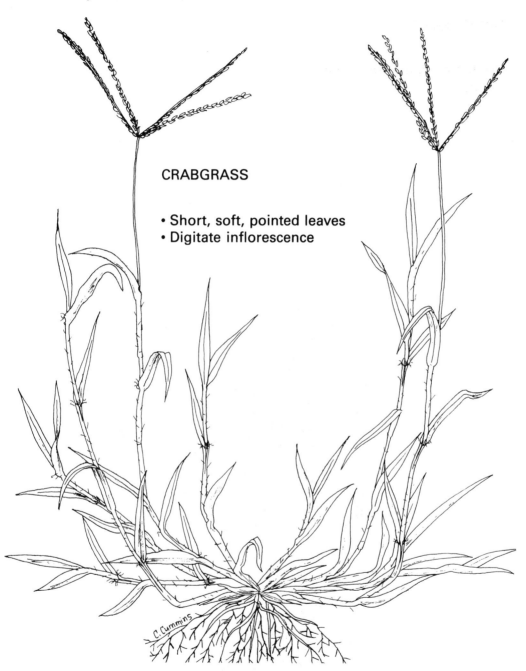

CRABGRASS

- Short, soft, pointed leaves
- Digitate inflorescence

Figure 5-4 Crabgrass *Digitaria sanguinalis* (L.) Scop.
Short, soft, pointed leaves.
Hairy blades and sheaths.
Rooting at decumbent lower nodes.
Digitate inflorescence.

DALLISGRASS

- Wide, flat blades with rough edges

Figure 5-5   Dallisgrass *Paspalum dilatatum* Poir.
   Wide, flat blades with rough edges and prominent midvein.
   Hairy near the ligule.
   Spike-like racemes.
   Spikelets fringed with hairs.

TALL FESCUE

- Coarse, long leaves with prominent veins
- Forms flat clumps on lawns

Figure 5-6 Tall fescue *Festuca arundinacea* Schreb.
Long, coarse leaves with prominent veins and rough edges.
Forms flat clumps.

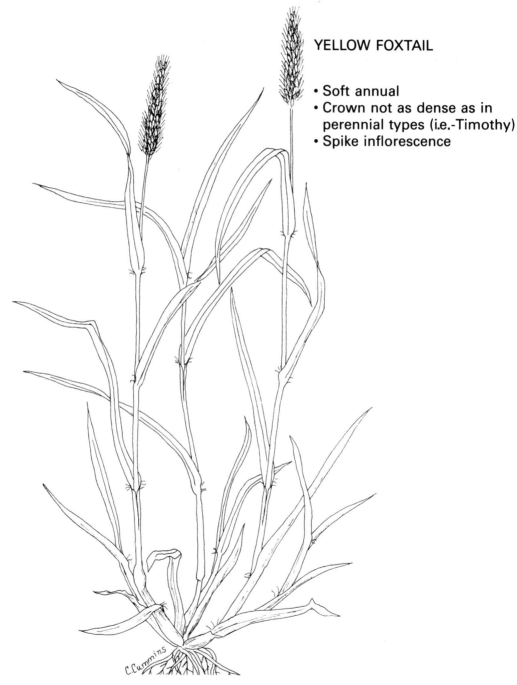

YELLOW FOXTAIL

- Soft annual
- Crown not as dense as in perennial types (i.e.-Timothy)
- Spike inflorescence

Figure 5-7   Yellow foxtail *Setaria glauca* (Weigel) Hubb.
  Soft annual.
  Crown not as dense as in perennial types, such as Timothy.
  Hairy ligule, no auricles.
  Bristled, spike inflorescence.

- Often lies flat like spokes in a wheel
- Digitate inflorescence

GOOSEGRASS

Figure 5-8 Goosegrass *Eleusine indica* (L.) Gaertn.
Dark green annual.
Often lies flat appearing like spokes of a wheel.
Close spikelets in two rows along one side of digitate inflorescence.

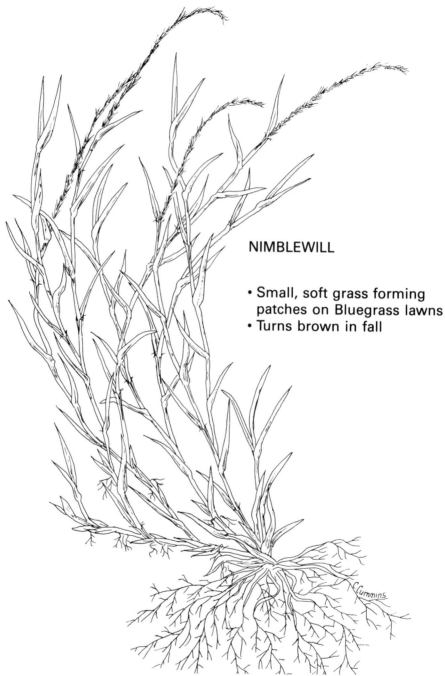

NIMBLEWILL

- Small, soft grass forming patches on Bluegrass lawns
- Turns brown in fall

Figure 5-9 Nimblewill *Muhlenbergia schreberi* Gmel.
Small, soft grass with short, flat, pointed blades similar to those of Bentgrass.
Annual, turning brown in fall.
Possibly weak stoloniferous or rhizomatous.
Inflorescence tight, a spike-like panicle.

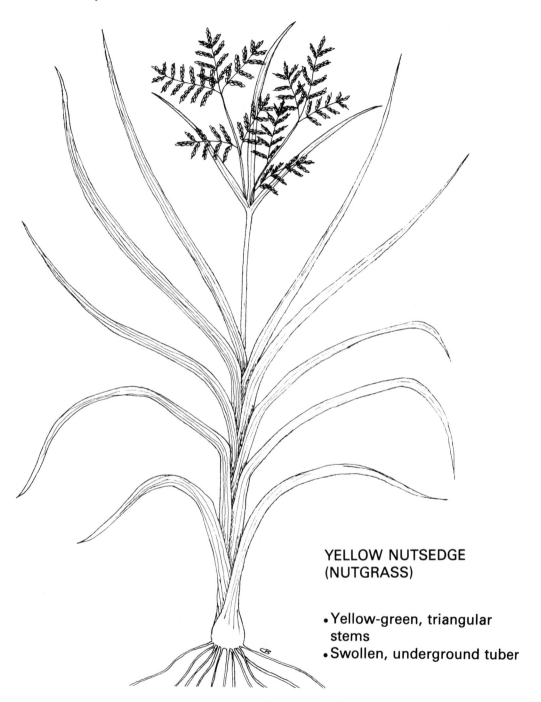

Figure 5-10 Yellow nutsedge (nutgrass) *Cyperus esculentus* L.
Erect, yellow-green, triangular stems.
Leaves grass-like but sheaths not obvious.
Underground base of plant is a perennial, swollen rootstock or tuber.

- Long, membranous ligules
- Does not have bulbous base
  like Timothy

ORCHARDGRASS

Figure 5-11 Orchardgrass *Dactylis glomerata* L.
Bunchgrass.
Stems do not have a bulbous base like Timothy.
Long, membranous ligules.
Inflorescence a panicle with compressed spikelets.

QUACKGRASS

- Clasping auricles
- Vigorous rhizomes
- Spike inflorescence

Figure 5-12 Quackgrass *Agropyron repens* (L.) Beauv.
Aggressive grass with vigorous rhizomes.
Blades wide, pointed, rough on upper surface.
Clasping auricles.
Spike inflorescence.

SANDBUR

• Spikelets surrounded by a spiny bur

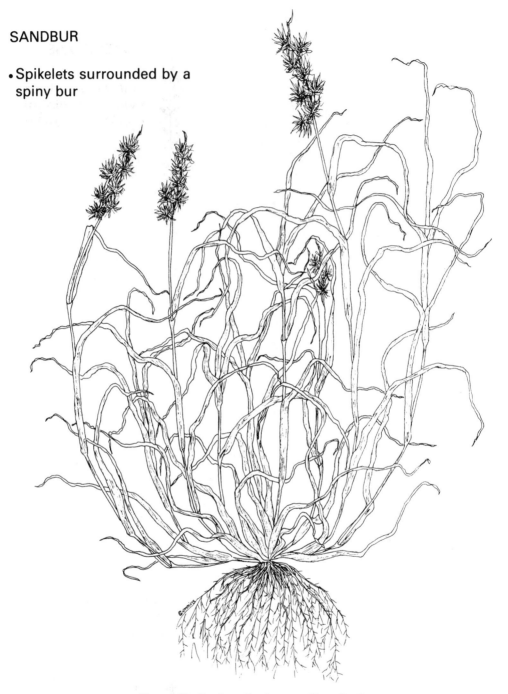

Figure 5-13   Sandbur *Cenchrus pauciflorus* Benth.
Widespread annual on sandy soils.
Spikelets surrounded by a spiny bur.
Inflorescence a raceme of six or more burs.

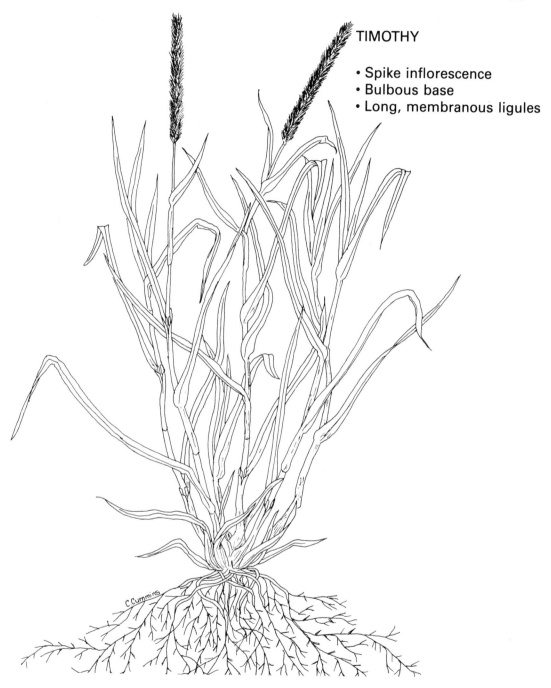

TIMOTHY

- Spike inflorescence
- Bulbous base
- Long, membranous ligules

Figure 5-14 Timothy *Phleum pratense* L.
Base of stems swollen, bulbous.
Long, membranous ligules similar to those of Orchardgrass.
Inflorescence a dense spike.

Broadleaf Weeds

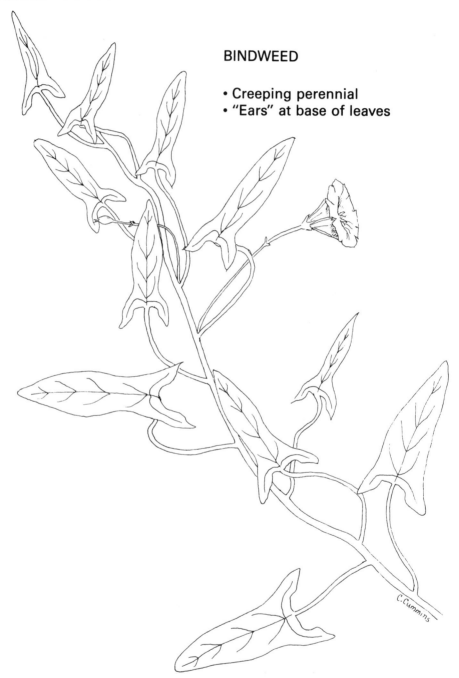

BINDWEED

- Creeping perennial
- "Ears" at base of leaves

Figure 5-15 Hedge bindweed *Convolvulus sepium* L.
Creeping perennial with extensive root system.
Large, alternate leaves with basal lobes, or "ears."

COMMON CHICKWEED

- Creeper with opposite, small, pointed leaves and hairy stems
- White petals are notched

Figure 5-16 Common chickweed *Stellaria media* (L.) Cyrillo.
Creeper with small, opposite, pointed leaves.
Small, white petals are notched.

MOUSE-EAR CHICKWEED

- Creeper with opposite,
  oblong ("mouse-eared"),
  hairy leaves

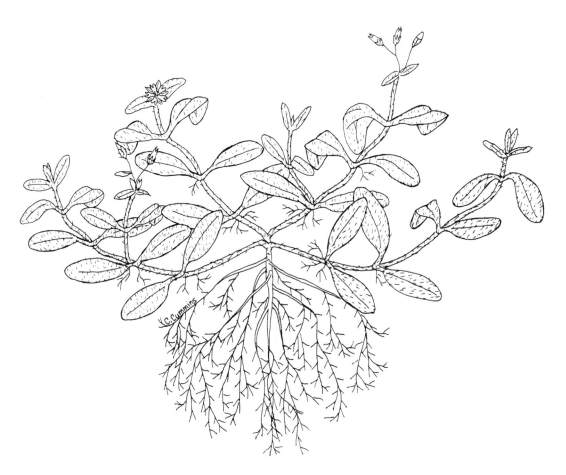

Figure 5-17 Mouse-ear chickweed *Cerastium vulgatum* L.
  Creeper with opposite, oblong ("mouse-eared"), hairy leaves.
  Roots wherever leaf nodes touch moist soil.
  Notched, white petals.

WHITE CLOVER

- Each leaf composed of three
  leaflets often having white
  "watermark"

Figure 5-18   White clover   *Trifolium repens* L.
   Low growing, creeping perennial with white flowers, fading in hot weather.
   Leaf composed of three leaflets often with white "watermark."

DANDELION

- Basal rosette
- Puff-ball type inflorescence

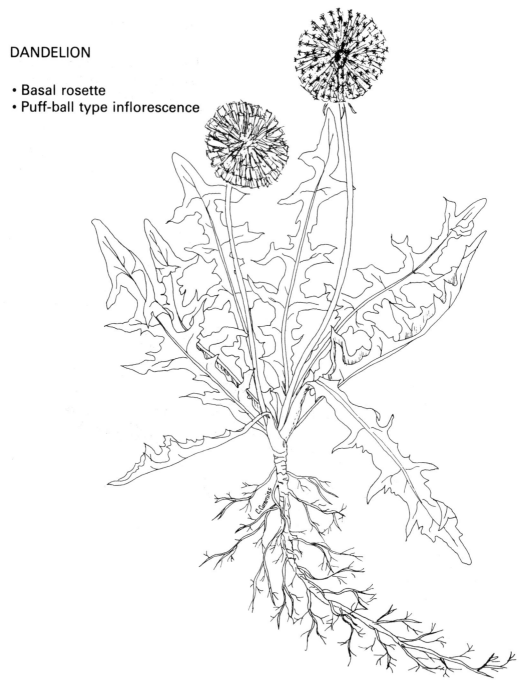

Figure 5-19 Dandelion *Taraxacum officinale* Weber.
Hardy perennial with taproot.
Basal rosette of leaves.
Yellow flower head, fluffy puff-ball seed head.

DICHONDRA

- Creeping stems
- Opposite, kidney-shaped
  leaves

Figure 5-20 Dichondra *Dichondra repens* Forst.
  Creeping, rooting stems.
  Opposite, kidney-shaped leaves.
  Sometimes used as a lawn in warm areas.

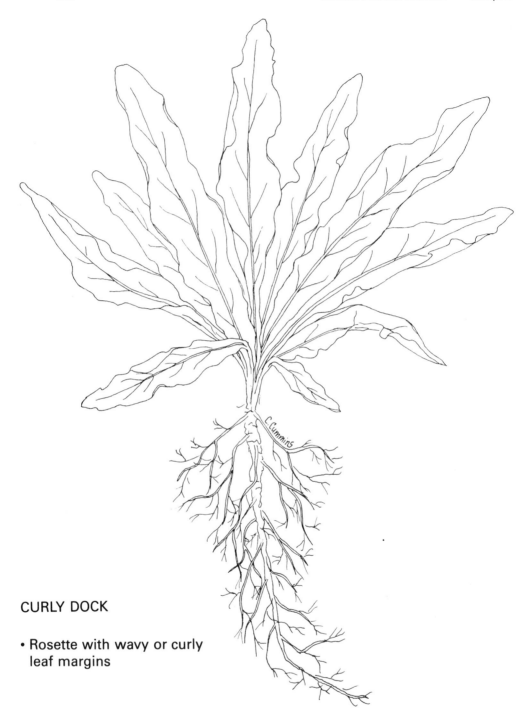

CURLY DOCK

• Rosette with wavy or curly
leaf margins

Figure 5-21   Curly dock   *Rumex crispus* L.
Rosette plant with wavy or curly leaf margins.
Deep taproot that keeps it dark green in summer.

GROUND IVY

- Long-stemmed leaves deeply notched at base
- Like mallow but square stems and opposite leaves

Figure 5-22   Ground ivy *Glechoma hederacea* L.
Creeping stems that root at the nodes.
Long-stemmed leaves deeply notched at the base.
Similar to mallow but with square stems and opposite leaves.

HEAL-ALL

- Square stems
- Opposite leaves with blue to purple flowers arranged in short spikes

Figure 5-23   Heal-all *Prunella vulgaris* L.
Perennial with square stems and opposite, stalked leaves that are sparsely hairy. Blue to purple tubular flowers arranged in short spikes.

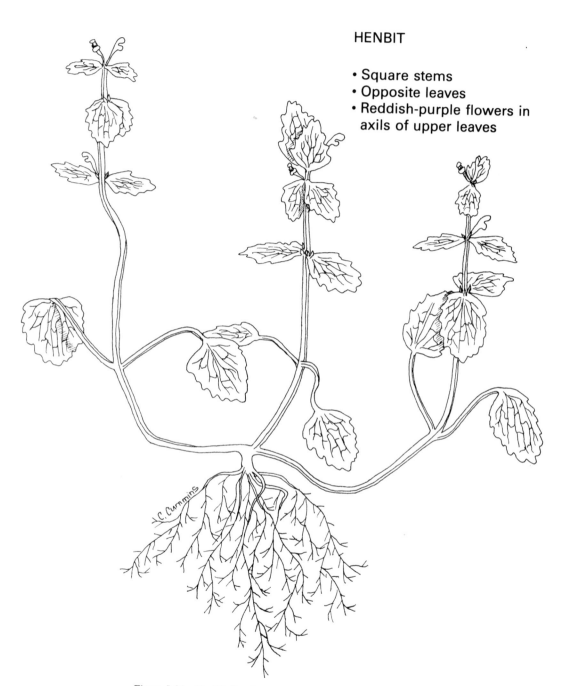

HENBIT

- Square stems
- Opposite leaves
- Reddish-purple flowers in axils of upper leaves

Figure 5-24 Henbit *Lamium amplexicaule* L.
Early spring plant with square stems and opposite leaves.
Leaves rounded, toothed, and sparsely hairy.
Reddish-purple flowers borne at bases of upper leaves.

KNOTWEED

- Prostrate mat former common in compacted areas
- Small pink flowers at junction of leaf and stem

Figure 5-25 Knotweed *Polygonum aviculare* L.
   Annual, prostrate mat former common on compacted soils.
   Blue-green leaves about an inch long.
   Small, pink flowers at the junction of leaf and stem.

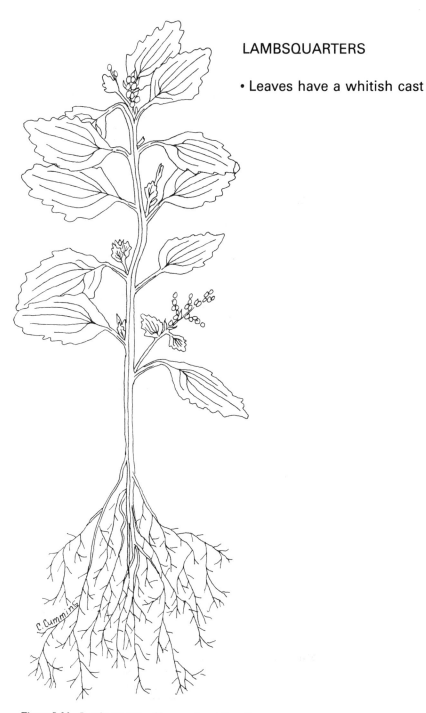

LAMBSQUARTERS

• Leaves have a whitish cast

Figure 5-26 Lambsquarters *Chenopodium album* L.
Leaves broad based, blunt tipped, and coarse toothed with a whitish cast.
Seeds in clusters at leaf bases.

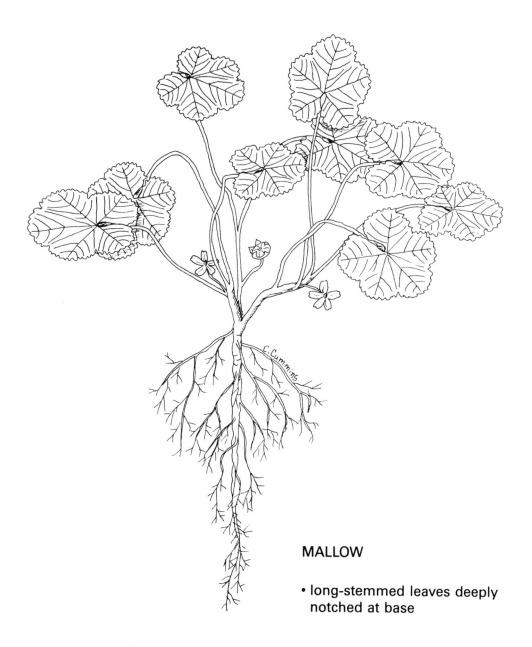

MALLOW

• long-stemmed leaves deeply
  notched at base

Figure 5-27   Mallow *Malva neglecta* Wallr.
   Long-stalked leaves deeply notched at their bases.
   Sprawling but does not root at the nodes like ground ivy.
   Pinkish-white flowers borne on stalks arising at leaf bases.
   Seed pods round and thick.

BLACK MEDIC

• Leaves composed of three
leaflets like clover but no
watermark and having small
tooth at leaflet tip

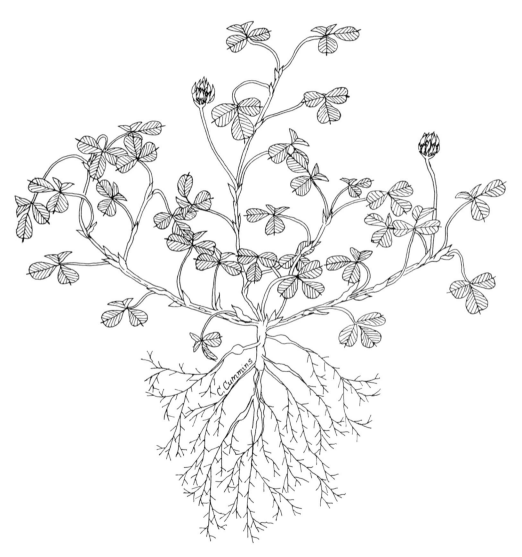

Figure 5-28   Black medic   *Medicago lupulina* L.
Leaves with three leaflets like clover but with a small bristle at leaflet tip and without the
watermark.

PARSLEY PIERT

- Parsley-like leaves
- Large lobed stipules

Figure 5-29   Parsley piert *Alchemilla microcarpa* Boiss. & Reut.
Small, much branched annual with parsley-like leaves.
Each leaf with a pair of broad lobed stipules at the base.
Minute, green flowers.

BUCKHORN PLANTAIN

- Rosette of long, narrow, curled leaves
- Spike-like inflorescence borne at top of long stalk

Figure 5-30 Buckhorn plantain *Plantago lanceolata* L.
Rosette of long, narrow, curled leaves.
Deep taproot.
Spike-like inflorescence borne at the top of a long stalk.

COMMON OR BROADLEAF PLANTAIN

- Rosette of egg-shaped leaves
- Long, spiked flower stalks

Figure 5-31   Common (broadleaf) plantain *Plantago major* L.
Rosette of egg-shaped leaves lying flat.
Long, spiked flower stalks.

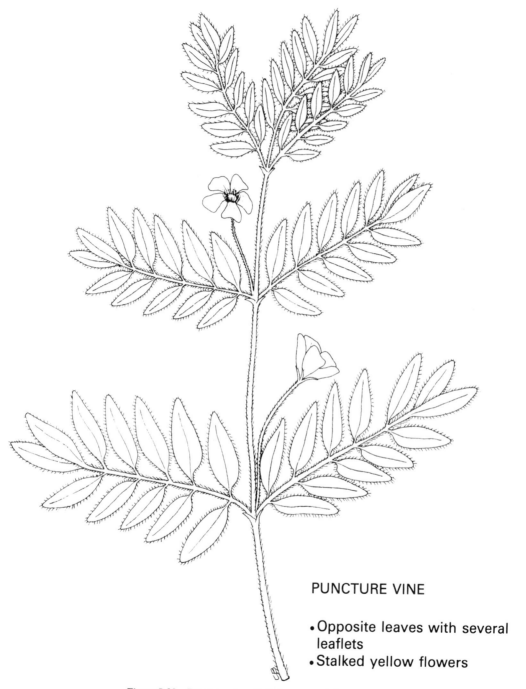

PUNCTURE VINE

- Opposite leaves with several leaflets
- Stalked yellow flowers

Figure 5-32 Puncture vine *Tribulus terrestris* L.
  Prostrate, branched annual with spiny burs.
  Opposite leaves each with several leaflets.
  Hairy stems and leaves.
  Light yellow flowers borne on stalks arising at leaf bases.

PURSLANE

- Thick, fleshy stems and leaves

Figure 5-33 Purslane *Portulaca oleracea* L.
Thick, fleshy stems and leaves.
Adapted to hot, dry summers.

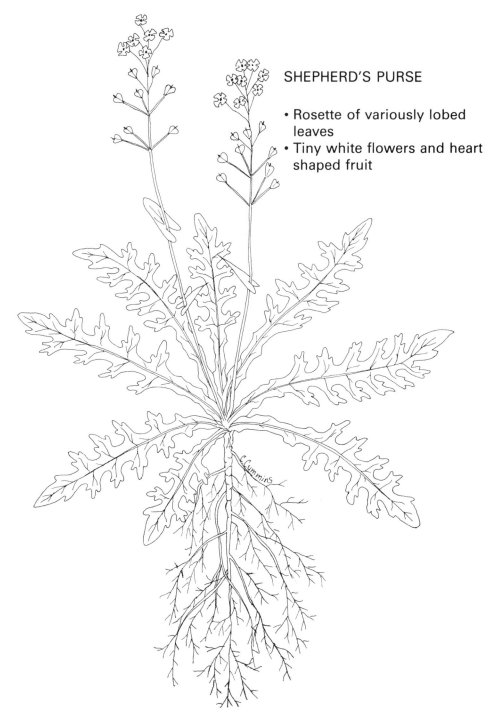

SHEPHERD'S PURSE

- Rosette of variously lobed leaves
- Tiny white flowers and heart shaped fruit

Figure 5-34 Shepherd's purse *Capsella bursa-pastoris* (L.) Medic.
Widespread winter annual with rosette of variously lobed leaves.
Heart-shaped seed capsules in a raceme.
Flowers are small with four white petals.

SHEEP OR RED SORREL

- Arrowhead-shaped leaves

Figure 5-35   Sheep (red) sorrel *Rumex acetosella* L.
Arrowhead-shaped leaves with sour taste.
Spreads by vigorous rhizomes.
Male and female flowers grow on separate plants.

THYMELEAF SPEEDWELL

• Creeper with opposite, oval leaves

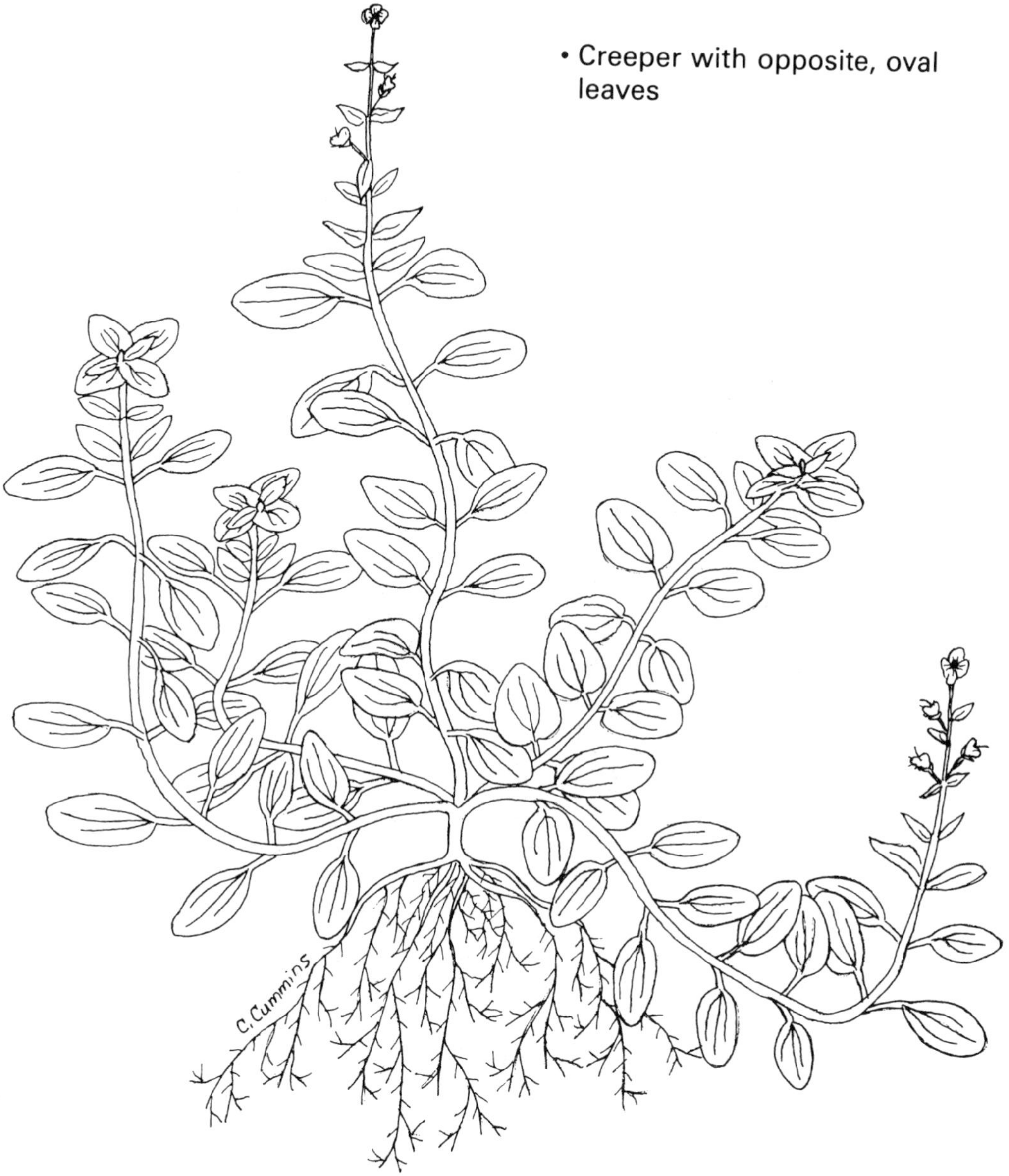

Figure 5-36 Thymeleaf speedwell *Veronica serpyllifolia* L.
Creeper with opposite, oval leaves, forming dense patches.
Tiny, irregular shaped flowers with four purple-white petals.

SPOTTED SPURGE

- Opposite leaves with purple-brown spot on upper surface
- Milky sap

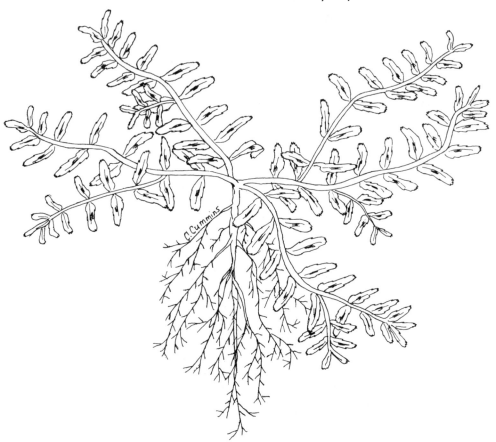

Figure 5-37   Spotted spurge *Euphorbia maculata* L.
Low growing, spreading annual.
Opposite leaves are less than 1 in. long with a purple-brown blotch on the upper surface. Stems exude milky sap.

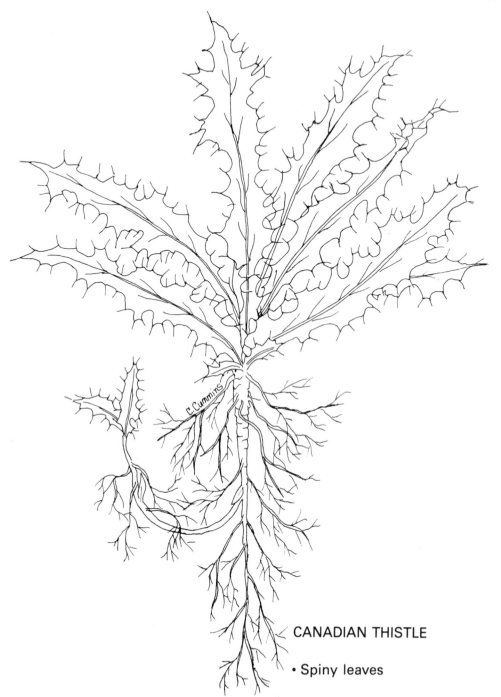

CANADIAN THISTLE

• Spiny leaves

Figure 5-38 Canadian thistle *Cirsium arvense* (L.) Scop.
Difficult perennial; spreads by rhizomes.
Lobed leaves with crinkled margins and sharp spines.
Lavender flower heads.

WOODSORREL, YELLOW SORREL

• Each leaf composed of three heart-shaped leaflets with notch at its apex

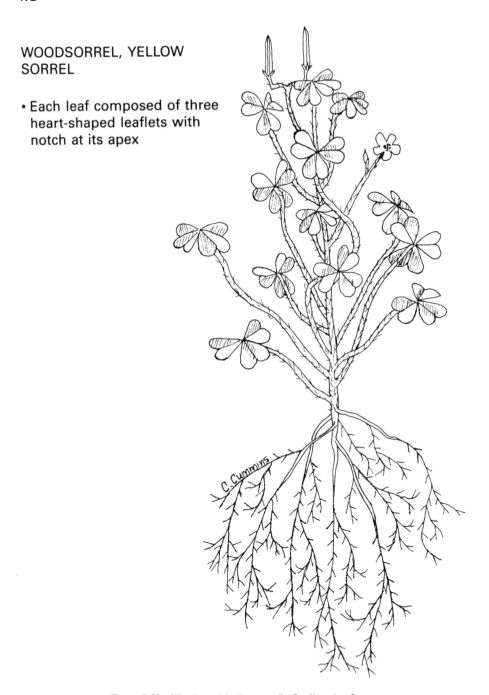

Figure 5-39 Woodsorrel (yellow sorrel) *Oxalis stricta* L.
Resembles clover but is lighter green.
Leaf is composed of three heart-shaped leaflets, each notched at the tip.
Leaves sour to the taste.
Yellow flower.

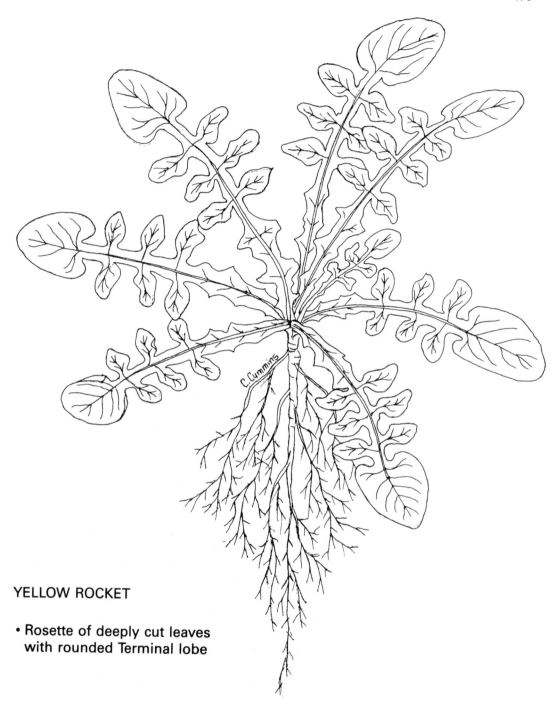

YELLOW ROCKET

• Rosette of deeply cut leaves
  with rounded Terminal lobe

Figure 5-40 Yellow rocket *Barbarea vulgaris* R. Br.
Early spring weed with rosette of deeply cut leaves having rounded terminal lobes.
Small flowers with four yellow petals.

6

Insects and Their Control

RAPID REPRODUCERS

Somewhere between 70% and 80% of all the known kinds of animals are insects. Nobody knows exactly how many kinds of insects there are, but estimates of those that have been discovered, described, and named approach a million. Several million more probably remain to be discovered. They are a fantastically variable and adaptable group of animals. By survival of the fittest, nineteenth-century biologist Charles Darwin actually meant those animals that are the most prolific reproducers, and by this standard insects as a group are without peers in the animal world. If all the descendants of a pair of houseflies survived, in just one season the total number of descendants would reach about 200,000,000,000,000,000,000. The estimated number of insects and mites in grassland has ranged up to several hundred million per acre. Fortunately, nature is also blessed with birds, other predatory insects, disease, unknown weather, and even insecticides, all of which keep this giant group in check.

Some of the most striking examples of insect damage are recorded in descriptions of the migrating swarms of grasshoppers in the Great Plains of the 1870s, as indicated in the following passage from *Insects**: "The locusts are said to have left fields as barren as if they had been burned over. Only holes in the ground showed where plants had been. Trees were stripped of their leaves and green bark. One observer in Nebraska recorded that one of the invading swarms of locusts averaged a half mile in height and was 100 miles wide and 300 miles long. In places the column, seen

---

**Insects, In The Yearbook of Agriculture, 1952.* (Washington, D.C.: United States Department of Agriculture, 1952), p. 4.

through field glasses and measured by surveying instruments, was nearly a mile high. With an estimate of 27 locusts per cubic yard, he figured nearly 28 million per cubic mile. He said the swarm was as thick as that for at least 5 miles an hour. He calculated that more than 124 billion locusts were on the move in that one migration."

ONLY A FEW CAUSE DAMAGE

Of the vast number of insects, fortunately only a few to date cause extensive damage in turf. Perhaps the most devastating is the chinch bug, whose populations can kill extensive areas of turf in only a few days, causing a dilemma for the turf manager. Some lawns on a suburban street will show extensive damage in a seemingly random pattern, and some will be completely spared. Under the same weather and insect population conditions, an unknown factor protects certain lawns. Often there is a marked boundary between affected and unaffected areas.

INSECTS HAVE THREE PARTS

Technically speaking, the giant Class Insecta consists of those animals with a body composed of three main divisions: head, thorax, and abdomen. An insect also has antennae and usually has wings and three pairs of jointed legs. If the body has only two main parts (a fused head and thorax and an abdomen), four pairs of jointed legs, and no wings or antennae, the "bug" belongs to another class, the Arachnida—spiders, ticks, mites, and scorpions. Centipedes, millipedes, and sowbugs, all of which are common in the turf environment, are not, strictly speaking, insects either, yet to the layman, they are all known as "bugs." (True bugs are insects belonging to the Order Hemiptera.)

INSECTS MAKE DRAMATIC CHANGES IN THEIR LIFESTYLE . . . METAMORPHOSIS

Insects begin their development from eggs, which in the case of most grass-feeding insects are laid in or on the plant or nearby in the soil. In some insects the eggs hatch into *nymphs*, which are usually similar to but smaller than the mature adult. Then a series of about 4 to 8 changes called *molts* occurs, during which the old *cuticle*, or skin, is shed after a new and larger one is produced. The nymphs thus develop into adults, the sexual stage. Eggs are formed and laid, and the cycle is completed. This is called a *simple metamorphosis* and is shown, for example, in the chinch bug in Figure 6-1.

Those insects that have a *complete metamorphosis* develop from an egg into a *larva* (variously called grub, worm, caterpillar, or maggot); this is the stage that frequently causes turf damage. The larva will transform into a *pupa,* which is typically a nonfeeding, inactive stage. The pupa often becomes covered with a protective mate-

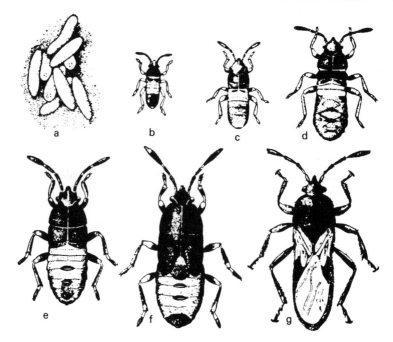

Figure 6-1   The simple metamorphosis of the chinch bug. Source: USDA.

rial, forming a *cocoon* in which it passes the winter. At the end of this stage (for example, the next spring), the adult emerges, has a brief sexual life, lays eggs, and the cycle is completed. Various grubs, sod webworms, armyworms, and cutworms have this type of life cycle. The complete metamorphosis of the Japanese beetle is shown in Figure 6-2.

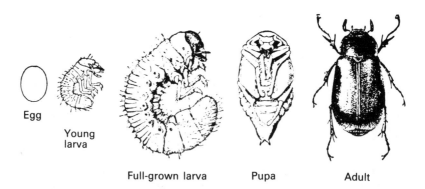

Figure 6-2   The complete metamorphosis of the Japanese beetle. Source: USDA.

INSECTICIDES—THE AMMUNITION . . . USE ONLY WHEN NEEDED

Insects have been on the scene over 200 million years longer than humans, and the first humanoids without a coat of hair probably resorted to mud and dirt to protect themselves. As humans forsook the nomadic life and developed agriculture, they tried everything to protect their homes and crops, usually with only minimal success: Solutions of nicotine or pepper or both, soapy water, vinegar, turpentine, and fish oil were tried. It was noticed that chrysanthemums repulsed insects, and these were often planted near or around vegetable gardens. Extracts of the mums were made, and a group of compounds known as pyrethrums were isolated and became one of the best natural controls. They are still widely used today.

It was not until about the time of World War II that the chemical industry developed a new weapon for insect control: synthetic organic pesticides. Insecticides are by and large the most toxic of the pesticides. Many of them are related to the "nerve gases" by chemical structure and mode of action, which consists of inhibiting important enzymes of the nervous system. There are basically three types of insecticides: *chlorinated hydrocarbons* such as DDT, lindane, chlordane, among others, which contain carbon, hydrogen, and chlorine; *organophosphates,* which contain carbon, hydrogen, and phosphorus; and *carbamates,* which are derived from carbamic acid ($HO—C—NH_2$) and therefore contain carbon, hydrogen, and nitrogen.

The most famous and widely used insecticide ever developed was a chlorinated hydrocarbon known as DDT. It was first synthesized by a German graduate student in 1873 and rediscovered in 1939 by Dr. Paul Muller while searching for an insecticide that would control the clothes moth. It was so successful in controlling mosquitoes in areas of malaria and yellow fever that Dr. Muller was awarded the Nobel Prize in Medicine in 1948. A few years later, however, its harmful effects on wildlife and its persistence in the environment were recognized and the once mighty bug killer was greatly restricted in use. The same fate has also befallen another chlorinated hydrocarbon and popular turf insecticide, chlordane.

Insecticides should be used with care and deliberation. Some important cautions regarding their use are:

1. Use them only when a definite need has been established! These highly toxic chemicals should not be randomly or routinely spread around the environment. Most of them are toxic to beneficial insects such as bees and insect predators as well as to turf-damaging organisms. Some of them also retard grass seed germination and growth of new seedlings or soddings. Overuse also increases the risk of insecticide resistance in the target organisms.

2. Read the labels thoroughly if you are not completely familiar with the insecticide! Many insecticides cannot be mixed with lime, iron, copper, and other compounds containing heavy metals. Their effectiveness is often limited in alkaline solutions. Many are highly toxic to bees, fish, ducks and geese, and other wildlife.

3. Keep them away from streams and all other kinds of water supplies! Toxic chemicals are becoming increasingly common in reservoirs and drinking water supplies.

4. Keep them away from houses and automobiles! Avoid spraying on a windy day. Some pesticides may cause spotting on automobile finishes (wash immediately).

5. By and large, do not mow for 24 hours after an insecticide has been applied! This gives time for the material to take effect and avoids the problem of disposal of pesticide-contaminated clippings.

A list of some insecticides that are relatively common in turf management follows. The first name given is the one by which the pesticide is most widely known in the turf business (usually the trade name). Other commonly used names, if any, are given next in parentheses. The chemical class of the pesticide, whether chlorinated hydrocarbon, organic phosphate, or carbamate, is given next. The LD_{50}, stated in milligrams of the chemical per kilogram of body weight, is the dose that is lethal to 50% of the population of experimental animals on which the chemical was tested.

Carefully study all labels for recommended rates. Rates are most conveniently given in pounds of active ingredient per acre, or ai/A. An acre is 43,560 sq ft or 4840 sq yd. These are commonly used figures in the turf industry—memorize them! To convert the rate per acre to ounces per 1000 sq ft use the following formula:

$$\text{ounces per 1000 sq ft} = \frac{\text{lbs per acre} \times 16}{43.5}$$

Aspon (an organic phosphate)

Origin: Stauffer Chemical Co., 1963. LD_{50}: 2710 mg/kg. Used largely for chinch bug control. Control lasts 60 to 90 days. Usually 95% kill within 48 hours. Irrigate immediately.

Baygon (Propoxur) (a carbamate)

Origin: Farbenfabriken Bayer, Germany and Chemagro Corp., U.S., 1963. LD_{50}: 100 mg/kg. Used for chinch bugs, ants, ticks, aphids, sod webworms, billbugs. Do not use in fiberglass tanks. Highly toxic to bees.

Bendiocarb (Turcam) (a carbamate)

Origin: FBC Ltd., 1968. LD_{50}: 40 mg/kg. Short soil life. Used to control chinch bugs, sod webworms, mole crickets, leafhoppers, and ants.

Dasanit (Fensulfothion) (an organic phosphate)

Origin: Farbenfabriken Bayer, Germany and Chemagro Corp., U.S., 1964. LD_{50}: 2.2 mg/kg. This is a long-persisting organophosphate used largely to control nematodes.

Diazinon (Spectracide) (an organic phosphate)

Origin: Geigy Chemical Co., 1952. LD_{50}: 150 mg/kg. A broad-spectrum insecticide particularly effective against sucking and leaf-eating insects; probably the most widely used turf insecticide. Also used against ants, ticks, fleas, chiggers, and mosquitoes. Highly toxic to ducks and geese.

Dursban (Chloropyrifos) (an organic phosphate)

Origin: Dow Chemical Co., 1965. LD_{50}: 163 mg/kg. Effective against chinch bugs and sod webworms. Persists in soil 2 to 4 months.

Dylox (Proxol) (an organic phosphate)

Origin: Farbenfabriken Bayer, Germany, 1952. LD_{50}: 450 mg/kg. Used against cutworms, armyworms, sod webworms, and leafhoppers.

Ethion (an organic phosphate)

Origin: FMC Corp., 1959. LD_{50}: 208 mg/kg. Used to control chinch bugs and sod webworms. Toxic to fish and bees.

Ethoprop (Mocap) (an organic phosphate)

Origin: Mobil Chemical Co., 1963. LD_{50}: 62 mg/kg. Used to control nematodes as well as chinch bugs, sod webworms, and mole crickets. Rats and dogs received 100 mg/kg in their diet daily for 90 days with no effect other than depression of cholinesterase levels. Toxic to fish; not toxic to bees if used as directed.

Malathion (an organic phosphate)

Origin: American Cyanamid, 1951. LD_{50}: 2800 mg/kg. Toxic to fish and bees. Cholinesterase inhibitor but considered of low toxicity to mammals. Used widely to control mosquitoes, in dust form to control human body lice. As much as 5000 mg/kg was placed in the daily diet of rats for 2 years with no ill effect detected apart from its effect on cholinesterase activity.

Nemacur (Fenamiphos) (an organic phosphate)

Origin: Farbenfabriken Bayer, 1969. LD_{50}: 15 mg/kg. A systemic nematicide. Toxic to fish. No effect on soil bacteria. Soil residual 4 to 6 months.

Oftanol (Isofenphos) (an organic phosphate)

Origin: Farbenfabriken Bayer, Germany and Mobay Chemical Corp., U.S., 1981. LD_{50}: 28 to 38.7 mg/kg. This is a new 50W granular insecticide used for the control of white grubs, billbugs, chinch bugs, and sod webworms. Does not tie up in the thatch layer and does not leach in heavy rains. The manufacturers claim that it provides longer grub control than any other available product. Was fed to dogs and rats at 1 mg/kg for 3 months with no effect. Toxic to fish.

Orthene (an organic phosphate)

Origin: Chevron Chemical Co., 1969. LD_{50}: 945 mg/kg. For greenbug aphid control. Residual activity 5 to 6 days. Apply when bugs or signs of damage first appear.

Sevin (Carbaryl) (a carbamate)

Origin: Union Carbide, 1956. LD_{50}: 500 mg/kg. A broad-spectrum insecticide with a long residual. May retard the germination of grasses; should not be mixed with lime. Highly toxic to bees.

Trithion (Carbophenothion) (an organic phosphate)

Origin: Stauffer Chemical Co., 1956. LD_{50}: 79 mg/kg. Used primarily to control the bermudagrass scale and mite. In combination with petroleum oil it has a long residual activity. Toxic to fish and bees.

IDENTIFYING INSECTS—SAMPLING TECHNIQUES

With a little experience, you'll soon get an almost intuitive feeling for destructive insect activity on a lawn. A touch of brown, the season of the year, a jerkily flying moth—your mind will immediately click . . . sod webworms!

To make sure, however, before you call for the insecticide ammunition, it would be wise to back up your intuition with a closer inspection. There are four main ways to take a sample:

1. Simply get down on your hands and knees, part the grass with your fingers, and concentrate your attention on the edge of a damage area. Like fungi, insects tend to proceed with their damage from a center point outward; they are most active on the outside edge, where the damage area grades into the healthy grass. Part the leaves and look into the thatch layer. Concentrate your eyes on a specific area for several seconds and watch for specific insect movements.

2. A second time-honored technique for recognizing many types of turf insects is to take both ends out of a metal 2-lb coffe can and file or otherwise sharpen one edge of the can. Insert this a short distance into the soil and fill it with water. Insects such as chinch bugs that are otherwise hidden from view will float to the surface in a few minutes.

3. A third method of insect detection is to use a so-called *disclosure solution*. That is, use an irritating chemical such as a pyrethrum insecticide or a liquid detergent mixed in the water in the can of the previous method or applied with a watering can directly to a square yard of turf. Use 1/2 teaspoon of a 2% to 3% pyrethrum solution or 1 tablespoon of detergent per gallon of water. Most of the insects should be on the surface in 5 minutes.

4. Still another technique is to take a sod lifter, a cup cutter for golf greens, a sturdy knife, or a trowel and cut out a small piece of sod. Slowly peel the sample—soil,

thatch, and grass—apart over a sheet of newspaper or, preferably, a sheet of white butcher's paper. Against the white background, all kinds of life in the top few inches of the turf should be detectable.

GRUBS

Turf-damaging insects can be conveniently divided into (1) those that feed on grass roots, such as grubs of various kinds, mole crickets, wireworms, and ground pearls, and (2) those that feed on the grass shoots or stems, such as chinch bugs, billbug adults, sod webworms, cutworms, armyworms, greenbug aphids, frit flies, leafhoppers, and scale insects.

Many of the root-feeding insects that damage grasses are the larvae, or grubs, of various beetles that hatch from eggs laid in the ground by the female beetle. Typically, they spend 10 months to 3 years in the ground, at depths that fluctuate depending on the weather. When the weather is mild, they exist rather close (1 to 3 in.) to the surface of the lawn; they go deeper as it gets colder. They are whitish or grayish with darker heads and hind parts and are usually found in a curled position in the soil. Figure 6-3 shows the *rasters* of several kinds of grubs, as an aid to their identification.

Grubs inflict their damage to turfgrasses by feeding on the grass roots an inch or so below the soil surface. An indication of their presence is often the increased activity of moles, skunks, or birds searching for them in the sod. In areas where damage is extensive, the sod, with its roots cut off, can be easily pulled back by hand to expose the little coiled grubs. If this state of damage has not been reached, yet a few small, isolated brown patches in the turf lead one to suspect grub activity, a flat spade can be used to slip under and lay back a piece of sod. Dislodge the soil in the overturned sod or search the soil surface with a trowel and count the number of grubs. Repeat this in several other parts of the lawn, being careful to replace the sod and tamp it down. The rule of thumb is that if your calculations indicate a grub population of three or more per square foot, you should prescribe an insecticide.

TURF-DAMAGING INSECTS

The following section consists of descriptions of the various turf-damaging insects, with symptoms on turf and methods of control. A listing of insecticides that have been recommended for insect control is presented in Table 6-1.

DAMAGING LARVAE

Japanese Beetle (Figure 6-4)

This beetle was first found in the United States in New Jersey in 1916. Entomologists at the New Jersey Experiment Station felt at the time that they could eradicate it and asked the New Jersey legislature for a few thousand dollars to support a control pro-

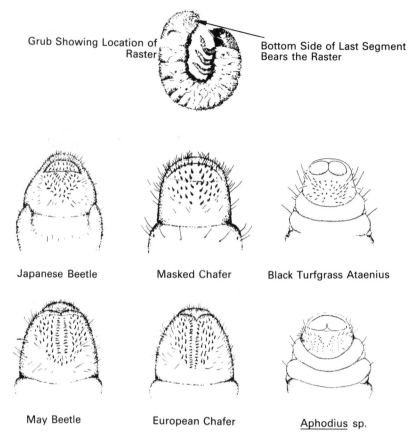

Grub Showing Location of Raster

Bottom Side of Last Segment Bears the Raster

Japanese Beetle   Masked Chafer   Black Turfgrass Ataenius

May Beetle   European Chafer   Aphodius sp.

Identification is an essential step in achieving control of grubs. Examination of the raster with a 10-power hand lens will identify the common species.

Figure 6-3   The rasters of some common turfgrass grubs. Reprinted from Dr. Harry D. Niemczyk, *Destructive Turf Insects*, 1981, H.D.N. Books, Wooster, OH.

gram. The money was denied, and now the beetle is a nuisance from Maine to Georgia and west to the Mississippi River.

The beetles are distinctive: about 1/2 in. long, and shiny metallic green with coppery-brown wing covers. They have six small patches of white hairs along the sides and back of the body. The beetles appear in early summer and are abundant for 4 to 6 weeks. After breeding, the female burrows a few inches into the soil, usually in turf areas, and lays eggs. The grubs develop quickly, becoming 1 in. long when full grown, and spend the rest of the summer and the next spring feeding on grass roots. If abundant, they can severely damage turf areas.

TABLE 6-1. Insecticides Recommended for Control of Turf-damaging Insects

	Aspon	Baygon	Bendiocarb	Dasanit	Diazinon	Dursban	Dylox	Ethion	Ethoprop	Malathion	Nemacur	Oftanol	Orthene	Sevin	Trithion
Damaging Larvae															
Japanese beetle					X		X					X			
May or June beetle					X		X					X			
Masked chafer					X		X					X			
Black turfgrass *Ataenius*					X		X					X			
Hyperodes weevil					X		X					X			
Frit fly					X										
Billbug larva					X										
Sod webworm	X	X			X	X	X					X	X	X	
Armyworm					X	X									
Cutworm					X	X	X							X	
Damaging Nymphs and Adults															
Chinch bug	X	X	X		X	X		X	X			X		X	X
Billbug		X			X	X						X		X	
Greenbug aphid													X		
Mole cricket		X	X*		X	X*			X	X*		X		X*	
Leafhopper		X			X								X	X	
Ant		X			X	X					X				
Chigger, tick					X						X				
Scales															
Ground pearls						No effective control									
Bermudagrass scale					X										X
Rhodesgrass scale					X						X			X	X
Mites															
Bermudagrass stunt mite					X										X
Clover mite					X										
Winter grain mite					X										
Others															
Nematodes				X					X		X				

*Bait is recommended.

As an alternative to use of the chemical controls indicated below, effective biological control of Japanese beetle grubs can be achieved using milky spore disease (see Chapter 4). The disease, caused by the bacterium *Bacillus popilliae,* kills the larvae a month or more after infection. It may take several years for disease spores to build up in the soil to a level sufficient to provide complete beetle control, and infestations of the grubs should be tolerated during this time. A spore suspension of milky spore disease is applied to the turf as a dust.

Symptoms: Patches of turf appear wilted and dying, especially in April to May and

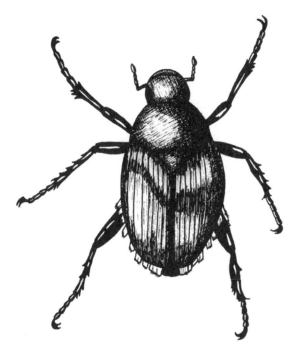

Figure 6-4 The Japanese beetle.

October to November. Turf can be peeled back since roots have been cut off. Moles and skunks are active on the lawn. Bird feeding activity increases.

Controls: Immediate heavy watering to reroot the sod. Apply diazinon, Dylox, Oftanol. Water heavily and continuously. Insecticide must be washed through thatch to make contact with grubs. Effective biological control can be achieved with the use of milky spore disease. Apply as a dust (at any time except when ground is frozen) at the rate of about 12 lb dust per acre. This can be done by applying 1 teaspoon of dust in spots 4 ft apart in rows 4 ft apart.

May or June Beetle (Figure 6-5)

Sometimes called "white grubs", these are the larvae of the May or June beetle found all over the United States but most abundant in the eastern half of the country. They are hard-shelled beetles commonly seen flying around lights on warm nights in the late spring. The bugs remain in the soil 2 to 3 years (3-year cycle north of the Ohio River, 2-year cycle in the South). The adult beetles emerge in May and June, they mate, and the female deposits an average of 50 eggs in the soil. These hatch into grubs in 2 to 3 weeks. For the first season the grubs or larvae feed mostly on decaying vegetable matter. In the second summer they feed on grass roots and cause most of the turf damage. They go deeper into the soil as the weather gets colder. In the third spring the grubs feed for only a short time, and in June they move down into the soil and change into the

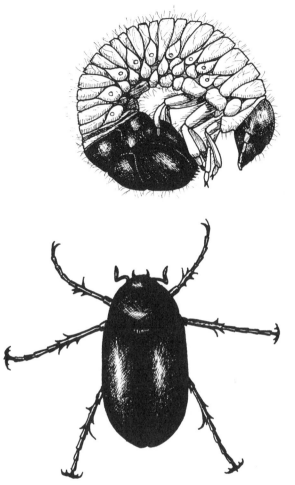

Figure 6-5   The larva (*top*) and adult (*bottom*) of the May-June beetle.

pupal stage. Although they metamorphose into the adult beetle in about a month, they remain in the pupae until the following May or June.

Symptoms: Patches of turf appear wilted and drying, especially in April to May and October to November. Turf can be peeled back since roots have been cut off. Moles and skunks are active on the lawn. Bird feeding activity increases.

Controls: Diazinon, Dylox, Oftanol.

Masked Chafer (Figure 6-6)

The damaging larvae of masked chafers are known as annual white grubs. The adults, which are about 1/2 in. long and brown, emerge at night in June and July and are strongly attracted to light. They eat no food, since their mouthparts are nonfunctional. The annual white grub, which completes its life cycle in one year, is distin-

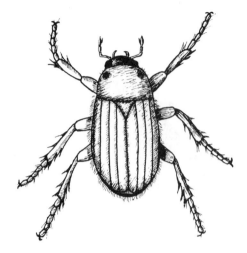

Figure 6-6   The masked chafer.

guished from the white grub larvae of the May or June beetle by spines on the under-side of the *last* body segment.

The northern masked chafer ranges from Connecticut south to Alabama and west to California. The southern masked chafer is common in the southeast up to Kentucky and Ohio, Indiana, and Illinois.

Symptoms: Patches of turf appear wilted and dying, especially in April to May and October to November. Turf can be peeled back since roots have been cut off. Moles and skunks are active on the lawn. Bird feeding activity increases.

Controls: Diazinon, Dylox, Oftanol.

Black Turfgrass *Ataenius* (Figure 6-7)

The larvae, or grubs, of the widespread black turfgrass *Ataenius* cause damage largely to northern golf courses, though they have been found in other areas also. The small black beetle lays its eggs in late spring in the thatch layer or soil. The larvae that hatch are tiny white grubs, smaller than a grain of rice, with brownish heads and dark poste-riors. The larvae feed on the roots of bluegrass, bentgrass, and particularly annual bluegrass on irrigated fairways. They are less common on home lawns. Where infesta-tions are heavy, several hundred larvae can be found per square foot. Treatment should be considered if grub populations are greater than 30 to 40 larvae per square foot. By midsummer the adult beetle lays a second generation of eggs, which develop into larvae by late August and early September. They produce a second round of dam-age, which is recognized by the wilted appearance of the turf and eventually dead patches. Then pupation occurs, with beetles emerging during the same fall in latitudes including Ohio. The beetle overwinters a few inches into the soil or under leaf debris, always near its primary food source.

Symptoms: Turf appearing dry or wilted, then brown and dead. Most obvious in July and again in August.

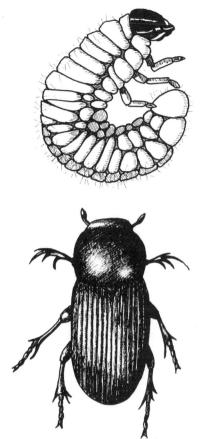

Figure 6-7 The larva (*top*) and adult (*bottom*) of the black turfgrass *Ataenius*.

Controls: Diazinon, Dylox, Oftanol. Timing and watering are important. For control of adults, apply diazinon in spring when they are laying eggs (this coincides with blooming of horse chestnut and black locust); water only lightly so that material does not penetrate below thatch layer. For control of grubs, apply Oftanol from late May on; water in thoroughly to reach grubs. Control may not be effective after damage is severe, as grubs will have finished feeding.

Hyperodes Weevil

This insect is a small (1/8 to 1/4 in. long), black-snouted beetle that causes significant damage to annual bluegrass on golf courses in the Northeast. Most of the damage is done by larvae feeding in and on grass stems and leaves. The grub is also small, about 3/16-in. long, crescent-shaped, and white with a brown head. The adult weevil over-winters in leaf debris. In April and May the female deposits small clusters of eggs in tiny holes chewed in the grass leaf sheaths. The eggs hatch into larvae, which begin feeding on the stems and leaves, chewing out U-shaped areas and working their way down to the base of the plant. This damage can be detected with a hand lens. Eventually, when mature, the larvae burrow into the soil and pupate. In 8 days a young adult emerges, completing the cycle, of which there may be two per year. Most of the damage occurs in mid-June.

Symptoms: U-shaped, V-shaped, or crescent-shaped chewing marks or notches on stems and leaves. Yellowing of the central leaf of the plant.

Controls: Diazinon, Dylox, Oftanol.

Frit Fly

This tiny black fly, about 1/16 inch long, is a pest of golf greens and collars. It is attracted to white—golf balls and white shirts. If present in abundance, the flies can be detected by placing a white handkerchief on the turf. The adult fly feeds on the exudate from young grass shoots and lays its eggs in the leaf sheaths. The eggs hatch into maggots, which tunnel into and feed on grass stems, causing them to turn yellow. Like in the *Hyperodes* weevil, yellowing may occur in just the central leaf of a plant, with surrounding tissue remaining green. The maggots have unusual mouth hooks.

Three or four generations may be produced each season. The frit fly also infects rye, oats, and wheat, on which the larvae consume young developing grains and leave an empty kernel, or "frit."

Symptoms: Yellowing of at first just the central leaves of plants.

Controls: Diazinon.

Billbug (Figure 6-8)

Both the adult beetle and its larvae, or billbug grubs, feed on and cause damage to grasses. The adult beetle is clay yellow to reddish brown to black, measuring 1/5 to 3/4 in. long, with a long snout tipped with a pair of strong jaws used for chewing food. During the first warm days of spring, the beetle comes out of hibernation and begins feeding on turfgrasses, burrowing into the stems at the crown, where the eggs are laid. In a week or two the eggs hatch into tiny grubs, which at maturity are 1/2 to 3/4 in. long, white, and legless, with a hard brown or orange head. The grubs feed on the crown and on the roots of grasses slightly below ground level, making it easy to pull up individual grass plants.

After several weeks of feeding, the grub changes into a pupa, usually in a cell in the soil. Within a few days the pupa produces an adult, which may either remain in the soil for the winter or else may emerge and become active until hibernation for the winter.

Various species of billbugs attack bermudagrass, zoysiagrass, and also bluegrass. The damage is not always localized as much as with other grubs, but it appears as a general thinning of the turf. Sometimes dead, yellow, circular or irregular patches occur; these are easy to confuse with fertilizer burns, except that the grass pulls up easily.

Symptoms: Thin areas of dead patches in turf; damaged turf is easy to pull up. Look for evidence of larvae feeding at base of stem or among roots (fine sawdust-like residue

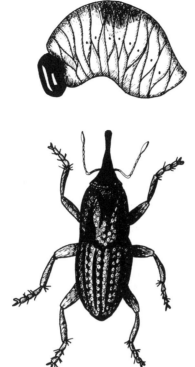

Figure 6-8 The larva (*top*) and adult (*bottom*) of the billbug.

is left by root-feeding larvae). Adults frequently seen on sidewalks, driveways, and gutters in spring and fall indicate that larval infestation may occur in July and August.

Controls: The larva is controlled with diazinon, whereas Baygon, diazinon, Dursban, Oftanol, and Sevin have been recommended for control of adults.

Sod Webworm (Figure 6-9)

The sod webworm is the larval stage of a lawn moth (sometimes called a miller) that is dingy brown with an open wingspread of about 3/4 in. When the insect is at rest, the wings are folded tightly against the body. During the day the moths are inactive and hide in shrubbery or other protected spots. In the early evening, however, they become active and fly in a jerky, zig-zag pattern over the lawn, dropping and scattering eggs while in flight.

The eggs hatch in about a week to produce the larvae, which begin to feed on grass plants almost immediately. At maturity the sod webworm is 1/2 to 1 in. or more long, is greenish-brown, and has stiff hairs arising from dark brown, round patches on the body. Like the moth, the webworms are active only at night, chewing grass leaves, severing the entire plant at the crown, and feeding on roots. During the day they tend to retreat to silk-like tunnels (hence the name webworm) that they have constructed in thatch or just below the soil surface.

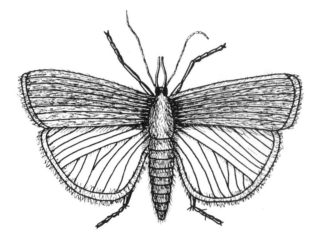

Figure 6-9   The larva (*top*) and adult (*bottom*) of the sod webworm.

Slightly below the soil surface the sod webworm builds a loosely woven cocoon in which it pupates and later changes to the adult, or moth, stage. The entire life cycle may be completed in less than 6 weeks; hence there may be two or more generations over the summer season.

Sod webworms seem to prefer newer lawns, which is probably a function of their arrival with a fresh-cut batch of sod. They seem to attack any type of turfgrass, but they cause the most damage in bluegrass and bentgrass. As with chinch bugs, the damage appears as irregular brown patches, but since the moth has scattered its eggs across the lawn, webworm activity does not necessarily start in the sunny, warm areas, as with chinch bugs. It has been our experience, however, that chinch bugs and sod webworms tend to go hand in hand, frequently appearing together on a damaged lawn.

Symptoms: Irregular brown patches across turf. Peel back sod on edge of damaged area and look for webworms. As with grubs, if three or more per square foot are found, consider use of an insecticide.

Controls: Aspon, Baygon, diazinon, Dursban, Dylox, Oftanol, Orthene, and Sevin.

Armyworm (Figure 6-10)

Like sod webworms, armyworms are the larval stage of several kinds of moths. The worms are about 1/2 to 1 1/2 in. long, with stripes along each side and the back of a light green to dark brown body. The middlestripe running down the back is often yellowish

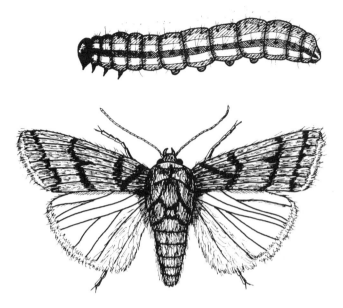

Figure 6-10   The larva (*top*) and adult (*bottom*) of the armyworm.

white and ends as an inverted V on the head. The body of the armyworm is segmented, with three pairs of stubby legs and additional projections along the bottom segments. They feed on grass leaves mostly at night.

The adult moth is brownish gray, with a wingspan of about 1¹/₂ in.—a good-sized moth. Egg masses are laid at night in the grass or in nearby shrubs. Hatching occurs in about a week, and larvae begin feeding immediately. At the rare moments when conditions are ideal, thousands of armyworms may become active in a small area, and as the name implies, the insects travel in hordes, leaving badly damaged or even bare turf behind.

Symptoms: Brown patches, frequently with probe holes left by birds looking for the worms. Damage often recognizable by grass blades that have been unevenly chewed along the edges, skeletonized, or completely severed. Green excrement pellets (*frass*) may be present in feeding areas.

Controls: Diazinon, Dursban.

Cutworm (Figure 6-11)

Cutworms are the larval stage of various night-flying, brown to gray lawn moths with wing spans up to 1¹/₂ in. They look very much like armyworms, with segmented bodies, two pairs of legs, and additional projections along the abdomen. Their body stripes are lighter against a green, gray, brown, or even black body color. Some species are spotted. The caterpillar ranges in size from 1 to 2 in.

Only one generation per season is produced by most species of cutworms. The adult moths start to lay eggs in the late spring, depositing the eggs on grass leaves,

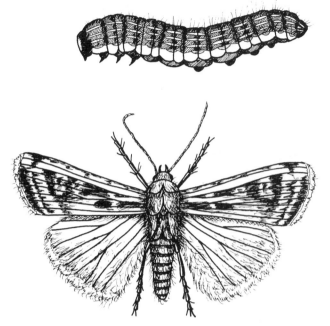

Figure 6-11 The larva (*top*) and adult (*bottom*) of the cutworm.

weeds, or other debris above the soil. The eggs hatch in about a week, and the larvae feed on grasses most of the summer. At maturity they dig cells in the soil like the sod webworm, where they propagate and overwinter, emerging as adult moths the next spring. Cutworms feed usually at night on grass leaves or cut-off grass near the soil. They have been noted to do severe damage to seedling leaves of ryegrass, bentgrass, and bermudagrass.

Symptoms: Brown patches, frequently with probe holes left by birds looking for the worms. Damage often recognizable by grass blades that have been unevenly chewed along the edges, skeletonized, or completely severed. Green excrement pellets (*frass*) may be present in feeding areas.

Controls: Diazinon, Dursban, Dylox, Sevin.

DAMAGING NYMPHS AND ADULTS

Chinch Bug (Figure 6-12)

Perhaps the most devastating of all turf insects is the chinch bug, which will reach population levels that can kill off extensive areas of turf in a matter of a few days. This sudden damage is a perplexing problem to the turf manager. On a typical suburban street some of the lawns will show extensive damage in what is almost a random pattern down the block. Many of the lawns will be completely spared, showing little or no damage. Given the same weather and the same general population, obviously some

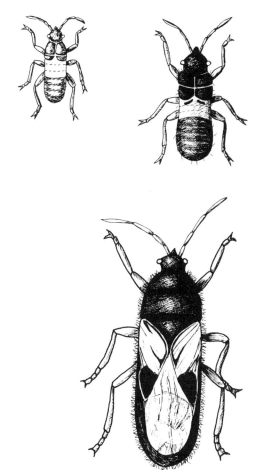

Figure 6-12 Nymphs (*top left and right*) and adult (*bottom*) of the chinch bug.

factor difficult to detect protects some lawns, which often show a marked boundary between the damaged and the protected ones.

Chinch bugs are tropical insects and hence are not active in the bluegrass region until the temperatures are well up in the 70s or above. The first symptoms are patches of dead grass in sunny areas, particularly on slopes, mounds, or terraces with a southern exposure or along sidewalks, driveways, or sides of buildings where heat is radiated. These first symptoms are often confused with drought or fungal damage.

The chinch bug has a slender beak, which it inserts into the grass plant along with a toxin to extract plant juices. The combination of the toxin and the extraction of vital juices frequently kills the plant or leaves it in a state of slow recovery.

Like most insects, the chinch bug is prolific—the female produces 15 to 20 eggs per day for about a month. The bug may produce two generations: one in early June and the more destructive second generation in August. Eggs are laid on grass leaves and stems, in the thatch layer, or in almost any protected and warm place. The eggs hatch in about a week into yellow, wingless nymphs which soon turn *red with a white band across the body.* As they enlarge, the nymphs turn orange-brown and then black at maturity. Adults are about $1/5$ in. long and black with white wings folded over their backs, so that on casual observation the insect appears to carry a *white cross on its back.* Frequently, the little white-cross bugs can be seen quickly scurrying around, annoyed by the disruption of their habitat and trying to avoid direct light by burying themselves in the thatch. As much as they prefer warm areas, they also seem to dislike light. Though small, they are easy to spot if one looks closely at a specific area.

Symptoms: Patches of dead grass in sunny areas, particularly on south-facing slopes, mounds, and terraces or along sidewalks, driveways, and the sides of buildings where heat is radiated. Look for insect by parting grass at border between dead and healthy grass. Usually late summer, early fall.

Controls: Aspon, Baygon, bendiocarb, diazinon, Dursban, Ethion, Ethoprop, Oftanol, Sevin, Trithion.

The chinch bug has two natural predators. The first is a fungus named *Beauveria* (see Chapter 4), which is particularly active when the soil moisture level is high. This may explain in part why chinch bug activity is noticeably reduced by watering. The second predator is an insect called the big-eyed bug, which looks not unlike the chinch bug itself; it is slightly larger with two prominent eyes and lacks the white-cross appearance of chinch bug wings. The big-eyed bug is much quicker and more active than the chinch bug. Given the right conditions, both this bug and the fungal predator *Beauveria* can significantly reduce chinch bug populations. For this reason alone one should proceed cautiously with the use of insecticides and fungicides.

Greenbug Aphid

This is a relatively new insect pest on turfgrasses. Serious damage was first reported in Dayton, Ohio, in the early 1970s and seems to have spread into Indiana, Illinois, and Wisconsin. The aphid is only $1/16$ in. long and light green with a darker green stripe down its back. It inserts its piercing mouthparts into a grass blade and sucks it dry. Salivary fluids are also injected, and the tissue around the hole dies. The turf acquires a burnt-orange coloration, and 50 or more tiny aphids can be seen on a single blade. The damage frequently occurs in a ring underneath a tree and spreads to more open areas. Ladybugs may also be present feeding on the aphids. Significant aphid populations begin to appear in late June, and they may persist well into a warm fall. Though the spring infestation may be largely due to migration from the South, eggs can overwinter in the North also. Damage can be quick and quite severe, often to the point where the turf must be replaced. Repeat applications of insecticide may be necessary to control the insect.

Symptoms: Yellow to dark orange damage, first obvious under the shade of trees. Clusters of light green aphids on grass blades. Ladybugs frequently present.

Controls: Orthene. Apply when greenbugs or their damage first appear in sufficient water to obtain good coverage (1 to 4 gal per 1000 sq ft). Do not mow for at least 24 hours after application.

Mole Cricket (Figure 6-13)

These skinny, beady-eyed, southern "ground puppies" can cause severe damage to grasses, flower beds, and vegetable gardens in Florida, Georgia, South Carolina, parts of Tennessee, Alabama, Mississippi, Louisiana, and eastern Texas. They burrow in the top few inches of the soil, feeding on roots and tubers, uprooting plants, and causing desiccation. Damage can be particularly severe on a new seeding or sodding. There are two main species of mole crickets: the southern and the Puerto Rican or Changa mole cricket. The Changa has a more restricted range, occurring in Florida, southern Georgia, Alabama, and southern coastal areas of South Carolina. Entomologists feel that both species were introduced at Brunswick, Georgia, in 1899.

The average southern mole cricket is 1¼ in. long and less than ½ in. wide, is brown often with a greenish tinge on top and a lighter shade underneath, and has large beady eyes and short but wide front legs adapted to digging. Males have a dark spot on the forewings. When the two species are compared from above, the Changa is larger, broader, and lighter brown than the southern mole cricket. (More distinguishing characteristics used by entomologists are that the southern has four distinct lighter spots on its prothorax and that the ultimate extensions [tibial dactyls, or furgers] on the forelegs are separated by a U-shaped space almost as great as the width of one dactyl. The Changa lacks the four distinct lighter spots, and its dactyls are separated by a V-shaped space that is less than the width of either dactyl.)

Adult mole crickets overwinter in underground burrows, digging deeper with increasing cold. When night temperatures reach 60 to 70°F in early spring, the insect comes out of its burrow for nocturnal mating and migrating flights, returning to the soil before daylight. Eggs are hatched in about 2 to 3 weeks, and nymphs resemble small adults with short wings. The nymphs mature into adults by the next spring, thus producing one generation per year.

Most of the feeding occurs at night on the soil surface during warm, damp weather after rainfall or irrigation. The insects have been observed to tunnel as much as 20 ft in a night, leaving the soil mounded much in the same way as ground moles or gophers do. Bahiagrass in Florida seems to be the top preference, followed by Bermudagrass. St. Augustinegrass is slightly more resistant, it is thought, because of its more coarse root system. Centipede and zoysia grasses have not been seriously damaged.

For detecting mole crickets, use a detergent disclosing solution as described earlier. If these insects are not located in this manner, peel back the turf and look for white grubs, which cause somewhat similar-appearing damage. If more than two mole crickets are found per square foot, treatment of the turf is recommended.

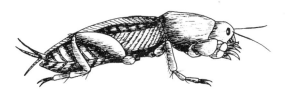

Figure 6-13 The mole cricket.

The optimum time for an insecticide application in Florida is during early July, as later treatments provide less control. Night temperatures should be at least 70°F so that the mole crickets will be out of the ground, and the insecticide should be applied in the late afternoon or early evening. Soaking the lawn *before* the spray application helps, and soaking is almost a necessity *after* the application. Even coverage is important—spray in one direction and then repeat at right angles. Some recommend a second insecticide application in 10 to 14 days.

If the damage to the turf does not occur until fall, baits that lure the crickets to the surface are considered more effective. The turf is watered as indicated earlier before the application, but *not after the application.* It is preferable to select a time when it is not likely to rain for 48 hours. The baits must also be applied evenly in two directions.

Recommended mowing heights should be maintained as follows: 3 in. for bahiagrass; 2 to 3 in. for St. Augustinegrass; 2 in. for centipedegrass; 0.2 to 0.5 in. for bermudagrass.

Symptoms: Patches of dying grass with partially destroyed root systems: mounds and 1/4-in. holes in soil that could be mole cricket tracks and tunnels; a certain "fluffiness" to the turf.

Controls: Baygon, diazinon, Ethoprop, Oftanol. Recommended bait formulations are Baygon, Dursban, malathion, Sevin, and Toxaphene.

Leafhopper (Figure 6-14)

These are common insects on lawns that fly and hop for short distances when they are dislodged by walking on or mowing the turf. Leafhoppers are usually less than 1/4 in. long and are green, yellowish, or brownish gray. They are usually not much of a problem, although they may alarm the homeowner mowing the lawn. They do suck sap

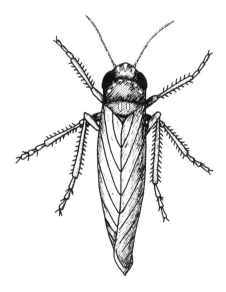

Figure 6-14 The leafhopper.

from the leaves and stems of grasses, and in considerable numbers they cause noticeable damage in the form of whitened patches often mistaken for drought or fungal disease. Leafhoppers have been known to extensively damage new seedings.

Symptoms: Whitened patches resembling drought in the turf.

Controls: Usually none necessary. Bendiocarb, diazinon, Orthene, Sevin.

SCALES, MITES, AND OTHERS

Ground Pearls

Ground pearls are the immature stage of a scale insect. A few days after hatching, the tiny nymphs, or crawlers, attach themselves to the roots of warm-season grasses, such as Bermudagrass, St. Augustinegrass, and particularly centipedegrass. With piercing mouthparts, they suck nutrients from the grass and secrete around themselves for protection a pearl-like shell or cyst. The shells are yellow-purple, varying in size from a pinhead to nearly 1/4 in. in diameter.

Apparently the mature insect leaves the protective, pearl-like cocoon and mates, moves a short distance, and then lays eggs. These develop into nymphs, completing a cycle from egg to adult that may require at least one and possibly two or more years.

The sucking insect attacks grass roots, essentially removing all the juices from them. The turf turns yellow and then brown in irregular patches. Detection can be verified only by digging through the root zone and confirming the presence of the pearls themselves. Since they can occur as deep as a foot in the soil, there is no practical or effective method to control these pests with an insecticide. The only recommendation at this time is to water and fertilize the turf to offset the injury.

Symptoms: Irregular yellow and brown patches.

Controls: None

Bermudagrass Scale and Rhodesgrass Scale

In addition to ground pearls, there are two other scale insects that damage southern grasses. The bermudagrass scale is about 1/16 in. long; has an oval, white, paper-thin protective covering; and is usually clustered along the grass stems at the nodes. The main body of the rhodesgrass scale is round, dark, and covered with a cottony secretion, about 1/8 in. in diameter, often with hair-like protections. This insect is usually found in clusters on the crowns of grass plants.

Like the ground pearl scale insect, the bermudagrass and rhodesgrass scales suck vital fluids from the plant, weakening the turf and causing it to turn yellow and brown. Coupled with the "moldy" appearance of these scale insects, the damage can easily be confused with a fungus disease.

Symptoms: Yellow and brown patches.

Controls: For bermudagrass scale, diazinon or Trithion. For rhodesgrass scale, also malathion and Sevin.

Bermudagrass Stunt Mite

Mites are arthropods related to the insects but differing from them in the form of the body. It is necessary to have a microscope to positively identify the tiny bermudagrass stunt mite, which is whitish and only about 1/25 in. long. It can complete a life cycle in about a week, producing hundreds of mites that suck the juices from the stem and leaves. All stages can be found together under the leaf sheath, where eggs are laid. Continued feeding results in light green leaves that are abnormally curled, shortened internodes, and rosetted or tufted plants resembling "witches' brooms." Browning and death may then occur. Control is difficult because of the short life cycle, reinfestation from untreated areas, and resistant strains of the organism.

Symptoms: Light green, yellowed, or dead leaves; plants tufted, rosette-like, and with shortened internodes.

Controls: Diazinon, Trithion.

Clover Mite

This organism is about the same size as the bermudagrass mite—about 1/25 to 1/30 in. long and requiring a 20 × hand lens or microscope for identification. Under a lens the mite can be identified by its relatively long front legs extending forward from the body. When crushed, the mite leaves a bright red stain. Eggs produced are also bright red. The mite overwinters in basements and along building foundations.

Symptoms: Silvery or frosted turf in spring, in areas 1 to 2 ft wide along the foundation of a building.

Controls: Diazinon.

Winter Grain Mite

The winter grain mite is unusual in that it is active in the winter and dormant in the summer. Its damage to cool-season grasses is easily mistaken for winter desiccation. Largely occurring west of the Mississippi River, there are only a few reports of extensive damage on golf course greens, fairways, and home lawns in Pennsylvania and Ohio. The mite is larger than the bermudagrass and clover mites and is visible to the naked eye; it has a dark body and eight reddish-orange legs. There are two silvery eyes on the front portion of the body, and on the back portion there is a reddish-orange spot surrounding the anus.

By late winter there may be several thousand mites per square foot feeding on grass blades. They damage the leaf surface, exposing the cell contents to winter wind and sun and causing the grass to dry out, or desiccate. The symptoms, then, are similar to winter desiccation, in which grasses dry out from excessive transpiration in wind and sun. The mite damage may also have the silvery cast associated with early spring frost damage.

Symptoms: Turf silvery, appearing desiccated.

Controls: Diazinon.

Nematodes

Nematodes are microscopic worms about $1/10$ to $1/75$ in. long. There are many genera and species that damage turf, causing conditions called by such names as "stubby-root," "summer dormancy," and "root-knot."

The life cycle typically takes about a month. Eggs are laid in the soil and the larvae develop there, sometimes remaining inactive and encysted for months or even years. The tiny worm does its first damage by puncturing the grass root with a hollow, needle-like stylet, causing some mechanical injury. But most damage occurs when the nematode secretes plant-digesting substances into the affected plant cells and liquefies them. This juicy food is then drawn back through the stylet. The result for the plant is either greatly reduced root growth, leading to the stubby-root syndrome, or else a sort of wound reaction of root cell growth, producing the characteristic root-knots.

The above-ground symptoms in turf areas are yellowing of leaves and a general failure to thrive, often in circular or irregular patches. The patches may wilt sooner than surrounding turf because of the root damage. If the grass root system is examined, it is seen to be stunted and sparse, discolored, or with small "galls" and swollen roots. Kentucky bluegrass, St. Augustinegrass, centipedegrass, bermudagrass, and zoysiagrass have been severely injured, and the damage is worst in heat, drought, and under conditions of low fertility.

If an infestation of nematodes is suspected, a soil sample should be sent to a laboratory for confirmation. The turf can be fertilized with potassium and phosphorus but the nitrogen rate should be reduced to $1/2$ lb per 1000 sq ft in order to reduce top growth on the weakened root system. Watering will help to prevent wilting. Two types of nematicides are available: Fumigants usually give broad control, but they must be applied before grass is planted; nonfumigants are more species-specific and can be applied to turf. Aeration prior to use of the nonfumigants is helpful, and the turf should be heavily watered after their application. Both types of nematicides are more effective on sandy soils low in organic matter.

Symptoms: Turf yellowed and wilting in patches. Stunted root system, sometimes with root-knots.

Controls: Dasanit, Ethoprop, Nemacur.

7

Fungi and Diseases

THE FUNGI

Although the turf manager may think of the fungi only in terms of their ability to cause disease, we should all understand the way they live and the many ways in which they benefit humans. The fungi are a diverse group of nongreen organisms that are unable to manufacture their own food through photosynthesis because they lack chlorophyll. This is in contrast to the green plants such as algae, mosses, ferns, grasses, and others, which are able to produce their own sugars, starches, and other nutrients from inorganic raw materials via photosynthesis. The fungi obtain their food by decomposing organic matter. They are called *saprophytic* if they decompose dead organic material and *parasitic* if their food source is living material. It is the parasitic fungi that give turf managers the most trouble.

A few fungi such as yeasts are one-celled organisms, but the typical fungus is filamentous, growing as a mass of filaments called a *mycelium* (plural, *mycelia*) as shown in Figure 7-1. Think, if you will, of a cotton ball: The whole mass of fibers is like the mycelium. Each individual filament is called a *hypha* (plural, *hyphae*); and a hypha that penetrates host cells is called a *haustorium*. Sometimes the mycelium forms a tight, hard mass of hyphae called a *sclerotium*; this is a resistant structure by which the fungus can overwinter.

All fungi produce tremendous numbers of either sexual or asexual spores, which are widely dispersed by wind, water, animals, and other vectors. The spores are very common in soil and in the air, and unless you are in a sterile chamber at this reading, you are probably inhaling and exhaling innumerable fungal spores at this moment. They are responsible for "hay fever" in many people—especially those fungi known as mildews, which become prolific spore producers in a warm, moist atmosphere.

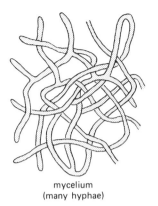

mycelium
(many hyphae)

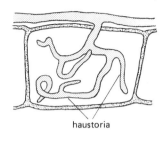

haustoria

Figure 7-1 The growth of a typical fungus. Adapted from T. Elliot Weier, C. Ralph Stocking, and Michael G. Barbour *Botany: An Introduction to Plant Biology*, 4th ed., 1970, p. 483. Copyright © 1970 by John Wiley & Sons, Inc. Reprinted by permission.

"GARBAGE COLLECTORS"

The greatest contribution of fungi to humanity is their ability to cause decay and deterioration (see Chapter 1). They have been called the "garbage collectors of the plant world" because they can decompose and destroy wood, fibers, leather, rubber, even glass lenses and some plastics, and almost anything in the living world. In most instances the effect is beneficial, since they rid the earth of fallen trees and leaves, dead organisms of all sorts, and organic trash that would otherwise collect and cover the earth in an ever-deepening layer. At other times their ability to break down organic matter can be annoying, as they decompose our foods and our homes and cause a number of plant and animal diseases ranging from irritating skin diseases such as athlete's foot to plant diseases of great economic importance such as wheat rust.

THE FIRST CULTIVATED PLANTS

Besides their usefulness in decay and their role in disease, the fungi are important in several other ways. One of these is the production of alcohol and carbon dioxide by certain one-celled fungi called yeasts. All beer and wine lovers should understand that these beverages are the product of a yeast *fermentation* reaction, in which sugar is broken down to alcohol and carbon dioxide. Yeasts are, in fact, considered the first cultivated plants: Always present in the environment, they began to grow in the drink that the caveman no doubt prepared from water and whatever fruits and grains he could collect. If the pot of fruit juice sat near the warm fire for a few days, fermentation occurred and the first brew was invented. Without knowing what had happened, the cavedweller probably had the good sense to maintain and "cultivate" this starter beer or wine, using a little bit of it to get new cultures of fruits and grains going.

If the alcohol produced in yeast fermentation is useful in the brewing industry (and in production of other industrial alcohols), the carbon dioxide produced is the basis of the baking industry. Yeasts were cultivated, maintained, and passed from person to person in the form of starter dough known as "sourdough" to the prospectors of the Yukon. When dough is put in a warm place, yeasts become active in producing carbon dioxide, which causes the dough to rise.

Various organic acids and antibiotics such as penicillin, as well as such delectables as mushrooms and cheese, are products of the fungal world. In fact, when you enjoy a loaf of bread, a jug of wine, and a piece of cheese you are sampling just a few products of the ubiquitous fungi.

ONLY A FEW CAUSE DISEASE

There are between 85,000 and 100,000 species of fungi and innumerable strains and races. Most of them are beneficial to us, and only a few cause problems to the turf manager, but that is more than enough, as any golf course manager will attest. Many varieties of turfgrasses have been selected and more recently bred for their disease resistance, but this characteristic is often ephemeral, or at least seldom universal. Thus a particular variety of bluegrass, for example, may be resistant to a particular fungus in one area of the country but may do poorly against the disease when tested in another part of the country. The reason for this is couched in the science of genetics, but it can be stated in simplistic terms. The fungus species consists of many strains, largely unidentified but each ecologically adapted to a specific region of the country. The bluegrass cultivar, on the other hand, may be an apomict (producing a high proportion of the seed asexually), hence it is genetically very uniform across the country in its disease resistance. In essence, the grass may lack the genetic variability or plasticity of the pathogen, and somewhere under some conditions a particular strain of the disease may have a damaging effect on the grass.

The significance of this to the grass breeder is far reaching, but its effect on the turf manager is one of knowing what grasses perform best under local conditions. This is frequently determined by the state agricultural experiment station or the state university in an area, which observes and tests new grass varieties as they are developed and released by various breeders around the world. You should make it a habit to check the latest turf bulletins issued by your state turf researchers and attend their field days and turf conferences. No amount of reading will substitute for this opportunity to observe turfgrasses in plots designed to compare their attributes and to measure their effectiveness under the local environmental and ecological conditions.

CIRCULAR PATTERNS AND FAIRY RINGS

Most fungi tend to grow in circular patterns, forming concentric rings. This is a useful attribute to remember when you have to make a decision on whether turf damage is fungal, insect-related, or otherwise. Often by the time the fungal damage is apparent, however, the circular patterns have merged or coalesced and the damage takes on an irregular pattern easily confused with insect or other damage. Streaks and crescents of damage are formed in response to the drainage pattern or to washing of the spores.

The circular or concentric growth of fungi is most dramatic in the formation by mushrooms of *fairy rings,* as shown in Figure 7-2. The mushroom itself is actually the *fruiting body* of the fungus, composed of a dense mass of filamentous hyphae. The rest of the mycelium—the great bulk of the fungus—is underground, producing on its leading edge the spore-bearing structures that we find so delicious in edible species.

The rings of mushrooms that form each year grow progressively larger and are sometimes a quarter of a mile or more in diameter (and as much as 300 years old). The reason the rings are clearly visible is that the young mycelium with its mushrooms apparently exudes some nitrates as it grows. This stimulates the grass around the mushrooms in a band as much as a foot wide to grow thicker, higher, and darker green than the surrounding turf. The older mycelium in the center of the fairy ring dies, and grass growing in this area often appears slightly stunted due to depletion of nutrients, as shown in Figure 7-2. Over fairly flat areas these large green circles can be seen clearly from a low-flying airplane. Fairy rings are said to arise in the footsteps of elves and witches or where lightning strikes, and one, of course, never steps inside a ring or even looks at one after dark!

Once the novelty of seeing them wears off, fairy rings can be rather annoying pests in turf, as indicated later in this chapter.

GOOD TURF MANAGEMENT IS GOOD *STRESS* MANAGEMENT

By and large grasses are most susceptible to disease when they are stressed. Good disease control, then, starts with sound cultural practices. Fungicides are used only as a last resort—when the disease overwhelms intelligent turf management. Stress and

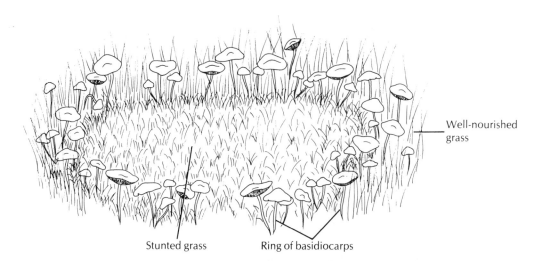

Well-nourished grass

Stunted grass   Ring of basidiocarps

Figure 7-2   A fairy ring formed by the mycelium and fruiting bodies of a mushroom. Reproduced by permission from: Hayden N. Pritchard and Patricia T. Bradt, *Biology of Nonvascular Plants*, p. 362, St. Louis, 1984, Times Mirror/Mosby College Publishing.

disease are not an association unique to grasses but are universal principles of biology. Think of your own system: Good nutrition, adequate sleep, and exercise all go a long way toward keeping you healthy and vital. Be on the alert for turf difficulties other than fungal diseases. Diseases are frequently the manifestations of other problems, and solving those problems will keep the turf healthy and avoid disease.

The following practices will help to prevent disease by reducing stress to the grasses:

1. Water deeply in the morning. Many fungal diseases are favored by dark, wet conditions. On established turf it is usually wiser to soak the grass heavily (1 in. of water or more) but infrequently instead of using smaller, frequent waterings. (New seedings, however, usually require more frequent soaks.) If the grass is watered during the morning, the turf has a chance to dry out before sundown and so does not remain constantly wet.

2. Don't fertilize when it is hot and the soil is dry. Grasses need soil moisture to metabolize fertilizers. Under dry, hot conditions fertilizers may actually weaken the grass, and some fungi like it hot and dry.

3. Don't use herbicides when it is hot and the soil is dry. Weed controls can weaken grasses at any time, and under hot, dry conditions the stress is compounded. Furthermore, the weeds are probably not growing under those conditions anyway, and the weed controls are ineffective. Whenever possible, spot-weed rather than apply herbicides over the entire turf.

4. Limit fertilizing in the shade. Grasses in the shade do not photosynthesize at full rate. Over-stimulating them with nitrogen causes them to overproduce proteins at the expense of their root reserves. The grasses are weakened, becoming more susceptible to disease.

5. Use herbicides in the shade with great care. If possible, avoid herbicides completely in shady areas or else spot-weed only. Weed controls can weaken grasses under the best conditions. In the shade, where most grasses are already struggling, herbicides can signal their death, weakening them to the point where they are susceptible to a wide range of fungal diseases.

6. Use a balanced fertilizer where soil phosphorus and potassium may be limiting. Both phosphorus and potassium are important "stress nutrients" in grasses (and in many biological systems).

7. Avoid mowing when the grass is wet. Several fungi have swimming spores that can easily be spread by mowing equipment when the grass is wet. Try to avoid mowing at this time. It is common to see disease streaks in turf cause by mowing tracks.

8. Try to reduce or eliminate thatch, poor drainage, and compaction (see Chapter 8). All of these conditions skew the biological struggle for existence in favor of the disease.

9. Mow sharp; mow high. Dull mower blades tear as they cut the grass leaves, exposing more damaged surface to fungal spores. Mow at the recommended height for individual grasses (see Chapter 8). For most bluegrass cultivars, for example,

the recommended cutting height is 2 to 2$^1/_2$ in. Cutting them suddenly at 1 in. will stress and damage the turf, making it more susceptible to fungal attack.

COMMONLY USED TURF FUNGICIDES

If too much shade, poor air circulation, poor drainage, excessive watering, dull mowers, close mowing, over-fertilization, and so forth are out of your control, it may be time to consider fungicides. Most plant diseases yield to this chemical treatment, although it may be necessary to repeat the applications two or more times.

In general, fungal diseases are more difficult to control with chemicals than are insects, simply because of the way in which fungi grow in the infected plants. They are able to penetrate inside the plant and proliferate there, which makes them hard to reach. In the last few years some successful *systemic* fungicides (including benomyl, chloroneb, fenarimol, thiophanate-M, and triadimefon) have been developed. These materials are slowly absorbed and translocated through the diseased plant to give more effective and lasting control.

With the exception of cycloheximide (LD_{50} = 2.2 mg/kg!), most fungicides are much less toxic to animals orally than insecticides are. Many fungicides, however, produce skin irritations and, like any pesticides, should be handled and used with great care. Everything else being equal and if you have a choice, use the fungicide with the *highest* LD_{50}.

In the list of fungicides that follows the first name given is the common name. This is followed by one or more trade names, which are often more widely known than the common name. The chemical type of the fungicide is then given in parentheses.

Check the turf bulletins from your state university or agricultural experiment station for specific fungicide recommendations, timing, and rates of application for your locality. Rates may be given in pounds of active ingredient per acre, or ai/A. (An acre is 43,560 sq ft or 4840 sq yd.) *Always study thoroughly the label of any pesticide formulation,* especially for rates and timing. Your state probably also has a plant disease clinic to which you can take or send diseased specimens of plant material for accurate diagnosis and fungicide prescription.

Anilazine (Dyrene, Dymec, Lescorene) (a chlorinated hydrocarbon)

Origin: Ethyl Corp. and Pittsburgh Coke and Chemical Co., 1955. LD_{50}: 2710 mg/kg. This is a popular turf fungicide used to control a wide variety of fungal diseases including leaf spot, dollar spot, brown patch, rust, and snow molds. It is not compatible with alkaline compounds. It is toxic to fish and may cause skin irritation.

Benomyl (Tersan 1991, Benlate) (a carbamate)

Origin: DuPont de Nemours & Co., 1967. LD_{50}: 10,000 mg/kg. This is a systemic foliar and soil fungicide used to combat brown patch, dollar spot, *Fusarium,* stripe smut, and pink snow mold. It has a long residual but a very low toxicity. There was no skin irritation or evidence of toxicity in 90 days after feeding rats 2500 ppm.

Chloroneb (Tersan SP, Proturf Fungicide II)
(a chlorinated hydrocarbon)

Origin: DuPont de Nemours & Co., 1965. LD_{50}: 11,000 mg/kg. This fungicide can be applied as a seed coating to prevent damping-off disease in new seedings. It does not leach and is highly effective in preventing damping off as the seedlings emerge. It is a systemic material, taken up by the roots. It has a low toxicity.

Chlorothalonil (Daconil, Bravo W-75)
(a chlorinated hydrocarbon)

Origin: Diamond Shamrock Co., 1965. LD_{50}: 10,000 mg/kg. Some people get allergic reactions to this chemical. It is toxic to fish and some varieties of roses. This is a broad-spectrum fungicide used largely in the turf industry to control leaf spot diseases. It has a long residual and is not broken down by UV light.

Cycloheximide (Acti-dione) (an antibiotic)

Origin: Upjohn Co., 1946. LD_{50}: 2.2 mg/kg. This highly toxic fungicide may cause skin irritation and will injure roses. It is actually an antibiotic that comes from a species of the actinomycete, *Streptomyces*. (Another species produces the more famous antibiotic, streptomycin.) Surprisingly, Acti-dione is inactive against bacteria, which fail to absorb it, but it is otherwise toxic to a wide range of organisms from algae and protozoa to mammals. It acts by inhibiting the synthesis of nucleic acids. It is frequently combined with Thiram (see later) and sold as Acti-dione Thiram, in which formulation it is used to control melting out, powdery mildew, rust, dollar spot, brown patch, and red thread. Do not combine with alkaline materials. NOTE THAT THE LD OF THIS FUNGICIDE IS VERY LOW. USE EXTREME CAUTION!

Ethazole (Koban, Ban-Rot)

Origin: Mallinckrodt Chemical Works, 1969. LD_{50}: 2000 mg/kg for mice. This fungicide is used to control *Pythium* blight or damping off on turfgrasses.

Fenarimol (Rubigan)

Origin: Eli Lilly & Co., 1975. LD_{50}: 2500 mg/kg. This systemic fungicide has been found effective against powdery mildew, brown patch, dollar spot, pink snow mold, stripe smut, and *Typhula* blight. It is toxic to fish but not to bees, and it has no marked effect on soil bacteria.

Iprodione (Chipco 26019, Proturf Fungicide VI)

Origin: Rhône-Poulenc. LD_{50}: 3500 mg/kg. Research has shown this fungicide to have both contact and systemic properties. It is labeled in turf for brown patch, dollar spot, leaf spot diseases, red thread, and *Typhula* blight. It is essentially nontoxic to bees and ducks.

Mancozeb (Fore, Dithane M-45)

Origin: Rohm and Haas & Co., 1961. LD_{50}: 8000 mg/kg. This fungicide is a combination of maneb and zineb. It may cause skin irritation. It is a protective fungicide effective against foliage disease including leaf spot, brown patch, rust, pink snow mold, slime molds, and algae in all turfgrasses.

Maneb (Tersan LSR, Dithane M-22) (a carbamate)

Origin: DuPont, 1950. LD_{50}: 6750 mg/kg. No ill effect was observed in rats receiving 250 mg/kg in their daily diet for 2 years. A protective fungicide recommended for use against leaf spot, brown patch, and rust.

Metalaxyl (Subdue, Apron)

Origin: Ciba Geigy, 1979. LD_{50}: 669 mg/kg. This compound is a systemic fungicide effective against downy mildew and *Pythium* diseases, in which it inhibits protein synthesis. It is not toxic to fish or bees.

PCNB (Quintozene, Terraclor, Turfcide) (a chlorinated hydrocarbon)

Origin: I. G. Farben, Germany, 1930s. LD_{50}: 12,000 mg/kg. This fungicide may cause skin irritation. It is recommended for use against brown patch and dollar spot.

Thiophanate-E (Cleary 3336)

Origin: Nippon Soda Co., 1969. LD_{50}: >15,000 mg/kg. This systemic fungicide has a wide range of activity. The designation E (for ethyl) distinguishes it from Thiophanate M (for methyl), which has slightly different properties. Its LD rate is over twice that of Thiophanate-M. It was fed for 2 years to rats and mice with no detectable ill effect.

Thiophanate-M (Fungo 50, Proturf Systemic Fungicide, Topmec)

Origin: Nippon Soda Co. and Pennwalt Corp., 1969. LD_{50}: 7500 mg/kg. This fungicide has some systemic activity. It has been recommended for use on powdery mildew, red thread, brown patch, dollar spot, and stripe smut. Dollar spot populations that are resistant to the fungicide have been noted after its continual use.

Thiram (Tersan 75, Arasan 50 Red) (a carbamate)

Origin: DuPont de Nemours & Co., 1931. LD_{50}: 565 mg/kg. This is an "old reliable" in the turf industry and is frequently combined with Acti-dione (see earlier).

Triadimefon (Bayleton)

Origin: Farbenfabriken Bayer, Germany and Mobay Chemical Corp., 1975. LD_{50}: 363 to 568 mg/kg. This fungicide should be treated with extra caution. It is claimed to have the broadest spectrum of disease control of any common turf fungicide. Used as a wettable powder, it has not only contact activity but is also systemic in action. It is used to prevent summer patch and many other turf diseases, including brown patch, dollar spot, powdery mildew, red thread, rusts, and gray and pink snow mold. It does not control leaf spot diseases or *Pythium* blight.

Vinclozolin (Vorlan)

Origin: BASF, Germany, 1973. LD_{50}: 10,000 mg/kg. This systemic fungicide is labeled for use on dollar spot, pink snow mold, leaf spot diseases, and red thread. It is not toxic to bees or earthworms.

Zineb (Dithane Z-78) (a carbamate)

Origin: Rohm & Haas Co., 1943. LD_{50}: 5200 mg/kg. A broad-spectrum fungicide, this material is also used on flowers and ornamental trees and shrubs. It is recommended for leaf spot diseases, rust, and slime molds. It is not compatible with alkaline or mercury compounds. It may cause irritation to the nose, throat, and skin.

SOME COMMON TURF DISEASES

On the following pages are described a number of turf diseases, with their diagnoses and methods of cultural control. Fungicides that are used to combat the diseases are also given (see also Table 7-1). The diseases are arranged for ease of reference alphabetically by common name. This is always a little bit dangerous, since several diseases have more than one common name. If the disease you are looking for does not arise alphabetically, check the index at the back of the book.

Familiarize yourself with the diseases that occur in your locality. This can be done by checking your state extension service turf publications or by checking with other turf managers. In order to determine the most effective control measures for the following diseases, *always check recommended fungicides with your state agricultural experiment station or state university. Read carefully the label of every material to be applied.*

```
┌─────────────────────────────────┐
│                                 │
│       COOL-SEASON GRASSES       │
│              SUMMER             │
│                                 │
└─────────────────────────────────┘
```

Anthracnose (*Colletotrichum graminicola*)

Anthracnose is a common disease of tomato and many other plants worldwide. On turfgrasses it appears as a leaf disease, and under favorable conditions it also infects grass crowns and roots. It is most severe on annual bluegrass, and it seems to be very host specific. In some locations it will attack just *Poa annua* in bentgrass; in other locations it attacks just the bentgrass. In a mixture of bluegrass and fescue it may infect just the fescue. In cool, wet weather it produces stem lesions; in warmer, wet weather reddish-brown lesions appear on the grass leaves. The turf becomes blighted and turns yellow to brown in irregular patches a few inches to several yards wide. Tiny black, hair-like fruiting bodies clustered on the epidermis of dead tissue help to identify the disease. Like many fungi, anthracnose attacks when the turf is stressed, particularly during periods of high humidity.

Diagnosis: Irregular patches of blighted, reddish-brown to yellow turf several inches to several yards wide. Ruptured lesions of dead leaves have clusters of tiny black, hair-like fruiting bodies. Dry soils but hot, wet, humid conditions.

Cultural Control: Avoid fertilizing when hot and dry. Make sure soil has adequate phosphorus and potassium. Water deeply in the morning.

Fungicides: Benomyl and chlorothalonil (both approved only in selected states), thiophanate-M, and triadimefon.

```
┌─────────────────────────────┐
│                             │
│          BENTGRASS          │
│           MIDWEST           │
│                             │
└─────────────────────────────┘
```

Bacterial Wilt
(*Xanthomonas campestris* pv. *graminis*)

This is the only turf disease that is not caused by either fungi or a virus. Recently a bacterial wilt disease capable of causing severe damage was identified on Toronto creeping bentgrass. It gained sudden prominence in 1980, when Toronto greens at Butler National were destroyed two weeks before the Western Open golf tournament. Bacterial wilt has since been found on annual bluegrass and Nimsilia creeping bent-

TABLE 7-1. Fungicides Recommended for Control of Various Fungal Diseases

Disease	Anilazine (Dyrene)	Benomyl (Tersan 1991)	Chloroneb (Tersan SP)	Chlorothalonil (Daconil)	Cycloheximide + Thiram (Acti-dione + Thiram)	Ethazole (Koban)	Fenarimol (Rubigan)	Iprodione (Chipco 26019)	Mancozeb (Dithane M-45)	Maneb (Tersan LSR)	Metalaxyl (Subdue)	PCNB (Terraclor)	Thiophanate-E (Cleary 3336)	Thiophanate-M (Fungo 50)	Thiram (Tersan 75)	Triadimefon (Bayleton)	Vinclozolin (Vorlan)	Zineb (Dithane Z-78)
LD 50 mg/kg	50(!)	10,000	11,000	10,000	2.5(!)	2000	2500	3500	8000	6750	669	12,000	15,000	7500	565	363	10,000	5200
Anthracnose		Xs		Xs										X				
Brown patch		X		X	X		X	X	X	X		X	X	X	X	X		
Copper spot	X			X	X				X				X	X		X		
Dollar spot	X	X		X	X		X	X	X	X		X	X	X	X	X	X	
Drechslera diseases[a]	X			X	X			X				X	X				X	
Gray leaf spot								X										
Necrotic ring spot[b]							X											
Powdery mildew					X		X									X		
Pythium blight			X			X					X							
Red thread				X	X			X	X	X			X	X			X	
Rust diseases	X			X	X				X							X		X
Slime molds[c]																		X

Snow molds
  Coprinus snow mold[d]
  Pink snow mold[e]
Snow scald
Typhula blight
Spring dead spot
St. Augustine decline[f]
Stripe smut
Summer patch[b]
White patch[g]
Yellow tuft[h]

NOTE: Xs means fungicide is approved for use only in certain states. Read the label.

NOTE: Anilazine and cycloheximide + thiram have very low LD 50s! We advise using other fungicides whenever possible.

[a] *Drechslera* diseases were formerly the *Helminthosporium* leaf, crown, and root diseases: leaf spot, melting out, net blotch, zonate leaf spot.

[b] Necrotic ring spot and summer patch were formerly included in *Fusarium* blight.

[c] Slime molds can usually be controlled by mowing.

[d] Check your state agricultural experiment station recommendations.

[e] Pink snow mold is same as *Gerlachia* patch.

[f] Best control of SAD at present is to use resistant varieties.

[g] No effective control known at this time.

[h] Yellow tuft is same as downy mildew, most likely controlled by those fungicides labelled for *Pythium*, which is very similar (both produce motile spores).

grass. All of the Toronto greens at the Muirfield Country Club in Dublin, Ohio, home of the Memorial Tournament, were fumigated and reseeded to Penneagle bentgrass.

Electron microscope studies at Michigan State University showed a bacterium that plugged conducting tissue (xylem) in the grass plants, resulting in their rapid wilting, desiccation, and death. The only long-term recourse is to fumigate and reseed or resod with resistant (at the moment) varieties.

The disease has been identified on turfgrasses in eight states—Pennsylvania, Ohio, Indiana, Illinois, Michigan, Minnesota, Wisconsin, and Kansas—and appears to be spreading both geographically and to other grasses, possibly including Kentucky bluegrass. A few years down the road this disease could be a major problem in turfgrass management.

Diagnosis: Very rapid wilting. Leaf blades become shriveled, twisted, and blue-green in color. For positive identification mail sample overnight express to Plant Diagnostic Clinic, 141 Plant Biology, Michigan State University, East Lansing, MI 48824–1312. Call ahead at (517) 355–4536 or 353–9082.

Cultural Controls: Disease can be suppressed with the antibiotic oxytetracycline for a short term. Raise nitrogen rate. Mow slightly higher. Make weekly applications of iron with regular fungicide. Eventually turf will have to be fumigated and replaced unless more effective control is found.

```
              WARM- AND COOL-SEASON GRASSES
              LATE SPRING THROUGH EARLY FALL
```

Brown Patch (*Rhizoctonia solani* and Others)

This highly variable fungus causes a major turfgrass leaf disease recognized countrywide. The fungus overwinters as sclerotia or as a soil saprophyte, living on dead or decaying organic matter. The fungus starts growing at 64 to 68°F and dies if the air temperature drops below 62°. When the average air temperature reaches 73°F, the fungus penetrates leaves through mowing wounds. After penetration it remains relatively inactive until the day temperatures rise above 80° and night temperatures remain above 70°. If coupled with high humidity, the fungus can blight a lawn in 6 to 8 hours. It again ceases activity if the temperature reaches 90°F. Moisture on grass leaves greatly increases the rate at which the organism spreads.

The disease affects all turfgrasses in all areas of the country. It has been reported on 85% of samples sent in for disease diagnosis. St. Augustinegrass, zoysiagrass, and ryegrass are particularly susceptible, but all grasses can be severely damaged. In the North it can severely affect bluegrasses, bentgrasses, ryegrasses, and fescues when warm and moist. The disease is less severe in the Northwest, where it is cooler.

Brown patch first appears as circular to irregular patches a few inches to 2 ft in diameter on areas mowed low, such as golf greens, and up to 50 ft in diameter on areas that are mowed higher, such as bluegrass. Blighted areas are purplish green at first, fading rapidly to light brown. Mycelium of the fungus can be observed as white tufts early in the morning while the grass is still wet. Sometimes there is a "frog-eye" effect: A small patch of healthy grass is surrounded by a ring of yellow, scorched, diseased turf. One of the chief diagnostic features is dark purple "smoke rings," 1 to 2 in. wide, which border diseased areas. These are more prominent in the early morning on closely mowed turf. The smoke rings are new areas of infection, since the fungus grows in a circular fashion, and they quickly fade as the morning gets drier and disappear altogether as the weather becomes cold or dry. Usually only the leaves are affected, and the turf recovers in 2 to 3 weeks; however, if the weather remains favorable, the fungus attacks the crowns and may kill the grass. Bermudagrass and bluegrass show a higher degree of recovery, since they can regenerate from underground rhizomes.

Diagnosis: Moist period with temperatures in the 80s, late April through October. Circular to irregular patches of blighted turf a few inches to many feet in diameter. Some "frog eyes." Dark purple smoke rings 1 to 2 in. wide bordering diseased areas and prominent in the early morning. Leaf tips look scorched, twisted, remain upright.

Cultural Control: Adequate amounts of soil phosphorus and potassium are essential for control. Do not apply excessive nitrogen in summer. Remove dew from golf greens in morning. Reduce thatch. Water deeply in the morning. Increase penetration of light and air circulation if possible. Improve drainage.

Fungicides: Many fungicides are labeled for control, including benomyl, chlorothalonil, cycloheximide + thiram, fenarimol, iprodione, mancozeb, maneb, PCNB, thiophanate-E, thiophanate-M, and thiram.

```
BENTGRASS, BERMUDAGRASS, ZOYSIAGRASS
                 SUMMER
```

Copper Spot (*Gloeocercospora sorghi*)

This is primarily a disease of bentgrasses, but it also causes a zonate leaf spot disease on bermudagrass and zoysiagrass. It appears as small round patches a few inches in diameter that are pink to copper colored. Infected leaves have small, reddish lesions that exude copper-colored spores that contrast sharply against a white handkerchief. The disease spreads rapidly in warm, wet weather from 65 to 85°F. It appears about the same time as dollar spot and is most severe on acid soils of low fertility.

Cultural Control: Apply fertilizer and lime.

Fungicides: Anilazine, chlorothalonil, mancozeb, thiophanate-E, thiophanate-M, and triadimefon.

WARM- AND COOL-SEASON GRASSES
SPRING AND FALL

Dollar Spot *(Sclerotinia homoeocarpa*)*

This disease overwinters as dormant mycelium or sclerotia in the grass roots and crowns. Spores and mycelia are easily spread by maintenance equipment. The fungus begins growing at 60°F and peaks at 70 to 80°F under conditions of high humidity. Periods of quick change in temperature—warm days and cool nights—favor the disease. It begins to appear in late spring, tends to be less active over summer, and becomes more active in early fall. It is more severe under conditions of low fertility, excessive thatch, and moisture stress.

On low-growing grasses such as bentgrass and bermudagrass, bleached, dead spots the size of silver dollars are characteristic of the turf. In time they merge to form large, irregular patches. A fine white, cobwebby mycelium can be seen in the morning dew. The effect is different on bluegrass, with its higher mowing: A general scorched effect starts with yellow-green blotches that become large, irregular, and straw-colored; the effect is easily confused with drought or fertilizer injury. The best symptom is the leaf lesion, a white hourglass-shaped infection with red to brown borders. (*Pythium* blight is similar but lacks the colored border.) The lesions typically extend across the entire leaf.

Most turfgrasses except those in the deep South are affected, and the disease is particularly bad on bentgrasses. There is a pronounced increase in the disease under conditions of low soil moisture. The damage is also considered greater if there is a nitrogen deficiency, but this is probably related to a faster recovery of the grass during periods when the fungus is inactive. The severity of the disease is apparently not affected by soil pH or by levels of soil phosphorus.

Diagnosis: Bleached dead spots starting at about the size of a silver dollar on bentgrass but less defined on bluegrass. Leaf lesion is a white hourglass with red to brown borders.

Cultural Control: Adequate nitrogen and potassium are important during periods of disease activity. Maintain adequate water levels. Water deeply in the morning. Select resistant cultivars.

Fungicides: Many fungicides are labeled for control of dollar spot, including anilazine, benomyl, chlorothalonil, cycloheximide + thiram, fenarimol, iprodione, PCNB, thiophanate-E, thiophanate-M, thiram, triadimefon, and vinclozolin.

---

*This is the traditional scientific name for dollar spot, but the taxonomy is not clear. See Richard W. Smiley, *Compendium of Turfgrass Diseases* (St. Paul, MN: American Phytopathological Society, 1983), p. 14.

```
┌─────────────────────────────────────────────┐
│                                             │
│         WARM- AND COOL-SEASON GRASSES       │
│             SPRING THROUGH FALL             │
│                                             │
└─────────────────────────────────────────────┘
```

Drechslera Diseases (Formerly *Helminthosporium* Leaf, Crown, and Root Diseases: Leaf Spot, Melting Out, Net Blotch, Zonate Leaf Spot)

Drechslera diseases comprise many of the diseases older turf workers learned as *Helminthosporium* leaf spot, melting out, or crown rot. Most of the diseases are prevalent on festucoid grasses, but one, zonate leaf spot, occurs on bermudagrass. The symptoms are manifested by leaf lesions, which vary on each turfgrass, as indicated in Table 7-2. As the diseases advance, the lesions coalesce and girdle the leaves, which then die. The turf weakens, turning chlorotic and yellow or tan and, in the case of bluegrass and bentgrass, taking on a reddish cast. As the infections become more severe, most of the leaves and tillers die back. The turf thins out—the melting out stage. Eventually, if conditions are favorable and the diseases progress, the crown and roots of the grass are infected and the plants are destroyed—the *crown or root-rot phase.*

Cultural Control: Do not overfertilize in the spring. Water deeply in the morning. Mow high. Be careful with herbicides, especially in the shade. Select resistant cultivars.

Fungicides: Many fungicides are labeled for control of *Drechslera (Helminthosporium)* diseases, including anilazine, chlorothalonil, cycloheximide + thiram, iprodione, mancozeb, maneb, PCNB, thiophanate-E, vinclozolin, and zineb.

TABLE 7-2. Symptoms of *Drechslera* Diseases on Various Turfgrasses

Turfgrass	Leaf Spots or Lesions
Bentgrass	
Red leaf spot	Small, round, reddish, some with tan centers; turf has reddish cast
Bermudagrass	
Zonate leaf spot	Brown with lighter centers that become elongated
Bluegrass	
Leaf spot	Straw-colored with reddish-purple margins; turf has reddish cast in advanced stages
Ryegrass	Small, brown with light centers and dark brown streaks parallel to leaf axis
Tall fescue	
Net blotch	Brown streaks in irregular patterns or nets

```
┌─────────────────────────────────────────┐
│                                         │
│           ALL AREAS OF THE COUNTRY      │
│                ALL SEASONS              │
│                                         │
└─────────────────────────────────────────┘
```

Fairy Rings *(Various Mushroom Species)*

As we learned earlier, fungi tend to grow in a circular pattern. This is most clearly seen in the growth of a "fairly ring" (Figure 7-2). The darker green area constituting the ring, a band that may be a foot or so wide, represents the active mycelium of the new season. As it decomposes organic matter, this new growth exudes nitrates, which stimulate and fertilize the grass in that region, forming the dark green band. The mycelium keeps expanding in diameter each season, forming a series of ever larger concentric circles. It is in the band of active mycelium that the fungus produces fruiting bodies, the spore-bearing stalks of packed mycelium that we know as mushrooms, toadstools, or puffballs.

Though fairy rings can grow to great size, on the typical home lawn they are just getting started and measure only a few feet in diameter. When one ring touches another in the same turf area, both stop growing in the area of contact and the growth begins to take on an irregular pattern.

Not all fairy rings are harmful. Some barely stimulate the grass, and others stimulate it with no apparent damage, but a third type badly damages turf and is of most concern to the turf manager. It is not easy to control harmful fairy rings. Recommendations usually include fumigating the soil with formaldehyde or methyl bromide. Both compounds are difficult to apply and should be handled only by someone with experience. Call your county extension agent for details. Another alternative is to try to drown the fungus and possibly encourage antagonistic microorganisms. Holes are punched 4 to 6 in. deep into and around the stimulated area with a garden fork or steel pin. The area is then flooded and kept soaked for 4 to 6 weeks. A wetting agent might help.

Diagnosis: Dark green rings of various diameters in the turf. At cetain times of year the band may produce fruiting bodies (i.e., mushrooms).

Cultural Control: No easy control. Infested turf can be dug out, replaced with clean soil, and sodded or seeded. Turf can also be fumigated with methyl bromide or formaldehyde, but this kills turf.

```
┌─────────────────────────────────┐
│                                 │
│         ST. AUGUSTINEGRASS      │
│             SUMMER              │
│                                 │
└─────────────────────────────────┘
```

Gray Leaf Spot (Blast) *(Pyricularia grisea)*

An important disease of rice, gray leaf spot occurs largely in St. Augustinegrass but has been reported to cause damage on bermudagrass, centipedegrass, ryegrass, and fescues. It occurs during periods of high humidity and high nitrogen fertilization, with optimum temperatures of 80 to 90°F, and produces round gray to brown spots with purple margins. The disease is usually more severe in shade when turf is wet from rain or irrigation for lengthy periods. It can severely damage plantings that are stressed by drought, excessive nitrogen, overzealous applications of herbicides, or soil compaction. Eventually the leaf spots enlarge and girdle and kill the grass; the turf area becomes weakened and yellow.

Diagnosis: Yellowing turf that looks drought-stricken. Gray to brown leaf lesions with brown to purple margins.

Cultural Control: Use nitrogen carefully. Water deeply in the morning. Reduce soil compaction. Avoid shade. Improve drainage. Use resistant varieties.

Fungicides: Chlorothalonil and cycloheximide + thiram.

```
┌─────────────────────────────────┐
│                                 │
│       COOL-SEASON GRASSES       │
│         SPRING AND FALL         │
│                                 │
└─────────────────────────────────┘
```

Necrotic Ring Spot *(Leptosphaeria Korrae)*
(Formerly Included in *Fusarium* Blight)

This disease is another split-off from the *Fusarium* blight syndrome. It is very similar to summer patch and difficult to distinguish from it. The main differences seem to be these: necrotic ring spot is more active at cooler temperatures—as early as April and as late as November; infected leaves have a reddish-purple cast; and the physiological responses of bluegrass cultivars are different.

As with summer patch, perennial ryegrass and tall fescue are resistant, thus providing the cultural control that comes from interseeding these grasses into susceptible bluegrasses. Colonial bent is susceptible; bluegrasses, creeping bent, and fine fescues vary in their susceptibility. The disease is severe on mixtures of bluegrass and fescue. Merion, Touchdown, and A-34 are more susceptible than Adelphi and A-20 cultivars.

Unlike summer patch, the disease appears to be more prevalent on drought-stressed turf and on soils that are organic rather than mineral.

Necrotic ring spot also produces "frog-eye" patterns, that is, small circles of dead grass surrounding a tuft of green and apparently healthy grass. The disease is active at relatively low temperatures, 58 to 82°F, but, as in summer patch, dead spots in the turf may not become apparent until warm, dry periods of summer, when they suddenly appear.

Diagnosis: "Frog-eye" pattern. Infected leaves turn reddish-purple. Like summer patch but active in cooler weather.

Cultural Control: Nitrogen fertilization in fall helps recovery of grass. Some biologically active products such as Ringer's Lawn Restore seem to promote recovery.

Fungicides: Fenarimol or iprodione, with applications of nitrogen.

```
COOL-SEASON GRASSES
SPRING THROUGH FALL
```

Powdery Mildew *(Erysiphe graminis)*

This fungus infects a wide variety of cultivated cool-season plants, most noticeably lilac, on which leaves are often covered with the benign powdery, grayish mycelium. It is not a major problem on turfgrasses except under shady conditions, when the fungus can severely weaken and even kill the turf. It overwinters as dormant mycelium or as spores contained in small black fruiting bodies in the turf debris. Spores are disseminated by the wind and quickly infect new leaves, producing germ tubes that grow directly through the cuticle and epidermis into the interior of the grass leaf. When the germ tube comes in contact with a cell in the grass leaf, it produces a specialized absorptive structure (called a haustorium) and sets up a parasitic association, living off the grass leaf without killing it.

The fungus is present during most of the growing season, but it is most active in cool, humid, cloudy weather with temperatures of 60 to 70°F. It is especially active in shady turf areas where the air circulation is poor and humidity is high. The disease is particularly prevalent on overfertilized bluegrass and fescue in these areas.

Powdery mildew is easily recognized by its gray to white, powdery mycelial growth over the surface of the grass leaves. When the growth becomes dense, the infected areas look as though lime has just been spread or the area has been sprayed lightly with white paint. The grass is weakened and lower leaves turn yellow, leaving the turf in a state of easy destruction by drought or other diseases.

The disease cycle is very rapid—spores that land on a susceptible plant germinate quickly and spread in a few days.

Diagnosis: Powdery, gray to white mycelial growth on leaves in shady areas where air circulation is poor and humidity is high. When growth is dense, turf looks as though lime has been spread over it.

Cultural Control: Use shade-tolerant cultivars. Avoid excessive nitrogen fertilization and herbicide applications in shade. Mow high. Use selective pruning to increase air circulation and admit more sun.

Fungicides: Cycloheximide + thiram, fenarimol, and triadimefon.

WARM- AND COOL-SEASON GRASSES
ESPECIALLY NEW SEEDINGS
SUMMER

Pythium Blight
(Damping Off, Cottony Blight, Grease Spot) (*Pythium* spp.)

These are extremely destructive plant pathogens that under optimum conditions can completely destroy a turf area in a matter of hours. They infect all turfgrasses and are particularly destructive on new seedings, especially overseeded ryegrasses in the South. The fungi survive the winter as soil saprophytes or as dormant mycelia in plants infected the previous winter. They become most active with temperatures of 85 to 95°F, high humidity, and warm nights. In the North *Pythium* appears in mid to late summer in conjunction with hot, moisture-laden Gulf air or excessive soil moisture caused by overwatering; it spreads quite rapidly if the temperatures rise above 95°F. The diseases are worse on poorly drained soil, and they have been noted at temperatures as low as the 60s in cases where overwatering for rapid germination of seedings has resulted in high humidity.

The first indication of the disease is small, irregular patches a few inches in diameter. The grass leaves appear water soaked, soft, and slimy, hence the name "grease spot." The blades soon wither and fade to light brown or straw color, sometimes reddish brown, particularly if the weather is sunny and windy. Then the patches coalesce to form large damaged areas often several feet in diameter, which assume various shapes sometimes corresponding to the drainage pattern. The white, cottony mycelium of the fungus can be seen on the leaves of diseased plants in the early morning.

Leaf lesions like those in dollar spot disease may be present on the edges of diseased turf—hour-glass bleached areas—except that they lack the reddish-brown margins of dollar spot. As well, grass that is infected with *Pythium* tends to lie flat, unlike the case in brown patch disease, in which affected leaves remain upright.

Diagnosis: Very high humidity, wet soil, with temperatures above 80°F. Shriveled leaves appear water soaked, soft, and slimy. Possible problem in dense new seedings that are being heavily watered. Cottony mycelia evident in the early morning. Leaf lesions white and hourglass-shaped but lacking reddish-brown margins. Infected turf appears flat or matted.

Cultural Control: Avoid overwatering, especially new seedings. Newly seeded areas should have good drainage. Water deeply in the morning. Do not mow wet grass in hot weather. Do not exceed recommended seeding rate. Use treated seed.

Fungicides: Chloroneb, ethazole (Koban), and metalaxyl (Subdue).

```
COOL-SEASON GRASSES
SPRING AND FALL
```

Red Thread *(Laetisaria fuciformis)*

This distinctive fungus causes damage particularly in the spring and fall when the temperatures are 68 to 75°F and humidity is high. It attacks cool-season turfgrasses that are deficient in nitrogen, and it can be particularly severe on fine fescues. It overwinters as reddish sclerotia or as dormant mycelium in leaves and in debris.

The disease is confined to leaves and leaf sheaths, forming irregular blighted areas several inches to several feet in diameter. The patches have a ragged appearance, and not all leaves in an area are infected. The first and least obvious symptoms of the infection are small spots that appear water soaked; these enlarge rapidly and cover a large portion of the leaf or leaf sheath. As they dry out the leaves fade to a light brown or tan. Under humid conditions diagnosis becomes easier in the final stages of the disease when red or pink finger-like structures—the "red threads"—form at the tips of grass leaves. These are actually gelatinous sclerotia approximately 1/4 in. long. The red threads can be abundant enough to give the turf a reddish cast that is easy to recognize.

The red threads are easily broken off the leaf and carried by the wind to spread the disease. Thus the disease tends to move on—that is, although it may occur year round and be severe for several weeks, the next year it is likely to move to another location.

Diagnosis: Ragged, blighted patches a few inches to several feet in diameter, late spring or fall, particularly on nitrogen-deficient turf. Later stages are thin red or pink finger-like sclerotia on the leaf tips. Reddish cast to infected turf.

Cultural Control: Maintain adequate nitrogen levels. Water deeply in the morning. Maintain soil pH of 6.5 to 7.0.

Fungicides: Many fungicides are labeled for control of red thread disease, including chlorothalonil, cycloheximide + thiram, iprodione, thiophanate-E, thiophanate-M, triadimefon, and vinclozolin.

WARM- AND COOL-SEASON GRASSES
SUMMER

Rust (*Puccinia* spp.)

There are many species and races of this disease, widely regarded as one of the most difficult and complex in the plant kingdom. It is a constant threat to our grain crops, and a great deal of agricultural research has been required to combat it. Most famous is the species that attacks wheat. It has a very complex life cycle, including an alternate host, the wild barberry. This was recognized early in the history of our country, and stern measures were taken to outlaw and eradicate common barberry plants (not to be confused with the ornamental Japanese barberry used in landscaping).

The disease was relatively unimportant on turfgrasses until the first widely acclaimed premium bluegrass, Merion, was introduced. Superior to common bluegrass in most qualities, Merion was unfortunately highly susceptible to rust, a factor that somewhat limited its usefulness.

Over a dozen species and races of rust fungi are known to infect turfgrasses, and all widely used turfgrasses are affected in varying degrees by this omnipresent fungus. Some turf species have their own specific rust that attacks them only—that is, the rust is species- or *host-specific*. For example, the rust species that attacks bermudagrass will not infect zoysiagrass or bluegrass or other turfgrasses. Some rusts even have races that infect only certain cultivars, and some rusts infect only certain parts of their specific host—stem rusts with round pustules, stripe rusts with linear pustules, and leaf rusts with round pustules.

The important rusts that infect turfgrasses can survive mild winters as spores, which reinfect the next spring, or as mycelia. When temperatures reach 70°F or above, the spores of the fungus begin to penetrate the grass through leaf pores, or stomates. The fungus becomes most active in cloudy weather with temperature ranges above 80°F, when growth of many of the turfgrasses is slowing. Severe infections occur especially when the turf is stressed from drought or low fertility and when leaf surfaces remain wet for long periods.

The symptoms of the disease are very obvious: yellow, orange, or reddish powdery pustules of spores often oriented in parallel rows along leaves and stems. If the infection is severe, the entire turf area has a yellow-orange cast, and anything moving through the area, such as shoes, clothing, or turf equipment, will be colored by the abundance of spores.

Diagnosis: Obvious yellow to red round or linear pustules on leaves and stems; often quite extensive. Midsummer or when temperatures rise above 80°F, particularly in cloudy weather on turfs of low fertility.

Cultural Control: Fertilize and mow regularly to sever infected leaf tips and retard spore formation. Use resistant cultivars.

Fungicides: Anilazine, chlorothalonil, cycloheximide + thiram, mancozeb, maneb, triadimefon, and zineb.

```
            WARM- AND COOL-SEASON GRASSES
              WET PERIODS—ALL SEASONS
```

Slime Molds (Various Species)

These interesting fungi cause little or no damage to turfgrasses and possibly are bene-ficial. However, the sudden appearance of their fruiting bodies on leaves and stems can cause concern to uneasy lawnowners. The fruiting bodies, of pinhead size, come in various colors—typically white, but sometimes pink, purple, or other colors. They usually occur only in very wet weather, and they give the turf a "slimy" appearance. In abundance they probably weaken the turf, but mowing is usually sufficient to control them.

Germinating spores of the slime molds become amoeba-like and feed on other fungi and bacteria, possibly exerting some biological control over turf pathogens. They also decompose organic material that might otherwise contribute to thatch formation.

Diagnosis: Patches of "slimy" turf. Fungal fruiting bodies of pinhead size, various colors. Wet weather.

Cultural Control: Mowing.

Fungicides: Unnecessary.

```
              COOL-SEASON GRASSES
             WINTER AND EARLY SPRING
```

Snow Molds: Coprinus Snow Mold, Pink Snow Mold, Snow Scald, and Typhula Blight (Gray Snow Mold)

Coprinus snow mold (Coprinus psychromorbidus)

Some turf scientists feel that this fungus consists of two strains: The first (called the LTB, or low temperature basidiomycete) does not produce sclerotia, and the second strain (called the SLTB, or sclerotial LTB) does. Both strains produce whitish-gray, cottony mycelium in patches a few inches to 1 ft or so in diameter. The non-sclerotial LTB strain is slightly more vigorous.

The sclerotia of the SLTB strain first appear as white bumps as large as 1/4 in. in diameter on grass leaves; they then begin to darken as they mature. Light-brown lesions with darker margins can be found on infected leaves. Long periods of deep snow with temperatures ranging from freezing to 58°F in late winter and spring encourage the spread of the disease. Like the other snow molds, the disease becomes inactive as temperatures rise above 60° and the turf becomes warmer and drier.

Diagnosis: Whitish-gray, cottony mycelium in patches of a few inches to 1 ft or more. One strain produces dark sclerotia. Light-brown leaf lesions with darker margins.

Cultural Control: On golf greens, charcoal, ashes, or fine sand can be used to speed the melting of snow. Landscaping or snow fencing can be used to reduce deep snow-drifts. Fungicides usually applied in late fall or early winter. Check with your state agricultural experiment station for fungicide recommendations. Some bluegrass and fine fescue cultivars may be resistant to the disease.

Pink snow mold (*Gerlachia* patch) *(Gerlachia nivalis)* (formerly *Fusarium* patch and *Fusarium nivalis*)

This is a disease complex that looks like the gray snow mold except that the mycelium on the edges of patches may be pink or pale red and sclerotia are absent on infected leaf tissue. Like the gray snow mold, the fungus is active under a snow cover, particularly on unfrozen ground. Light yellow patches a few inches to 1 ft or more in diameter become apparent with the first thaw. They enlarge and coalesce until large areas of turf are damaged. These may have a green to black perimeter. The color of the affected areas changes to whitish gray, with leaves having a bleached appearance and feeling slimy when wet. The mycelium in the diseased areas takes on a faint pink color as it is exposed to light. In severe cases not only the leaves but also the crown of the plants are infected, resulting in a complete loss of the turf stand.

The fungus is most active when the humidity is high and the temperature is about 32 to 45°F. It is still active up to about 65° and then goes dormant at 70°, surviving the summer as a dormant mycelium. Spores are again produced when conditions become optimal in the fall. They germinate on leaves, and the hyphae penetrate to the interior of the leaf through the stomates. The disease is not limited just to snow-covered turf, and it is not always pink or pale red. It is most severe on bentgrass greens and on perennial ryegrass. Bluegrass and red fescue usually survive.

Diagnosis: Circular brown patches in fall, 1 to 2 in. Larger circular patches up to 2 ft, white to pink, in late winter and spring. Patches may have green to black margins. Sclerotia not present as in gray snow mold. Symptoms resemble copper spot, but that disease occurs at much warmer temperatures (over 80°).

Cultural Control: Avoid high nitrogen fertilization in last 6 weeks of season. Adequate levels of potash and low pH seem to suppress the disease. Avoid poor drainage and matted leaf debris. Mow to normal height at end of season. Lightly fertilize turf in early spring to encourage the grass.

Fungicides: Many fungicides are labeled for control of pink snow mold, including benomyl, cycloheximide + thiram, fenarimol, mancozeb, PCNB, thiophanate-M, triadimefon, and vinclozolin. Chlorothalonil and iprodione are labeled in certain states.

Snow scald *(Myriosclerotinia borealis)*

This fungus infects all North American turfgrasses, particularly on frozen ground covered with deep snow for long periods. Gray to white patches a few inches to 2 ft in diameter appear after snow melt. As in the gray snow mold, black sclerotia appear in the mycelium in warmer weather and provide the means for oversummering. Infected grass leaves are bleached white. Optimum growing temperatures for the disease are 40 to 80°F, but there have been some reports of growth at temperatures in the low 20s.

Diagnosis: Gray to white patches up to 2 ft in diameter appearing after melt of deep snow. Black sclerotia present on grass blades that are bleached white.

Cultural Control: As in gray snow mold, plus placement of snow fence to impede drifting over golf greens.

Fungicide: Cycloheximide + thiram.

Typhula blight (gray snow mold) *(Typhula incarnata* and *T. ishikariensis)*

This fungus, as the name implies, is active in the cool, humid regions of North America, particularly under snow cover. It is most conspicuous as the spring thaw exposes light yellow grading to grayish-white patches, at first a few inches in diameter and then coalescing into large, irregular, matted areas of damaged grass. A border of grayish-white mycelia an inch in width can sometimes be discerned on the margins of the infected areas. As the grass dies the patches become silvery-white. Scattered over the surfaces of leaves and crowns of infected plants are hardened dark sclerotia that are the size of pinheads or larger.

The mold begins to grow at temperatures just above freezing. Optimum growth has been reported from 48 to 55°F, with sclerotia produced at these temperatures in 5 to 10 days. The fungus survives the heat of summer as sclerotia, and it is ready to germinate and produce mycelia in the late fall or winter under the reduced light of a snow cover on unfrozen ground. It coexists with pink snow mold (*Gerlachia* and other fungi in this complex) and is separated visually by the presence of dark sclerotia. Creeping bentgrass and perennial ryegrasses are the most susceptible to the disease. Late-season applications of nitrogen promote the disease, and turf should be mowed at normal height at the end of the season to prevent matting under the snow cover.

Diagnosis: Light yellow to grayish-white patches of diseased turf at time of spring thaw, border of grayish-white mycelia an inch wide. Sclerotia scattered over infected plants.

Cultural Control: Avoid fertilizing within 6 weeks of dormancy. Mow to normal height for winter. Rake the grass in early spring to break up matting and promote drying. Fertilize lightly in early spring to stimulate grass.

Fungicides: Many are labeled for control of *Typhula* blight, including anilazine, chloroneb, chlorothalonil, cycloheximide + thiram, fenarimol, iprodione, PCNB (phytotoxic to Cohansey bentgrass), thiram, and triadimefon (only effective against *T. incarnata*).

```
          BERMUDAGRASS
          SPRING AND FALL
```

Spring Dead Spot
(Possibly species of *Leptosphaeria*)

This serious disease of bermudagrass does not appear until the turf is 3 or more years old. It first appears in the spring as patches of bleached, dead grass. At first just a few inches in diameter, the patches reappear in the same spot for 3 to 4 years and expand in this time to rings several feet in diameter. The grass in the patches becomes rotted and stunted, and subsequent regrowth is sluggish and often weedy. A persistent soil toxin has been isolated. Sclerotia have been detected in some infected stolons and roots. Since sclerotia and toxins have been identified and the disease can be controlled by fungicides, it is thought that the causal agent is a fungus; however, the fungus has not yet been identified with certainty in the United States. In Australia spring dead spot on bermudagrass is caused by *Leptosphaeria korrae,* the same fungus that causes necrotic ring spot on cool-season grasses.

The fungus is most active in spring and fall when temperatures are cool and the soil is moist. Damage is most severe when the grass resumes growth in the spring, especially on turfs that are maintained at a high level of fertility. The disease appears to be confined to areas where average November temperatures are below 55°F.

Diagnosis: Patches of bleached grass up to several feet, appearing in the same spot for 3 to 4 years. Grass stunted and rotten. Cool temperatures and moist soil, spring and fall.

Cultural Control: Avoid heavy applications of nitrogen in late summer. Winter-hardy cultivars have shown greater resistance.

Fungicide: Benomyl (approved only in selected states).

```
        ST. AUGUSTINEGRASS
        SPRING THROUGH FALL
```

St. Augustine Decline (SAD) (*Panicum* Mosaic Virus)

Up to this point we have been dealing with diseases caused by fungi, or, in one case (bacterial wilt in bentgrass), a bacterium. St. Augustine decline is caused by a virus called the *Panicum* mosaic virus. (Mosaic refers to the mottled or blotched yellow coloration occurring in leaves on which the green chlorophyll has been destroyed. This pattern is a common symptom of plant viral diseases.) Over two dozen viruses have been noted in turfgrasses, but, other than SAD, none at this time have been observed to cause any serious damage. Viruses are probably transmitted, as in SAD, by aphids and leafhoppers or spread by mowing equipment.

As the disease progresses in St. Augustinegrass, the turf becomes yellow, stunted, and weak to the point where it is subject to winter-killing and other stresses. The grass may die in as little as 3 years.

Diagnosis: Leaves with mottled yellow coloration. Turf yellow and stunted.

Cultural Control: Care can be taken to prevent spread of the virus in leaf clippings and mowing equipment. Best control is use of resistant cultivars. No chemical controls available.

COOL-SEASON GRASSES
SPRING AND FALL

Stripe Smut *(Ustilago striiformis)*

This organism is a one of a group of fungi known collectively as smuts because of their production of masses of dark brown to black spores in clusters on leaves, stems, and flower parts. They infect a wide variety of grasses, including many of our grain crops. The fungus overwinters as dormant mycelia in infected plant parts or as spores in the soil or on seeds. The primary site of infection is through young seedlings or tillers; the symptoms are not very obvious until masses of spores rupture the epidermis of mature leaves.

Stripe smut is most troublesome on cool-season turfgrass in the spring or fall during periods when the temperature remains in the range of 50 to 60°F. The fungus decreases its activity as the temperature becomes warmer. The disease is most obvious in its final stages, when stripes or streaks of first light and then dark spore masses form along the surface of the leaf. The epidermis and cuticle are eventually ruptured; the leaves are split into ribbons, curl and die, and the grass plant becomes severely weakened. The fungus has the same effect on seed heads, making it of importance to growers of grass seed.

Diagnosis: Stripes or streaks of first light and then dark spore masses along leaf surfaces. Grass leaves split into ribbons.

Cultural Control: Use seed treated with fungicides. Reduce fertilization and watering on infected turf. Use resistant cultivars.

Fungicides: Benomyl, fenarimol, PCNB, thiophanate-E, thiophanate-M, and triadimefon.

```
COOL-SEASON GRASSES
SUMMER
```

Summer Patch *(Phialophora graminicola)*

For many years this distinctive summer disease of cool-season grasses was considered to be caused by *Fusarium roseum* and *Fusarium tricinctum,* but more extensive study has identified *Phialophora* at least as one of the causative organisms.

At certain stages the disease is easily recognized by the formation of small circles of dead grass surrounding a turf of green, apparently healthy grass. This pattern is frequently described as a "frog-eye" effect; in the case of summer patch it may not appear until the second year of infection, and the patches may later coalesce.

In the first year the disease is manifested by small wilted patches of turf, perhaps 1 in. to 1 ft in diameter. Small green tufts of healthy grass appear in the center of these wilted patches in subsequent years to give the frog-eye symptom. The fungus is active in the spring and fall, but no visible symptoms appear until temperatures climb above 85°F. The disease can then make a sudden, dramatic appearance, especially during dry periods preceded by heavy rains.

Colonial bentgrass and fine fescue are very susceptible to summer patch. Bluegrass cultivars vary in their resistance: A-20 and Touchdown have some resistance, Adelphi and Merion are intermediate, and A-34 is very susceptible. Perennial ryegrass and tall fescue are resistant, so if ryegrass is interplanted into a susceptible bluegrass, the turf gains resistance to the disease. Although a mixture of bluegrass and ryegrass is then resistant to the disease, a mixture of bluegrass and fine fescue is very susceptible. Fertilization at about 1/2 lb nitrogen per 1000 sq ft per month over the summer seems to reduce the severity of the disease. It is more severe on fumigated soils, on those treated with arsenicals, and on soils low in phosphorus.

Diagnosis: Small wilted patches of grass 1 to 12 in. in diameter before coalescing, followed in subsequent years by frog-eye patches. Usually June to September, temperatures over 85°, particularly in dry spells after heavy rains.

Cultural Control: Core-aerate to improve root growth. Fertilize with nitrogen. Interplant ryegrass or tall fescue.

Fungicides: Benomyl, fenarimol, iprodione, thiophanate-E, thiophanate-M, and triadimefon. Wet the turf the night before application. Triadimefon does not have to be watered-in but must be applied before the fungus becomes active in the season.

```
┌─────────────────────────────┐
│                             │
│        TALL FESCUE          │
│        SOUTHEAST            │
│                             │
└─────────────────────────────┘
```

White Patch of Tall Fescue *(Melanotus phillipsii)*

This disease has been elevated to significance because of the increasing use and popularity of the relatively new turf-type tall fescues. At present it has been found only on tall fescue and only in the Southeast. The disease can be very severe on newly seeded tall fescue.

Circular white patches a few inches in diameter, often with pinkish borders, are the first indication of the disease. In time the patches enlarge and overlap, and the grass leaves become blighted or yellow. Tiny white mushroom-type fruiting bodies can sometimes be seen on the grass blades.

The disease is most prevalent on dry soils during hot, humid weather of summer and early fall. It is most damaging when day temperatures exceed 85°F and night temperatures remain above 70°. Stress of any kind increases the severity of the disease. The crowns usually remain undamaged, and when cooler weather comes, the grass may recover completely.

Diagnosis: White patches of diseased turf, sometimes with pinkish borders. Small, grayish-white mushroom-type fruiting bodies sometimes apparent on grass blades. Hot, humid weather.

Cultural Control: Disease is reported to be more severe on dry soil, so soak down the soil if necessary. Use recommended seeding rates—do not increase.

Fungicides: No clearly effective fungicide has been identified at this time.

```
┌─────────────────────────────────────┐
│                                     │
│   NORTHEASTERN U.S. AND DEEP SOUTH  │
│        SPRING AND FALL              │
│                                     │
└─────────────────────────────────────┘
```

Yellow Tuft (Downy Mildew)
(Sclerophthora macrospora)

This is a widespread plant disease with white mycelium and sporangia, giving leaves a mildewed or "downy" effect, hence the name. However, this symptom in turfgrasses, is usually mowed off. What is seen instead as the disease becomes more severe are small yellow patches, typically a few inches in diameter. These form distinctive distorted, dense yellow tufts of leaves, stems, and tillers. If the turf is wet, one can see a downy white growth on the leaves. The disease occurs in spring and fall during wet periods.

In the Northeast yellow tuft occurs on bentgrasses, ryegrasses, fescues, and bluegrasses. The disease also occurs on St. Augustinegrass, on which it looks more like a viral disease, with white, slightly raised stripes or streaks on leaves. In wet weather the downy white mildew growth characteristic of the fungus can be seen on infected leaves. The fungus produces swimming spores that need lots of moisture to survive and spread, hence the disease is always more severe on wet or poorly drained soils.

Diagnosis: Downy white growth on leaves or slightly raised white stripes. Yellow patches a few inches in diameter. Plants showing distorted growth.

Cultural Control: Do not mow when wet. Improve drainage. No resistant cultivars available at this time.

Fungicides: Those labeled for *Pythium,* such as metalaxyl (Subdue), should also control this similar fungus.

8

Special Turf Practices

SEEDING

Bringing a fine turf seeding up to sod quality is one of the most satisfying experiences in turf management. It requires knowledge, patience, and skill. It is something of an art which, alas, is not widely practiced. Many builders encourage the incompetence . . . "Just give me something cheap, quick, and green" . . . often meaning a seed mixture laced with annual ryegrass. The quality of the lawn is often a reflection of the care and quality that go into the new building. The cost difference between cheap seeding and sodding or seeding with premium turfgrasses is usually paid for in extra care over the years, although the homeowner may not realize it.

The first rule of thumb in seeding, then, is *always use the best grass seed available,* selected from certified seed of labeled and certified varieties. This is one area of our economy in which there are no bargains! The seed bag or container should have a label on it. For example, the label shown in Figure 8-1 is from a bag of Merit Kentucky bluegrass sold by the Ohio Seed Company, West Jefferson, OH.

Note that the label gives the following information: the name of the cultivar, weed seed content, lot number, germination percentage, date tested, and place of origin. Obviously, the lower the weed content and the higher the percent germination, the better the seed quality. Many turf bluegrasses have as many as 2 million seeds/lb. A 5% increase in germination, then, would equal an increase of 100,000 seeds/lb. Do not buy seed unless it is properly labeled, as shown here.

The following is a list of the important characteristics that distinguish a professional seeding.

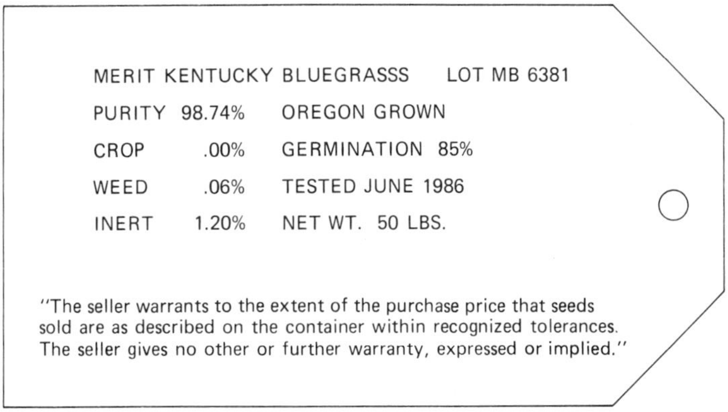

```
┌──────────────────────────────────────────────────────────────────────┐
│                                                                      ╲ │
│                                                                       ╲│
│         MERIT KENTUCKY BLUEGRASSS      LOT MB 6381                      │
│                                                                        │
│         PURITY  98.74%     OREGON GROWN                                │
│                                                                        │
│         CROP      .00%     GERMINATION  85%                            │
│                                                                    ◯   │
│         WEED      .06%     TESTED JUNE 1986                            │
│                                                                        │
│         INERT    1.20%     NET WT.  50 LBS.                            │
│                                                                        │
│                                                                        │
│        "The seller warrants to the extent of the purchase price that seeds  │
│        sold are as described on the container within recognized tolerances. │
│        The seller gives no other or further warranty, expressed or implied."│
│                                                                       ╱│
│                                                                      ╱ │
└──────────────────────────────────────────────────────────────────────┘
```

Figure 8-1 The label on a seed bag.

Preparing the seedbed.   The surface to be seeded should be finish-graded with blade and rake to exclude any debris and pockets and to lightly "fluff" the soil. One rule of thumb is that any rock bigger than a chicken egg should be removed. Finish-grading in itself is an art, and the tools vary according to the predilection of the grader. A simple blade, box blade, or tractor-mounted rake—all do an excellent job in the hands of a skilled operator proud of his work.

Prior to grading, any persistent noxious weeds such as quackgrass, coarse fescue, nutsedge, and common bermudagrass (if the seeding is to be an improved bermudagrass) should be treated with glyphosate (Roundup) so that there is no chance that they will re-root in the new seeding.

In warm-season grasses to be established with plugs, sprigs, or stolons, the site will require deeper tilling of 8 to 10 in. so that these vegetative parts can be properly planted and covered with sufficient soil.

Fertilizing.   Just prior to spreading the seed of cool-season grasses, an N-P-K fertilizer high in phosphorus, such as 10-20-10, should be applied to the seedbed at a rate of 1 to 2 lb phosphorus per 1000 sq ft. A soil test helps here, but if that is not available, one presumes that the phosphorus content of an excavated soil will be low. Phosphorus, of course, is an important inorganic nutrient in the germination and root growth of all higher plants. Lime and other nutrients may also be necessary, depending on the area of the country and the soil type.

Warm-season grasses are fertilized after the second or third mowing (rather than at the time of planting) with typically 1 lb of nitrogen per 1000 sq ft. Phosphorus, potassium, and lime are added, depending on the results of a soil test.

The mechanics of seeding.   For the typical home, golf course, or industrial seeding many professionals feel that the Brillion landscape seeder has no equal. If the fluff and moisture of the seedbed are right, its two alternating rows of cultipackers bury the seed, then cover it and compress, or roll, it. These actions are very important: Turfgrass seed germinates best if it is lightly covered with soil (1/8 in. is ideal) and if the soil is compressed all around the seed and touching all of its surfaces. Simply spreading the seed on the soil surface with a rotary spreader and covering it with straw or other mulch does not produce a high-quality seeding.

On small areas seed can be spread with a hand-type cyclone seeder or a lawn-type drop spreader. The seed should then be raked in by hand and rolled in a manner as close as possible to the action of a Brillion seeder. In any case, and by any method, covering the seed with a thin layer of fine soil and compressing it are the desired objectives.

Mulching.   Generally a new seeding is covered with a *mulch*—straw, shredded peat moss, pine needles, wood fibers, loose burlap, wood chips, or many other materials. A mulch is not always necessary if the seedbed is level, properly fertilized, and easily watered, and if the seed has been buried and rolled as with a Brillion seeder. Sod growers, for example, do not use a mulch, but if you have no control over the watering of the new seeding, a mulch is often worthwhile insurance.

Clean (weed-free) wheat straw is the mulch of choice for several reasons: It is usually inexpensive, readily available, and easy to spread. In addition there is a certain unexplained quality about straw aside from its maintaining soil moisture that seems to stimulate grass growth and retard weed seed germination. The straw helps to hold the soil in place and keeps it moist, and once it is soaked thoroughly, it tends to stay in place and resist movement by wind and rain.

Weedy straw, however, is to be avoided like the plague. It can carry some very noxious weeds like foxtail, quackgrass, Canadian thistle, and many others. If you are going to use a lot of straw over the years, try to locate a good farmer who will work with you. Weed-free straw is easily worth a few more cents per bale. If there are strawberry growers nearby, ask them about a straw source; they usually have several sources of clean straw that they use in late fall as a winter mulch.

It takes one to two 55-lb bales of straw to effectively mulch 1000 sq ft of new seeding (2000 to 4000 lb/acre). The upper figure is used on exposed, sloping ground, the lower figure on more protected locations that will be watered regularly. Emphasis should be placed on spreading the straw evenly over the surface. Any clumps of straw should be broken up to avoid smothering the young seedlings that begin to develop. The straw should be spread thick enough so that one can just barely see the soil through the pieces of straw. Some turf experts feel that 40% to 50% of the soil should show through the mulch.

On slopes where erosion is a concern, other measures may be necessary to protect the seeding from washing. The straw can be tacked down with asphalt emulsions or various organic glues. Alternatively, the straw may be omitted altogether and replaced by blankets manufactured from excelsior or various fabrics. Nettings of nylon, string, plastic, jute, or burlap can be placed over the straw and held in place with clothespins or with soft wire staples that disintegrate. Hydrograssing is also an alternative.

Hydrograssing (also called hydroseeding or hydromulching) is a popular and relatively new method of establishing a seeding, particularly on roadbanks and other areas that are too steep for safe use of a grading tractor. Everything needed for the grassing—seed, fertilizer, and mulch—is mixed together and agitated in a large tank of water mounted on a trailer or truck bed. The material is then sprayed as a slurry on the site. The mulch used in the slurry is usually wood or cellulose fibers or shredded cardboard that is dyed green to act as a marker. The fiber mulch is used at rates of 1000 to 3000 lb per acre, quantities slightly less than straw but more expensive. On the other hand, a wood fiber mulch is weed free. Asphalt emulsions, organic glues, or starch gels can also be included in the slurry to act as tacks or moisture absorbers, helping to bind and hold the seed and fiber to the site.

On very difficult slopes some people utilize elements of both systems: Straw is applied at the heavier rates and then this is hydrograssed with a slurry of seed, fertilizer, and a reduced amount (500 to 1000 lb) of wood fiber mulch. The wood fiber slurry acts as a binder, holding the straw in place for long periods, even on steep slopes.

Watering.   All the best preparations and operations are to no avail if the new seeding is subjected to a drought. New seedings need at least 3 in. of water per week, including any rain, for at least 3 weeks. Water as much as is necessary to keep the surface of the seedbed moist at all times! The seeding must be watched carefully until it is obviously on its way.

It is a poor choice to pay for an expert seeding and then try to economize on the watering. If a homeowner is not sure what constitutes an inch of water, suggest that an open-mouthed jar be placed in the path of the sprinkler and the time it takes to fill it to 1 in. (usually an hour or so at typical home water pressures) be clocked. After thorough watering of one area, the sprinkler should be moved to another site with as little disturbance of the wet soil as possible. Another important consideration in watering is to get the grass seedlings up and growing as densely as possible as quickly as possible, so that weeds will not have time or space to establish themselves. A dense population of turfgrass plants is an effective weed barrier.

Weed control.   As the soil is disturbed in seedbed preparations, long-buried weed seeds are brought to the surface, where they can germinate. Some are also brought in to the site if straw is used as a mulching material. With the watering of the new seeding, weeds acquire a new lease on life. Despite protests on the part of the typical homeowner to the contrary, this is a normal condition, and if the turfgrass seed has been well placed, fertilized, and watered, weeds are not a major problem in growing a fine turf. Most of the weeds are easily mowed out and the rest can be removed by appropriate herbicides.

The rule of thumb used by turf managers in applying a herbicide to a new seeding is to wait until the new turf has been mowed at least three times. Mowing encourages both the rooting and tillering of grasses, and after three mowings the turf should be established sufficiently to withstand the physiological shock of the herbicide. However, since herbicides do inhibit the growth of grasses (see Chapter 5) it is probably better to wait until the next spring or fall to apply the herbicide. That is, if the seeding is done in the spring, apply the herbicide in the late summer or fall; for a fall seeding, kill the weeds the next spring. One exception to this rule is the use of the preemergence herbicide Siduron. This material can be used with bluegrass seedings to inhibit the germination of a wide variety of nongrass weeds. It is most useful in spring seedings.

Siduron is photodecomposed and should therefore be watered or raked into the seed-bed before the seeding operation is done.

Mowing.   A common question asked after a seeding is done is, "When should I mow?" The answer is that a new seeding should be mowed at the same height and rate as an established lawn—weeds, gaps, and all. Mowing encourages the tillering and spreading of the new grass plants and eradicates some of the weeds. If the new turf is still being watered, it should be allowed to dry for a couple of days before mowing, lest the mower make ruts in the soft ground and kill the seedlings there. Mowing should follow at regular intervals sufficient to remove about $1/3$ of the grass leaf at a time.

Special mowings are required for new seedings in which the seed mixture consists in large part of ryegrass, for example on a northern playing field. The fast-germinating, vigorous ryegrass tends to smother slower-growing turfgrasses such as bluegrass. To compensate for this, a turf trick is to mow the new seeding at 1 in. for the first 2 or 3 mowings. This gives the slower-growing grasses a better chance to develop and to get established. This technique also will better maintain the composition percentages of the original seed mixture.

Subsequent fertilization.   A new seeding of cool-season grasses should be fertilized again in 2 to 3 weeks after the grass seedlings have begun to appear. High phosphorus starter-type fertilizer should be applied at a rate of 1 to 2 lb phosphorus per 1000 sq ft. Watering after the application is also recommended. The new lawn should then be placed on a regular fertilization program of balanced NPK until the turf is well established, usually after a year or more. Warm-season grasses are fertilized with 1 lb nitrogen per 1000 sq ft after the second or third mowing. Phosphorus and potassium are added only if indicated by a soil test.

The seeding blend or mixture.   Seedings on a home lawn or industrial site often consist of two or more types of seed, each included for a specific purpose, strength, or merit. A blend or mixture is recommended simply to give the potential turf a wider degree of environmental tolerance than could be afforded by a single type of grass. The blend or mixture has greater variability and hence a greater range of resistance to diseases, insects, and unfavorable weather conditions. For example, if a virulent strain of a fungus arrives on the scene, it is unlikely that all the grasses will fade out: It is hoped that at least one of the types will show some resistance. The blend (a seed lot consisting of more than one cultivar of a single grass species) or the mixture (a seed lot consisting of more than one species of grass) (see Chapter 3) is frequently designed for a specific function, such as for quick cover, for the wear-resistance necessary on a sports turf or playing field, or for shade. In order to design a blend or mix appropriate to the situation, one must know the key attributes of specific turfgrasses. These have been listed for many grass cultivars of both northern and southern species in Chapter 3.

Most warm-season grasses are seeded "straight," whereas most cool-season grasses other than bentgrasses are typically blended or mixed. For example, a typical cool-season multipurpose mixture might consist of the grasses listed in Table 8-1.

TABLE 8-1.   A Mixture of Cool-Season Grasses Suitable for General-Purpose Turf

10-20%	by weight of a turf-type perennial ryegrass for a quick start, wear resistance, and resistance to diseases such as summer patch
10-20%	fine fescue, in case the mix goes into some shady areas or is grown at low fertility
60-80%	Kentucky bluegrass, a component that may in turn consist of a blend of various bluegrass cultivars known to do well in your area as established by your Agricultural Experiment Station

The multipurpose mixture of cool-season grasses can be manipulated for optimum performance. For example, on a playing field or area where heavy traffic is anticipated, the turf-type ryegrass component is increased to 50%, the fine fescue is decreased, and an aggressive bluegrass (such as Touchdown, Sydsport, A-34, or Mystic) is included in the bluegrass blend. If the site is shady, the percentage of fine fescue is increased and shade-tolerant ryegrasses and bluegrasses are included. If healing is important, as on a golf tee, the percentage of aggressive, rhizomatous bluegrasses is increased. Where an open, sunny, fine turf is desired, the bluegrass component is increased to 100%. If faster-germinating bluegrasses are required, consider Monopoly and Park. If the mixture is to be used on a sloping site prone to erosion and under low maintenance, consider including 5% to 10% annual ryegrass.

Seeding rate.   By studying Table 8-2 you will see that just a little bit of seed goes a long way. One pound of bluegrass, for example, may contain as many as 2.2 million seeds. A professional sod grower will seed bluegrass at the rate of *1 lb per 1000 sq ft. or 15 seeds per sq in.* However, the sod grower is working under optimum conditions that are seldom met on home lawns and commercial sites. It is often difficult to "baby" a seeding on such sites, and a quicker, more dense cover is required before the homeowner becomes impatient. Hence the seeding rate is often increased to 2 to 3 lb of bluegrass per 1000 sq ft. If the mix is to include fine fescue and a fine-leafed perennial ryegrass, the seeding rate may approach 4 to 5 lb per 1000 sq ft, ensuring a fairly dense cover even under the most trying circumstances.

ESTABLISHING SOME WARM-SEASON GRASSES

Bermudagrass

Common bermudagrass seed can be obtained either hulled or unhulled. There are more hulled seeds to the pound, hence it is more expensive. It is seeded at a rate of 1 to $1\frac{1}{2}$ lb per 1000 sq ft, preferably in April or May. Unhulled seed is planted at twice the rate of hulled seed. The seed is raked-in lightly, rolled, and mulched with pine needles or straw (about two bales or 100 lb per 1000 sq ft). It should be possible to see the soil through the mulch. As with any seeding, watering should be provided in sufficient amount to keep the soil continually moist for 3 to 4 weeks ($\frac{1}{4}$ in. per day, minimum).

Bermudagrass takes 10 to 14 days to germinate. Mow when the grass is slightly above the desired mowing height, usually $\frac{3}{4}$ to $1\frac{1}{2}$ in. Fertilize after the second mow-

TABLE 8-2. The Approximate Number of Seeds Per Pound and Recommended Seeding Rate for Turfgrasses

	Approximate Seeds/lb	Seeding Rate (lb/1000 sq ft)
Bahiagrass	200,000	4–8
Bentgrass	6,000,000 to 9,000,000	1
Bermudagrass (hulled)	2,000,000	1–2
Bluegrass, Kentucky	1,000,000 to 2,220,000	1–2
Adelphi	2,200,000	1
Baron	2,200,000	1
Common	2,200,000	1
Fylking	1,100,000	2
Glade	2,100,000	1
Merion	1,600,000	1½
Park	2,200,000	1
Victa	940,000	2
Bluegrass, rough	2,000,000	1
Buffalograss (hulled)	300,000	2–6
Carpetgrass	1,200,000	1–3
Centipedegrass	875,000	1–2
Fescue, fine	500,000	2–3
Fescue, tall	200,000	5–10
Ryegrass, annual (Italian)	200,000	5–10
Ryegrass, perennial	200,000	5–10
Zoysiagrass	1,000,000	2–3

ing with about 1 lb nitrogen per 1000 sq ft. Apply phosphorus, potassium, and lime as indicated by soil test. The most favorable pH range for bermudagrass is 6.0 to 6.5.

Centipedegrass

This grass is best planted in May on soils with a pH range of 5 to 5.5 that are low in phosphorus. If a soil test reveals a pH higher than 5.5 or high phosphorus levels, other turfgrasses such as zoysiagrass should be considered. If the soil is poorly drained, bermudagrass should be considered.

Centipedegrass is seeded at a rate of 1/4 to 1/2 lb per 1000 sq ft. Mixing the seed with fine sand increases the ease of seeding. The seed should be raked-in lightly, rolled, and mulched with straw (about two bales or 100 lb per 1000 sq ft) or pine needles. Don't clump the straw. Some soil should be visible through the mulch. Centipedegrass seed takes 3 to 4 weeks to germinate.

This grass can also be established by *sprigging*. Sprigs or 2-in. plugs of sod are typically set on 1-ft centers (1000, or about 2 bu, of sprigs per 1000 sq ft). For best results one end of the sprig should be left exposed. As with seedings, spriggings are also rolled and mulched. Another technique is to broadcast the sprigs or stolons on top of the soil surface and then run over the area with a disk harrow with the blades set straight. This requires more sprigs—as many as 10 bushels per 1000 sq ft. The sprigs are rolled, mulched, and watered as with a seeding.

Mow when the grass is 1 to 2 in. high. Fertilize after the first or second mowing at a rate of 1 lb nitrogen per 1000 sq ft, then monthly from March through September. Once the turf is established, in about a year, the fertilizer rate should be dropped to about 2 lb nitrogen per year: 1 lb in March and 1 lb in September. Centipedegrass makes a low-maintenance turf requiring less fertilizer, lime, and mowing than other turfgrasses.

St. Augustinegrass

This grass is established by sprigging on 12-inch centers, or about 1000 sprigs per 1000 sq ft. Ideally each sprig should have 3 to 4 nodes and be soil-covered except for one exposed tip. The soil is rolled and the area mulched with straw, hay, or pine straw. Some soil should be visible under the mulch. The new grass should be mowed at 2 to 3 in. and fertilized with 2 to 6 lb nitrogen per 1000 sq ft per year.

Zoysiagrass

Seed is not yet readily available for this turfgrass, so it is usually established by using 2-in. plugs or sprigs placed on 1-ft centers. It takes about 3 sq yd of sod to produce enough plugs and 2 bu of sprigs to plant 1000 sq ft. The sprigs are placed in shallow furrows and covered lightly with soil, leaving at least one tip exposed. The plugs or sprigs are rolled and mulched with pine needles or straw (about two bales per 1000 sq ft); some soil is left exposed. One has to stay on the watering, keeping the soil continually moist for 3 to 4 weeks.

The sprigs or stolons, as in centipedegrass, can also be spread evenly on the prepared soil surface (about 10 bu per 1000 sq ft) and disk-harrowed with the blades set straight. The planting is then mulched, rolled, and watered as above.

Liming may be necessary to obtain an ideal pH of 6 to 6.5. The new planting is fertilized with 1 lb nitrogen about 3 weeks after planting, with potassium and phosphorus included at rates determined by a soil test. Too much fertilizer, particularly phosphorus, may be deleterious. Begin mowing when the turf grows to a height slightly above the desired permanent mowing height. With zoysiagrass, reel mowers usually give a cleaner cut than rotary mowers.

SODDING

Instant grass—sod—takes a great deal of the risk out of growing grass, and anyone who fights nature for a living much prefers it that way. Builders in particular often want that green color at times other than those most suitable for seeding. In addition, even the best seedings require several months of additional care and concern before they are well established. A sod is ready-to-go grass at costs that typically run 2 to 3 times that of a seeding.

These are the steps involved in installing sod on the site of a new home or building:

1. The new site is finish-graded, usually with a rubber-tired tractor and a blade. All finish graders have their own preferences regarding blades—flat blades, blades with wings, box blades, roll-over blades, blade-rake assemblies, and others. In the business there is a distinction between *rough grading* and *finish grading*. Rough grading is frequently done by the excavator or the general contractor with a small bulldozer. The rough grade is considered to be everything down to the final *1/10 ft or 1.2 in.* The finish grading is considered to begin *below 1.2 in.* The drainage patterns, then, should be set by the rough grader and maintained by the finish grader. Other than removing any small pockets or valleys and maintaining positive drainage, the finish grader's main concern is to prepare a suitable seed bed—preferably a fluff of 1 to 3 in. of soil into which the sod will root rapidly. If it is felt necessary to till the soil with a disk harrow or a rototiller, for example, this should be done before the finish grader begins his job. Usually working along with the finish grader are one or more "rakers," who pick up any debris and grade around trees and buildings that are too close for the grading tractor.

2. Cool-season sites are typically fertilized with a high phosphorus starter fertilizer, such as 10-20-10, at the rate of 1 to 2 lb phosphorus per 1000 sq ft. On warm-season sites the type of fertilizer applied should be based on a soil test. In some areas, especially in the East, it may be necessary to add lime before sodding, again based on the results of a soil test.

3. The sod is laid "butted up"—the pieces are put together as tightly as possible without overlapping. They are also staggered like bricks in a wall. The long axis of the rectangular sod strip is placed perpendicular to the drainage pattern of the site, or across the slope. On a typical lot this is parallel to the sidewalk and street. Small hatchets, sod lifters, or knives are used to cut and trim the sod to fit odd-shaped areas.

4. The sod is rolled to firm it against the graded surface and inspected for any gaps that need to be closed or for debris that needs to be removed.

5. In the handling and installation of sod, as with seeding, the most important consideration is water. The sod should be fresh, and once it is laid it must be kept moist for 2 to 3 weeks to encourage rooting. Depending on the season and the location, it may take as much as 4 in. of water per week to keep the sod moist and in optimum rooting condition. Some sod growers recommend that the sod be kept moist enough so that it is too wet to walk on; others say moist enough so that when a sod piece is rolled back its lower surface and the soil surface are both moist. The roots of the grass have been cut off during harvesting by the sod cutter, and there is a lag time before the grass plants making up the sod can regenerate new roots. The sod must be kept moist during this period, usually 2 to 3 weeks.

6. It is generally considered best to match as closely as possible the soil on which the sod has been grown with the soil on the site where it is to be laid. This is usually ensured by selecting a sod grown locally. In addition, a good local grower should be aware of those grasses that perform best in his area. Peat sods, for

example, often root poorly in clay soils and may show signs of deterioration after a few years. Poor rooting from mismatched soils can sometimes be easily alleviated by core aerating.

MOWING

The main principle of mowing is to do it frequently enough to maintain the desired height but without removing at any one mowing more than *1/3 of the leaf blade* and never more than *1 in.* On golf greens, where the grass may be kept as short as 1/8 in., this amounts to mowing almost daily. On home lawns, however, mowing once a week is almost a national ritual. It affords the opportunity for the weekend mower to take a week's worth of hostilities and frustrations out on the poor, meek, defenseless grass plants. And the weekend contribution to noise pollution in suburbia has encouraged many a soul to seek quiet solitude and isolation in a rural setting. Many a lawn has been scalped out of existence by a homeowner who wants his home lawn to look like the golf green at his country club.

By and large, warm-season grasses withstand closer mowing than cool-season grasses (see Table 8-3). Cool-season grasses mowed closer than 1 in. generally begin to sustain a decrease in root mass, become weakened, stress more readily, and deteriorate.

Many studies have shown that weeds can be controlled by mowing bluegrasses, for example, at least 2 in. high. A taller turf tends to shade the soil surface and prevent weeds such as crabgrass from germinating. Diseases, especially leaf spot, rust, and dollar spot, become more pronounced at low cutting heights. As one would expect, short-mowed bluegrasses are much less tolerant to drought, owing to their decreased root systems.

Another advantage in mowing higher is that the frequency of mowing is reduced. The first inch of leaf growth is the fastest. Bentgrass greens mowed at 1/4 in. require almost daily mowing, whereas a 2 in. cut in bluegrass may be required only once per week or less, depending on the weather and on fertilization practices.

TABLE 8-3. Recommended Mowing Heights for Various Turfgrasses (inches)*

Cool-season grasses	
Bluegrass	1 1/2–2 1/2
Fescue, fine	1 1/2–2 1/2
Fescue, tall	2–3
Ryegrass, perennial	1–2
Warm-season grasses	
Bahiagrass	2 1/2–3
Bermudagrass, common	1–1 1/2
Bermudagrass, hybrid	1/2–1
Centipedegrass	1–1 1/2
St. Augustinegrass	1 1/2–3
Zoysiagrass	1–2

*If weather is hot and dry, clip 1/2 to 1 in. higher.

Grasses should be mowed longer in shady areas (to provide more leaf surface for photosynthesis), but in general lawns going into winter should be cut at normal height or shorter rather than left long over winter. This prevents matting and decay of extensive leaf tissue; and the turf will have better color over the winter and quicker green-up in the spring.

New seedings should be mowed as soon as they are about an inch above the desired mowing height for the species used. Mowing affects the hormone balance and encourages the new grass to tiller and spread. In a bluegrass and ryegrass seeding the competitiveness of the bluegrass can be enhanced by mowing the first two or three times at $1/2$ to 1 in. This compensates for the extreme vigor of the ryegrass seedlings and allows the slower-growing bluegrass time to develop. More aggressive bluegrass cultivars such as Touchdown will also compete better against ryegrass with this mowing regime.

There is no question that a reel-type mower in good working order does the best job of mowing: This is particularly true at low cutting heights on zoysiagrass and on golf greens, where a reel mower is indispensable. The scissors action of the reel mower produces a cleaner cut than the more common home lawn-type rotary mower. On the other hand, rotary mowers are more versatile, cut closer to trees and other obstructions, and are usually easier and less costly to maintain. Reel mowers jam easily if the turf is too wet or too high. In either case, however, the mower must be kept sharp. This is particularly true of the rotary mower, whose action tends to mutilate grass leaves and expose more of the cut and sometimes shredded surface, providing a lot of germinating surface for disease spores. Most fungal diseases are spread readily by mowers, and the incidence of disease is aggravated if the leaves are mutilated when cut.

It is also preferable to mow when the grass is dry, not wet. The grass mows more easily and dries more quickly, there is less tracking and compaction, and the chance of spreading diseases is reduced. There is also less clumping of the clippings, which, when wet, form small, thick masses that can smother the turf, ferment, and contribute to the thatch layer.

Alternating the direction of mowing is also considered advisable to avoid a "grain" in the turf, or a tendency to grow in one direction. This practice also helps to reduce a path or compaction caused by the tracking of the mower wheels.

REMOVAL OF CLIPPINGS—PROS AND CONS

If the turf is mowed at regular intervals, the removal of the clippings is arbitrary. This is especially true if the fertilization levels are adequate. On the other hand, a turf grown at low levels of fertility probably benefits from leaving the clippings on the lawn. The clippings contain no small amount of nitrogen, phosphorus, potassium, and other elements, which are leached or acted on by microorganisms and returned to the soil. The clippings taken off a bentgrass golf green over a growing season, for example, may contain as much as 5 lb nitrogen per 1000 sq ft of mowing surface, 1 lb of phosphorus, and 2.5 lb of potassium. For each acre, this amounts to approximately 200 lb of nitrogen, 40 lb of phosphorus, and 100 lb of potassium. This is a significant amount of plant nutrients, and if fertilizer shortages occur in the future, clippings will have to be given due consideration for their contribution to soil fertility.

If the turf is mowed frequently enough so that the clippings at any one mowing are short (1 in. or less), their contribution to the thatch layer is kept to a minimum. Compared with stem sections, grass leaves have relatively little fibrous material (cellulose and lignin, which are highly resistant to decomposition), and therefore the leaves are more readily decomposed by decay organisms in the soil. They must come in contact with these organisms, however, and so any process such as core aerating, topdressing, or even dethatching that exposes the soil reduces the contribution of clippings to the buildup of thatch.

Clippings also contribute to the organic matter of the soil, always a desirable feature of any cropping system. Organic matter makes the soil more friable, increases cation exchange capacity of the soil (see Chapter 1), and in general enhances the quality of this medium in which the turf is growing.

Heavy clippings that tend to mulch the grass must be avoided. These essentially mat and then weaken or even smother the grass, contributing to thatch accumulation and helping to spread disease organisms. On the other hand, if the amount of clippings is small and especially if the turf is relatively thin or open as in a new seeding, the clippings serve as a soil mulch, conserve moisture, reduce soil temperatures in summer, and, through leaching and decomposition, return nutrients to the soil.

WATERING

Turfgrasses are watered when they need it. A need is established when you see any of the following:

1. Footprints remain in the lawn for a time after the impression has been made.
2. The soil is obviously dry.
3. The lawn has a bluish-gray cast.
4. The grass leaves are wilted and folded or rolled up as seen in the cross-sectional view in Figure 8-2.

The rule of thumb for watering established lawns is as follows: Always water at least 1 in. at a time, no more than once per week and preferably less often. One inch of water is usually sufficient to soak most turfgrass root zones on most soils—a sandy soil to a depth of 1 ft, a loam to 8 in., and a clay to 5 in. Light, more frequent waterings of less than 1 in. are generally considered inadvisable except on new seedings. This is because such watering practices keep the surface soil continually moist, which encourages shallower rooting of the turfgrass and also promotes the germination of surface-situated weed seeds.

The number of 1-in. waterings per period depends on the type of grass and the amount of seasonal rainfall. Learn the average annual rainfall and its distribution for your area. (Refer to Figure 1-7, the average annual precipitation in the United States.)

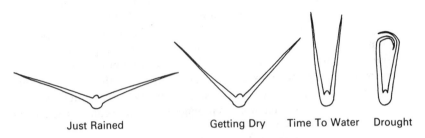

Figure 8-2   Cross sections of grass leaves showing varying degrees of wilting. *Left*, leaf fully expanded. *Center*, leaves wilting and folded. *Right*, leaf rolled up under drought conditions.

Uneven seasonal precipitation is made up by turning on one or more sprinklers. To determine the length of time it takes a sprinkler to deliver an inch of water, simply place a jar, can, or other container in its path and note the time it takes to fill the jar to 1 in. A typical time for a home sprinkler is 1 hr.

It should be kept in mind that cool-season grasses, especially bluegrass, undergo a dormant period in midsummer. Their rate of metabolism, hence their water-use rate, is reduced, and they may go slightly off color. Where a high maintenance turf is not necessary, it is probably advisable to use this normal adjustment to hot weather as an opportunity to conserve water. Depending on the frequency of thunderstorms, an occasional, deep, 1-in. watering is usually sufficient to keep the turf healthy during this period; the 1-in.-per-week rule of thumb becomes applicable again as the days become shorter in mid-August. In any case it is considered unwise to force the grass in and out of dormancy by irregular, heavy waterings.

By and large, most warm-season grasses can exist on less water or are more drought-resistant than cool-season grasses. An approximate grading of turfgrasses from excellent to poor drought tolerance would be as follows: buffalograss, bermudagrass, zoysiagrass, and bahiagrass are excellent; hard fescue, tall fescue, and creeping red fescue have relatively good drought resistance; Kentucky bluegrass, perennial ryegrass, and St. Augustinegrass are intermediate; and centipedegrass, carpetgrass, annual ryegrass, creeping bentgrass, rough bluegrass, and velvet bentgrass have relatively poor drought tolerance.

The actual daily amount of water that turfgrasses will use from the soil varies widely from about $1/10$ to $1/2$ in. per day. The $1/2$-inch rate occurs in warm regions under full sun, high temperatures, a slight wind, and low humidity. The plant uses only a small percentage of this water, often less than 5%, in its metabolism. Most of the water is evaporated off the leaf surface, providing a cooling effect. With the increasing concern over water resources nationwide, it is very important to identify cultivars of all turf species than can perform well on reduced water rates. In general, these will be grasses that have extensive deep root systems, such as the turf-type tall fescues. Even within a species of turfgrass there may be a significant variation in the rate at which separate cultivars use water. In Kentucky bluegrass, for example, cultivars such as Merion, Sydsport, Majestic, Nugget, Bristol, Fylking, and Park have high water-use rates, whereas Touchdown, Banff, Baron, Adelphi, A-20, and Enoble use water at relatively low rates.

Many cultural practices and environmental factors influence the rate at which grasses use water. Shade reduces water use: 50% shade will reduce it by as much as 50%. Each degree rise in temperature can increase water use by 1 to 2%. Nitrogen fertilization increases water-use rate and should be avoided in mid-summer when possible. On typical home lawns subject to periods of water stress, mowing higher and mowing less usually conserves water. On more intensely managed, irrigated turfs where the soil water supply can be maintained constantly at adequate levels, however, it has been shown that low cutting heights actually conserve water by reducing the amount of leaf surface exposed to evaporation.

LEAF LITTER IN THE FALL

The falling leaves of autumn have a nostalgic appeal, but they can present a difficult turf problem. If the leaves are allowed to accumulate on the turf, they smother it and may eventually kill it. A common cause of bare spots under or near trees is unraked leaves of the previous fall.

Fall is also an important time of growth for cool-season grasses. Trees that over the summer shaded, cooled, and protected these grasses are now bare, and the increased incidence of sunlight reaching the turf encourages cool-season grasses such as bluegrass to produce rhizomes and to build up their root reserves and winter resistance. These features should not be counteracted by a covering of dead leaves. In addition, tree leaf litter is often very acidic and detrimental to grasses that require a near-neutral pH for best growth.

Any leaf litter in a fall seeding should be removed very carefully, of course—lightly with a bamboo rake or with a blower or vacuum—so that the young, shallow-rooted seedlings are not dislodged.

The best guideline is to get the leaves off, put them in a compost bin, and winterize the lawn with an appropriate fertilizer.

SHADE

Lawns with more than 50% shade are beginning to stretch the capacities of most turfgrasses. Although some shade is often desirable and even beneficial in reducing heat and drought, especially on sunny, sloping ground, lawns with too much shade require special care and attention.

A lawn often looks weaker under the canopy of a big maple, for example, so there is a tendency to overfertilize it. Just the reverse should be done for several reasons. First, among cool-season grasses the dominant shady grass on older lawns is fine fescue, and this grass naturally requires only half the nitrogen fertilizer of bluegrass. When fertilized at full bluegrass rates, the fine fescue weakens and dies. Second, grasses in the shade photosynthesize at a reduced rate. If they are overfertilized, nitrogen metabolism is increased at the expense of the carbohydrate root reserves, subjecting them to increased stress, particularly in the winter. Third, fertilization also stimulates growth of fungi, which are naturally abundant and active in moist, shady areas. Fourth, grasses under a tree are competing with the tree roots for water; it is not an environment forgiving of overfertilization.

Herbicides should also be used with extreme caution on shady lawns. As discussed in Chapter 4, weed killers can stress grass, albeit imperceptibly. Applied in shady areas where the grass is already stressed, herbicides can be the final blow to a struggling lawn.

Shade is more of a problem in the older sections of a city, where the trees have had time to grow larger, their canopies broader. Lovely old trees can make a property more desirable, and combined with a fine turf, the effect is often one of the most pleasing in the world of landscaping.

Following are some guidelines for turf care in shady areas:

1. Adjust the fertilizer rate. Reduce it slightly, more if the dominant shade species is fine fescue. Try to avoid fertilizing during midsummer.

2. Use herbicides only sparingly. Spot weeding is usually wiser than making a broad herbicide application. As with fertilizing, try to avoid using herbicides in summer.

3. If the shade approaches 50%, some tree trimming might be useful. However, proceed with caution, since tree trimming is expensive. You want to be sure that it will solve the problem.

4. If the shade is so intense that there is little turf in sight, recommend that a ground cover such as ivy, *Ajuga, Pachysandra,* or creeping myrtle be considered. Ground covers are expensive, but they are both effective and attractive.

5. Water deeply but infrequently.

6. Mow the grass higher.

7. Remove leaf litter produced by trees overhead.

8. Have the soil tested. After years of leaf fall, the soil may be too acidic to support grass successfully.

9. If the grass is thin and struggling and no thatch is present, consider seeding or overseeding with some of the shade-tolerant cultivars named later.

Historically, of the warm-season grasses, bermudagrass has been considered intolerant of shade, whereas bahiagrass and zoysiagrass are moderately tolerant to shade, centipedegrass has good tolerance, and St. Augustinegrass has excellent shade tolerance. Of the cool-season grasses, rough bluegrass *(Poa trivialis)* and the fine fescues—creeping red, Chewings, and hard fescue—have dominated seed mixtures used in shade.

In the past few years, however, as mature lawns and landscapes become increasingly plentiful, there has been an emphasis on the breeding and development of cultivars with improved shade tolerance. This often means grasses with greater resistance to fungal diseases, particularly powdery mildew, but photosynthesis rate under low light conditions is also important. Bermudagrasses are being bred or selected for improved shade tolerance. St. Augustinegrasses with SAD resistance have been developed, enhancing the natural shade tolerance of this species.

Many new cool-season cultivars have been developed with improved shade tolerance. Among the Kentucky bluegrasses are A-34, America, Bristol, Eclipse, Enmundi, Glade, Mystic, Nugget, Ram I, and Sydsport. Sabre is an improved cultivar of rough bluegrass, *Poa trivialis;* it can be used alone in shady situations but should not be included in the standard mix given earlier of bluegrass, fine fescue, and turf-type ryegrasses. Some of the improved fine fescues include Boreal, Commodore, Dawson, Fortress, and Ruby rhizomatous fescues; Aurora, Biljart, Reliant, Spartan, and Waldina hard fescues; and Shadow Chewings fescue. Some of the newer turf-type perennial ryegrasses also show better shade tolerance when compared with older ryegrasses, including Birdie II, Cowboy, Gator, Palmer, Pennant, and Yorktown II.

Shade tolerance is a surprising feature of the new turf-type tall fescues such as Apache, Arid, and Mustang, whose leaves become more fine and soft. In shady turf plots at Ohio State University the tall fescue Falcon has been doing as well as or better than Bristol or Glade bluegrass over the past few years. An excellent cool-season mixture for shade, then, might consist of a tall fescue such as Falcon with 5% to 10% Bristol or other shade-tolerant bluegrass. Also recommended for shady lawns of the North and transition zone is 5% to 10% improved fine fescue mixed with tall fescue.

THATCH

The American Society of Agronomy defines thatch as "a tightly intermingled layer of living and dead stems, leaves, and roots of grass which develops between the layer of green vegetation and the soil surface." In other words, it is a mostly dead layer of organic material between the grass and the soil. It is a very poorly understood feature of turf and is in need of much research.

The extent of the thatch layer is often misinterpreted by the homeowner, who confuses it in the spring with the dead debris of winter. It cannot be ascertained by standing on the turf and looking down; a soil probe or other instrument should be used to obtain a plug of soil and sod so that the extent of the thatch layer can be accurately determined.

Various reasons have been advanced to explain the formation of excessive thatch:

1. Excessive fertilization: In theory, this builds thatch by stimulating the turf to produce more organic matter than can readily be decomposed. Several tests, however, show no relationship between the amount of nitrogen applied per 1000 sq ft and the amount of thatch.

2. The routine or continual use of pesticides: It is becoming more clear that many pesticides, especially herbicides and fungicides, destroy the activity of the microorganisms necessary to decompose thatch.

3. An acidic condition: Soil tests are misleading in that they indicate the pH of the soil rather than that of the soil–thatch interface, where decomposition occurs. Most microorganisms of decay do not function under acidic conditions.

4. Poor aeration and poor drainage: Wet, compacted soils lacking oxygen, like acidic soils, do not support a vigorous population of decay microorganisms. Many decomposition reactions are oxidations.

5. The use of vigorous turfgrass cultivars: Many of the premium turfgrasses currently in vogue have been selected in part for their increased vigor. These in turn produce greater amounts of dead organic matter that must be decomposed if an extensive thatch layer is to be avoided.

6. Mowing infrequently and producing large quantities of clippings at one time: Clumped masses of clippings are difficult to work into the soil for decomposition. Normal amounts of clippings, however, seem to contribute very little to thatch formation.

It is important to understand that turfgrasses are subjected to population stress: To provide a uniform turf we are growing the grass plants in dense populations never obtained in a natural situation. This alone enforces the need for extra nutrition and increases the effect of fungal diseases, insect activity, and the problem of thatch.

It is not uncommon for the thatch layer to eventually retard the penetration of water and nutrients into the soil. The grass plants may root in the thatch itself, such that the turf can be peeled back from the soil surface like a rug. This is similar to the condition following a grub attack, but the turf is still green. The thatch layer also harbors disease spores and detrimental insects.

The actual thickness of the thatch is probably not too important; rather, it is the quality of the thatch that determines whether or not the lawn is functioning in a healthy manner. A vigorous two-year-old sod may have a thicker thatch layer than a twenty-year-old lawn that has been maintained intensively. But in some way, undoubtedly very complex biochemically, the thatch layer changes and becomes fibrous, lignified, leached, very acidic . . . and biologically dead. The lawn, this dense population of grass plants, has passed its zenith and has no way to go but down.

To combat thatch it has been a standard practice for many years to whack away at it with machines known appropriately as *dethatchers*. Three types are commonly used: (1) The tine type, which is the most gentle in its action of combing dead material to the surface. Once the material has been removed it is difficult to see where the dethatcher has been. (2) The fixed-blade type, usually with triangular blades that have more of a slicing or cutting action. It is used to slice, cut, or vertically mow actively running grasses such as bentgrass and bermudagrass. Set a little deeper, it can also double as a soil slicer or groover in renovations and overseedings. (3) The flail type, with free-swinging steel blades that can provide the most severe dethatching.

If the thatch is extensive and the turf is poorly rooted, the flail-type dethatcher has the effect of almost stripping the lawn. Its action is not unlike that of a rototiller, and the lawn is left in an unattractive condition prone to weed invasion. Great quantities of material may have to be removed from the lawn, making the process costly.

Unless overseeding is the intent, severely dethatching a living lawn is probably unwise. In the case of an otherwise healthy, well-established, well-rooted turf, severe dethatching weakens the turf and disturbs the soil, allowing difficult grassy weeds such as coarse fescue to gain a roothold. Unless overseeding is contemplated, the dethatcher blades should be set so that the soil surface is disturbed as little as possible. It is better to do a mild dethatching frequently than to do a severe tearing or stripping that approaches rototilling.

A variation of the fixed-blade dethatcher is the *vertical mower*. Research on warm-season grasses has shown that the spacing of the vertical mower blades is important. For bermudagrass and zoysiagrass the blade spacing should be 1 to 2 in.; for bahiagrass and centipedegrass, 2 to 3 in.; and for St. Augustinegrass, 3 in. Penetration of the blades into the soil should be kept to a minimum of 1/4 in. or less, and dethatching in one direction works best.

Another method for reducing thatch on limited areas is *topdressing*. This practice consists of applying a thin layer of biologically active material (for example, topsoil) on top of the turf to promote decomposition of the thatch. As indicated above, thatch is acidic and biologically dead. In theory, then, applying lime combined with any material rich in decay bacteria and fungi and then moistening the turf should stimulate decomposition of thatch. In practice, however, the results have often been spotty and inconclusive. The method seems reasonable, however, and many (mostly organic) products claiming thatch-reducing properties have appeared on the market. Research and testing should eventually identify some material or combination of materials that will be effective.

Many turf workers have supplanted mechanical dethatching altogether with the simpler process of *core aerating*. In this technique cigar-shaped plugs of soil several inches long are removed by machine from the soil and deposited on the surface of the turf. Rain and subsequent mowing and raking will crumble these plugs of topsoil so that a thin topdressing is actually effected over the surface of the turf. In addition, holes are made by the core aerator through the thatch into the soil, reducing compaction and allowing deeper rooting and penetration of water and fertilizer.

To date, core aeration is probably the most effective and economical method for combatting excessive thatch formation. Unlike a mechanical dethatching, there is no great amount of material to be removed, the turf is not substantially weakened, and there appears to be little or no subsequent weed invasion. There are additional benefits of core aeration: Soil compaction is decreased, soil aeration is increased, and rooting and the penetration of water and nutrients are enhanced.

SOIL COMPACTION

Heavy clays characterize many United States soils, especially in the bluegrass region. They are good soils and they are fertile, but they have to be treated with special care. When they get wet they can easily be compacted into almost a brick-like consistency. Needless to say, this doesn't help the growth of grass or any type of plant. The oxygen is squeezed out of the root zones, root respiration is limited, and the roots themselves have difficulty penetrating the dense layers of the soil (see Chapter 1). In addition, it is the rare builder who sets aside the topsoil to be spread evenly back over the subsoil when the new home is ready for a lawn. Normally the sod or seed is placed on hard subsoil that has already been compacted severely by the equipment necessary for the construction of the home.

Rolling a turf area is seldom necessary, except when it is first planted. The frost heaving that occurs over winter is actually beneficial to the grass in that it aerates the soil. It should not be counteracted by rolling the lawn during a wet spring. Pockets, ruts, or undulations in a lawn are usually the result of poor grading before the lawn was established and are seldom removed by rolling, anyway. A wiser choice is to consider applying topsoil to these difficult areas in the lawn and reseeding or resodding.

There are two systems that have been used in efforts to help decrease compaction. One is topdressing—making a series of applications of gypsum (calcium sulfate) or sand (of particle size less than 1 mm), or both. Gypsum, which is chemically inert, as is sand, affects the physical structure of clay, making the soil more porous. As with lime, gypsum is relatively inexpensive, but it takes a great deal of it (at least 50 lb per 1000 sq ft) to be effective, hence a special spreader and some heavy labor are required. Sand rather than gypsum should be used west of Illinois, where soils tend to be more alkaline.

The sand or gypsum is sometimes worked into the soil with a *core aerator,* which in itself is used as another method of relieving soil compaction. The core aerator, or plugger, removes solid plugs of soil about 4 in. deep and typically 3/4 in. in diameter, brings them up, and deposits them on the surface of the lawn. There they are crumbled by subsequent mowing, forming a thin topsoil also useful in retarding thatch development. The holes are made on about 3- to 5-inch centers, and the action speeds the penetration of gypsum, sand, water, nutrients, and air into the soil and to the grass roots. Aerators that make slits in, or slice, the soil are to be avoided: They do not remove a core of soil and in effect actually compress and compact the soil even more.

Most experts feel that the best time of year to core aerate is late summer through early fall. The grass should still have 4 to 5 weeks of growth left to recover from the aeration. The topdressing is done after the cores are removed.

Some grasses tolerate compaction better than others. Of the cool-season grasses, perennial ryegrasses are more tolerant than tall fescues, which are more tolerant than Kentucky bluegrass. Some bluegrasses, however, such as Touchdown, Ram I, and Sydsport, are considered more tolerant of compaction than others. Touchdown and Sydsport are also considered aggressive bluegrasses, hence are frequently mixed with perennial ryegrasses for cool-season playing fields. The bentgrasses and fine fescues are the least tolerant of compaction. Of warm-season grasses, bermudagrass is the most tolerant of compaction, followed in descending order by buffalograss, zoysiagrass, centipedegrass, and St. Augustinegrass.

In summary, a badly compacted soil simply will not support a lawn, as is obvious where foot traffic makes a path around the side of a house. The soil is a living system teeming with life of all kinds. If the oxygen is reduced or too much water is retained, the soil microflora and microfauna cease functioning. Good turf management involves good soil management.

CLUMPS OF GRASSY WEEDS

Clumps of grassy weeds such as nimblewill, quackgrass, and coarse fescue can mar the beauty of an otherwise uniform turf. Standard broadleaf and preemergence herbicides have little or no effect on these grasses. The clumps can be eradicated with total killer-type herbicides such as Monsanto's Roundup. After spots are obviously dead and easy to discern, they are raked out vigorously and reseeded. For this purpose it is helpful to use a premix of seed and peat or topsoil and spread this liberally in the dead areas. These spots have to be watered carefully for 2 to 3 weeks, as with a regular seeding.

If the clumps are not so great in number as to practically dominate the lawn, it may be easier simply to slip them out with a sod lifter and replace them with pieces of sod. The action, however, must be done carefully so that the finish grade is not changed and does not cause any bumpiness in the lawn. Once again, the spots have to be kept continually moist for 2 to 3 weeks until the sod pieces are well rooted.

Still another technique, probably the most simple, is to use a hand-held wick applicator (commonly used in other horticultural crops). Quackgrass and coarse fescue, for example, grow faster and higher than bluegrass in a mowed turf. It is sometimes possible, with a steady hand, to brush their leaves with a wick applicator filled with Roundup *without touching the bluegrass* or other desired turf.

TURF RENOVATION

Renovating a lawn consists of killing the existing turf and replacing it with new grass. This has become an almost routine process for two reasons: the introduction of the herbicide Roundup by the Monsanto Chemical Co. and the development of a vast assortment of new and improved turfgrass cultivars. Roundup, or glyphosate, is a relatively safe chemical that interferes with amino acid synthesis in plants. A 2% solution will kill most lawns. The chemical is translocated into the root system, effecting a permanent kill even of difficult broadleaf and grassy weeds. Once in the soil, the Roundup is quickly inactivated.

Reseeding the dead turf can begin just a few hours later, but in practice one usually waits 1 to 2 weeks to assess the effectiveness of the Roundup application, making sure that no difficult weeds have been missed. The Roundup may be spot-applied a second time to weeds that may be difficult to eradicate, such as nutsedge, quackgrass, coarse fescue, and nimblewill.

Once the old lawn is dead, there are three ways to proceed. The choice is determined by the extent of the dead material, including the thatch, that covers the soil surface. In all three procedures, the primary concern is getting the seed past the dead material into the soil, where it will germinate properly.

1. If there is little or no thatch, the next step is simply to slice through the thin layer of dead material left on the lawn with a vertical mower, fixed-bladed dethatcher, overseeder, slit seeder, slicer, or groover—a variety of mechanisms, all of which cut through the material and make slits in the soil. The key is making good slits

$1/4$ in. or less in the soil and not more than 2 in. apart (preferably, 1 in.). The old lawn is now seeded with improved cultivars by using a box or rotary spreader, fertilized, and watered in the manner described earlier for seeding. The dead material is left on the lawn to act as a mulch.

2. If there is more than just a thin layer of thatch or dead material on the lawn (for example, from $1/4$ to $1/2$ in. of thatch), it is impossible to effectively slice through it and make good contact with the soil. In this case a severe dethatching may be in order, done with a flail dethatcher set just above soil level. The material is flailed into a fluff and raked or vacuumed off, leaving just enough for a mulch. The lawn is then sliced, seeded, fertilized, and watered as above.

3. If the thatch layer is so thick that even a severe dethatching is either ineffective or too costly, the old turf can be cut off with a sod cutter, rolled up, and trucked away (it makes good compost). The new soil surface is regraded, and topsoil, lime, and fertilizer are added as required. The site is then grooved with a slicer or slitter and seeded with appropriate cultivars. The new seeding is back-dragged to lightly cover the seed and mulched with straw or pine needles, as in a conventional seeding.

There are no easy guidelines one can give to help in making the decision whether to slit seed directly into the dead material, to dethatch severely, or to use a sod cutter. Like so much of turf management, good judgment comes with experience. If in doubt, use the next most rigorous procedure, remembering the ultimate aim of getting the seed into slits in the soil.

Removing the old turf is also a good time to correct any underlying problems that may have necessitated the renovation in the first place. Compaction, poor drainage, and bad original grading can all be dealt with more easily once the original soil is exposed. If an underground irrigation system has been contemplated, now is the time to install it.

OVERSEEDING—SLIT SEEDING

In the previous section on turf renovation, the turf is first killed with Roundup, excessive thatch is removed, and the dead lawn is slit seeded. The term *overseeding* is used to indicate the seeding of a turf that is living although possibly dormant, as in the case of winter overseeding of warm-season turfs.

Overseeding is typically accomplished by using machines that slice or slit the existing cover, allowing the seed to penetrate to the soil. An ordinary dethatcher or vertical mower can be used to make the slits prior to seeding. Special machines have also been manufactured that slit and seed in one operation: Typically a series of whirling dethatching blades slice through the existing cover, making slits in the soil into which seed is metered; coulters or drags then cover it slightly and firm it into the soil. As with a regular seeding, it is important that the seed have good contact with the soil and be slightly buried and lightly compressed.

The overseeding should be treated just like a renovation or a new seeding. It should be fertilized and limed as required and watered sufficiently to keep the soil moist for 2 to 3 weeks. An overseeding machine does not work if the thatch is too thick. The slicing blades will not penetrate adequately into the soil and the seed becomes hung up in the thatch layer, which is a poor place for it to germinate. In cases such as this the only alternative may be to do a complete renovation—to kill and strip off the old lawn and start over with a new seeding or sodding.

One drawback in overseeding is that the soil is slightly churned, allowing weed seeds that were buried long ago a chance to surface and germinate. This can be prevented to some extent in bluegrass turf by using the special preemergence herbicide Siduron, and it can be prevented in all turfs by preferably deferring the overseeding until fall, when weed seed germination is less of a problem.

Overseeding is sometimes performed in newly established turf (for example, after a year) that is weak and spotty. The general rule of thumb here is that if the desired grasses are stoloniferous or rhizomatous and present in at least 50% cover, it might be easier simply to continue mowing, to fertilize more heavily, and to kill weeds in a series of close applications until the turf closes up and becomes dense. With less than 50% cover, or with nonspreading grasses such as the ryegrasses and tall fescues, overseeding may be the appropriate way to proceed.

It has been common since the 1920s to overseed dormant warm-season grasses, particularly bermudagrass greens, with cool-season grasses such as ryegrass. Aside from the aesthetic appeal of having green winter greens, the overseeding of annual or perennial ryegrass, for example, also tended to limit the winter invasion of annual bluegrass. Many superintendents also felt that the green winter cover protected or reduced traffic wear on the dormant warm-season grass.

The practice of winter overseeding spread from bermudagrass greens to other grasses, such as St. Augustinegrass, centipedegrass, and zoysiagrass, and from Florida north into the transition zone. At first, annual ryegrass was the primary grass used for winter overseeding, but now the turf-type perennial ryegrasses are widely used as well as bentgrasses, the fine fescues, rough bluegrass *(Poa trivialis)*, and even Kentucky bluegrass. Several seed companies produce seed mixes and blends specifically for winter seeding, such as the Winterturf series by O. M. Scott & Sons, which is a blend of perennial ryegrasses, Northrup King's Medalist series, also a blend of perennial ryegrasses, and Dixie Green + Sabre from International Seeds, Inc., which is a mix of perennial ryegrass, fine-leafed fescue, and Sabre, a rough bluegrass. The ball-roll speed on a green can be reduced by including rough bluegrass in the overseeding.

Winter overseeding rates for perennial ryegrass in the Southeast run typically from 20 to 30 lb per 1000 sq ft. Fairways are seeded at rates of 300 to 450 lb per acre. The seeding rates are higher in the Southwest (35 to 40 lb per 1000 sq ft for greens and 400 to 700 lb per acre for fairways), where the heat initiates an earlier spring transition.

Prior to overseeding, the turf is mowed very low, almost scalped, then mowed with a vertical mower, which slices through the existing turf and makes slits in the soil. After seeding it is common to drag the turf with a piece of chain link fence to maximize the seed–soil contact, to fertilize with starter-type (high-phosphorus) formulations, to topdress with various materials where economical, and in all cases to water the young seeding sufficiently to keep the soil moist for a week or so. The young seedlings are mowed much shorter than the comparable species growing in a summer lawn of the North. Winter perennial ryegrass greens may be mowed *closer than 1/2 in.*, a shock to a northern turf manager, where ryegrasses, like bluegrasses, are typically mowed at 2 in. or even higher.

Overseeding is done as early as late September in the northern limits of warm-season grasses and as late as early December in Florida. The timing is important and must be gauged carefully for your locality. Generally, the overseeding follows the first sharp cold snap of the fall. Bentgrasses, which are slower to establish, are seeded earlier than ryegrasses.

Since the new seeding is so dense, a condition that encourages fungal damage, it is common to pretreat the seed with fungicides or to be prepared to apply fungicides in the early growth of the seeding. To keep the seeding dense, green, and playable over the winter, nitrogen is applied at regular intervals.

The newer, improved perennial ryegrasses have greater heat tolerance, which is good for the North but less attractive for winter overseeding. This is because the heat-tolerant perennial ryegrass will hang on longer into the warm spring. Ideally, when the warm-season grass begins to break dormancy, green-up, and grow, the cool-season overseeded grass will lose its competitiveness, die, and disappear. The transition back to warm-season turf proceeds naturally at about 80°F and can be stimulated by applying soluble nitrogen combined with vertical mowing.

Some turf managers prefer using *intermediate ryegrasses,* such as Oregreen, 3CN, and Agree, which make a sharper transition than the turf-type perennial ryegrasses. Intermediate ryegrasses, which are hybrids between annual and perennial ryegrass, are like annual ryegrass in that they germinate quickly yet lack heat tolerance. Their finer texture, deeper green color, and reduced shoot growth are similar to characteristics of perennial ryegrass. The lack of heat tolerance is an advantage in that these grasses will disappear as the bermudagrass begins to grow in the spring. They will not shade or otherwise retard the bermudagrass as much as will the more heat-tolerant turf-type perennial ryegrasses.

With the introduction of the new turf-type tall fescues, it may be possible, at least in the transition zone, to construct more permanent year-round turfs, obviating the overseeding of warm-season grasses altogether. This is especially true on lawns that have irrigation systems, where it is possible to maintain tall fescue, perhaps with 10% bluegrass, through the hottest periods of summer. Some selections of even more heat-tolerant tall fescues and bluegrasses would greatly increase the range of this turf combination, which, with the powdery mildew-resistant bluegrasses, is already showing promise for shady lawns.

SPOT SEEDING—PATCH AND STAMP

There are often bare spots in turf, caused in numerous ways, that have to be repaired but are simply too small in either number or size to warrant the use of an overseeding machine. These areas can be effectively *spot seeded.* A simple technique consists of raking out the spot with a steel rake and removing any dead grass or debris. The seed is pre-mixed with dry peat (or any weed-free, absorbent organic material) and a spot of fertilizer, placed in a bag, and kept on hand. At the time of seeding the required amount of premix is placed in a bucket or wheelbarrow and moistened. The moistened seed premix is applied by hand or by shovel about 1/2 in. thick, spread evenly with a rake, and stepped down or in some way lightly compacted. As with any type of seeding, subsequent watering is the key to a successful stand of grass.

If time is of the essence—for example, getting the torn-up areas of a football field ready for play in one week—the seed can be *pregerminated*. This consists of soaking the appropriate amount of seed in a bucket, barrel, or tank of water. The water should be drained off and changed at least once a day, and it helps to use water with a temperature above 60°F (but not so hot as to damage the seed or growing embryo). The seed should be given a final rinse *just before the roots are about to emerge* and then mixed with sand, calcined clay, peat, or any medium that facilitates its handling and spreading. The seed is spread on the regraded, damaged area, covered very lightly with peat or topsoil or a similar cover, and then remoistened. It is kept moist as close to game time as possible. Another procedure, used during cool weather, is to wet the seeding down and then cover it with plastic sheeting, which will keep it warm and moist, greatly enhancing germination and growth.

A Turf Vocabulary

Acre: 43,560 square feet, or 4840 square yards. A square approximately 208 feet on a side.

Apomixis: Reproduction without sex, including the production of seed without the intervention of sexual reproduction.

Auricle: An ear-like protrusion present in some grasses at the base of the leaf blade and projecting around the stem.

Blade: The extended part of a grass leaf that projects out at an angle from the stem.

Bunchgrass: A grass with a tufted growth habit that spreads only by tillers. It lacks rhizomes and stolons.

Cation exchange capacity (CEC): A measure, in milliequivalents (me) per 100 grams of dry soil, of the extent to which cation exchange can occur in a soil. One milliequivalent is 1 mg of hydrogen or the weight of any other ion that will combine with or displace it.

Chlorosis: A yellowing of a leaf or other green tissue resulting from the breakdown of chlorophyll synthesis.

Collar: The area where the leaf blade meets the leaf sheath.

Colloid: A particle, as in clay, that is so small that it remains suspended in a liquid or gel and does not settle out.

Cool-season grasses: Northern, temperate grasses that grow best in spring and fall at temperatures below 75°F. Principally bentgrasses, bluegrasses, fescues, and ryegrasses.

Core aeration: A mechanical process in which cores or plugs of material are removed from the soil and deposited on top of the turf.

Cultivar (cv):   A cultivated variety.

Culm: The botanical name for the stem of a grass.

Crown: The area in a plant, usually at ground level, where the root system joins the stem.

Dicot: Having at germination two seed leaves, or cotyledons.

Dolomitic lime: Lime that contains a high percentage of magnesium.

Floret: The flower of a grass.

Friable: A soil with an ideal consistency. When wet it crushes easily under gentle pressure between the thumb and forefinger, yet remains coherent when pressed together.

Green manure: A crop such as rye, oats, or soybeans that is plowed under while still young and succulent to build up the organic matter of a soil.

Humus: Organic matter that has decomposed to the point where it is no longer recognizable as having been originally either plant or animal but is resistant to further decay.

Inflorescence: A group of spikelets, each in turn composed of florets.

Inorganic: Lacking carbon.

LD$_{50}$:   An abbreviation for "lethal dose," used to indicate the amount of pesticide taken orally that is necessary to effect a 50% kill of test animals (usually laboratory rats). The lower the LD$_{50}$, the more dangerous the pesticide.

Ligule: A small flap of tissue or row of hairs on the inner surface of a grass leaf at the junction of blade and sheath.

Loam: A soil that contains roughly equal parts of sand, silt, and clay.

Meristem: A growing point on a plant, where cells are rapidly dividing.

Microelements: Trace elements, or those nutrients required by plants in very small quantities: chlorine, iron, boron, manganese, zinc, copper, molybdenum.

Monocot: Having at germination only one seed leaf, or cotyledon.

Monoculture: A turf composed of only one cultivar.

Mineral soil: A soil containing less than 20% organic matter.

Mycelium: The mass of filaments making up a typical fungus. A single filament is called a hypha.

Mycorrhiza: An association between a fungus and a plant root in which the fungal mycelium grows in and around the root, producing a greatly increased absorptive surface.

Nitrogen fixation: The combining of atmospheric nitrogen with oxygen or hydrogen to give nitrates, nitrites, or ammonia.

Node: A point on a stem where a leaf arises; in grasses, a growing point, usually swollen.

Organic: Containing carbon.

Organic matter: The decaying, decomposing remains of dead plants, animals, and microbes in a soil.

Organic soil: A soil comprised of at least 20% by weight organic matter.

Overseeding: The seeding of a living (though sometimes dormant) turf. Usually accomplished with a machine that slices through the existing turf and makes slits in the soil into which the seed is deposited.

Panicle: A compound, branched inflorescence.

pH: An abbreviation for "power of hydrogen." A means of designating the concentration of hydrogen ions (H^+) in a solution. A pH of 7 is neutral, a pH less than 7 is acidic, and greater than 7 is alkaline.

ppm: Parts per million, equal to mg/L, to 0.0001%, or to 0.013 oz in 100 gal. To convert ppm to lb/A, multiply the ppm reading by 2.

Preemergence herbicide: A turf chemical that inhibits or retards the germination of weed seeds.

Raceme: An inflorescence in which the spikelets arise individually from the main axis on small stalks, or pedicels.

Rhizome: A horizontal stem that grows underground.

Saprophyte: An organism that decomposes *dead* organic material, in contrast to a parasite, in which the food source is living.

Seed blend: Consists of seeds of two or more cultivars of the same species (e.g., Merion and Glade bluegrasses).

Seed mixture: Consists of two or more cultivars of different species (e.g., Merion bluegrass and Pennlawn fine fescue).

Sheath: The lower part of the grass leaf, enclosing the stem.

Spike: A grass inflorescence in which the spikelets are attached directly, without stalks or pedicels, to the main stem.

Sprig: A piece of a grass, usually of a stolon, which is planted to propagate a grass vegetatively.

Stolon: A horizontal stem that grows across the soil surface.

Surfactant: A wetting agent or chemical with special properties that decrease the surface tension of water, allowing it to spread out and wet more surface.

Synergism: The phenomenon in which the combined effect of two or more ingredients is greater than the sum of the ingredients acting alone.

Systemic pesticide: A pesticide that is absorbed by leaves or roots and translocated through the conducting system to all parts of the plant.

Thatch: A layer of compressed organic material composed of living and dead grass stems, leaves, and roots that develops between the layer of green vegetation and the soil surface.

Tiller: A grass shoot that forms from a bud at the base, or crown, of the plant.

Topdressing: The application of a thin layer of topsoil, organic material, or sand over a turf to improve its contour or to promote decomposition of the thatch.

Transition zone: That region of the United States in which cool-season grasses grade into or coexist with warm-season grasses.

Warm-season grasses: Southern, subtropical grasses that grow best in summer at temperatures above 75°F. Principally, bahiagrass, bermudagrass, carpetgrass, centipedegrass, St. Augustinegrass, and zoysiagrass.

A Turf Library

PROFESSIONAL MAGAZINES

Grounds Maintenance. P.O. Box 12901, Overland Park, KS: Intertec Publishing Corp.
Lawn Servicing. P.O. Box 12901, Overland Park, KS: Intertec Publishing Corp.
Weeds Trees & Turf. 7500 Old Orchard Blvd., Cleveland, OH: Harcourt Brace Jovanovich, Inc.

BOOKS

BEARD, JAMES B. *Turfgrass: Science and Culture.* Englewood Cliffs, NJ: Prentice-Hall, Inc., 1973. 658 pp.
COUCH, HOUSTON B. *Diseases of Turfgrasses,* 2nd ed. Huntington, NY: Robert E. Krieger Publishing Co., 1973. 348 pp.
DANIEL, WILLIAM H., AND R. P. FREEBORG. *Turf Managers' Handbook.* Cleveland, OH: Harvest Publishing Co., 1979. 424 pp.
DUBLE, RICHARD, AND JAMES C. KELL. *Southern Lawns and Groundcovers.* Houston, TX: Gulf Publishing Co., 1977. 91 pp.
HANSON, A. A., AND F. V. JUSKA. *Turfgrass Science.* Madison, WI: American Society of Agronomy, Inc., 1969. 715 pp.
HITCHCOCK, ALBERT S., AND AGNES CHASE. *Manual of the Grasses of the United States,* U.S.D.A. Publication #200. Washington, D.C.: U.S. Government Printing Office, 1950. 1050 pp.
MADISON, JOHN H. *Practical Turfgrass Management.* New York, NY: Van Nostrand Reinhold Co., 1971. 466 pp.

MADISON, JOHN H. *Principles of Turfgrass Culture,* 2nd ed. New York, NY: Van Nostrand
Reinhold Co., 1982. 420 pp.

SMILEY, RICHARD W. *Compendium of Turfgrasses Diseases.* 3340 Pilot Knob Rd., St. Paul,
MN: The American Phytopathological Society, 1983. 102 pp.

TURGEON, ALFRED J. *Turfgrass Management.* Reston, VA: Reston Publishing Co., 1981. 391
pp.

SPRAGUE, HOWARD B. *Turf Management Handbook.* Danville, IL: The Interstate Printers &
Publishers, Inc., 1982. 255 pp.

VARGAS, JOSEPH M., JR. *Management of Turfgrass Diseases.* Minneapolis, MN: Burgess Publishing Co., 1981. 204 pp.

VENGRIS, JONAS, AND WILLIAM A. TORELLO. *Lawns,* 3rd ed. Box 9335, Fresno, CA: Thomp-
son Publications, 1982. 247 pp.

Index